03092   02753

D0310359

J. H. PLUMB

In the Light of History

ALLEN LANE THE PENGUIN PRESS

Copyright © J. H. Plumb, 1972

First published in 1972

Allen Lane The Penguin Press
74 Grosvenor Street, London W I

ISBN 0 7139 0291 4

Printed in Great Britain by
Butler & Tanner Ltd, Frome and London
Set in Monotype Baskerville

TO T. AND JOYCE
WITH GRATITUDE

Contents

Contents

Part Three

OTHER TIMES, OTHER PLACES

Preface

Most of these essays, some in a shortened form, have appeared during the last ten years in a number of magazines and periodicals. To some of my more austere colleagues one or two of these may seem, perhaps, a little superficial, even light-hearted, but I feel that it is a historian's duty not only to pursue his own historical researches but also to attempt to lay bare to the largest possible public what may be the historical roots of some of our own problems – an attitude which I have argued at length elsewhere.

I am grateful to the editors of the following journals for permission to reprint: *American Heritage, Horizon, Saturday Review, New York Review of Books, Spectator,* and also the Director of the Clark Library, Los Angeles.

J. H. P.

Part One

THE EIGHTEENTH CENTURY

It is the duty of man to obtain all the knowledge he can and make the best use of it.

The Complete Works of Thomas Paine,
ed. Philip S. Foner
(New York, 1945), p. 810

I

Reason and Unreason in the Eighteenth Century: the English Experience*

Tom Paine's title, *The Age of Reason*, was an inspired piece of journalism. It has been adopted with alacrity by historians because it provides a wonderful basis for that game of affirmation and denial upon which our profession seems to thrive. At first glance it seems to fit like a glove the era which stretches from the end of Louis XIV's reign to the outbreak of the French revolution. The ancients had been defeated, the triumphs of Newton and Leibnitz had become a part of the mainstream of European intellectual life, the scepticism of Bayle had spread like dye throughout the culture of Western Europe, giving rise to the triumphant Encyclo-paedists. The early dawn of rational criticism fulfilled its promise in the acknowledged brilliance and versatility of Voltaire. Indeed the Western sky was studded with brilliant stars who had, or seemed to have, freed themselves from the myth-ridden universe of their ancestors. History in the hand of Gibbon, philosophy expounded by Hume, human economy described by Adam Smith, no longer looked to God for any answers. Human activity needed to be explained in

* I am not entirely happy about the title, for reasons that will be obvious, yet in some ways it covers the theme which I wish to explore better than any other. The providential world of the ordinary literate man of the seventeenth century was, of course, to him highly rational, if greatly mysterious. A sudden tempest or the death of a hog were indications not so much of disease or meteorology, but of the workings of providence whose hidden meaning had to be discovered. See Alan Macfarlane, *The Family Life of Ralph Josselin; an Essay in Historical Anthropology* (Oxford, 1970), pp. 180–81 and also Keith Thomas's masterly book, *Religion and the Decline of Magic* (London, 1971). It is the movement of the search for causation to the observable world and the spread of such an attitude with which I am concerned.

3

human terms. And these were not the only stars of the first magnitude. Nor were they the most uncompromising of rationalists of this century. Helvetius, d'Holbach and Condorcet, to name but a few, accepted the logic of an attitude which had lead beyond deism to materialism. And even if we allow that most of the *philosophes* believed in God, it was a highly generalized deism to which most of them subscribed; more a polite bow to the unknown than an act of faith. After all, Thomas Paine regarded himself as a deist and this was in no way incompatible with aggressive materialism.

And there can be little doubt that to whatever form of intellectual activity we turn, we find a heightened consciousness of the need for logical and experimental processes. Whether it be the Grimms' study of languages, Beccaria's inquiry into law or Bentham's consideration of the perfect prison, there is a similar faith in, and reliance on, man's capacity to study himself, his institutions, his history and his social relationships through his intellectual capacities working on the observable. Aware of ignorance, the eighteenth-century philosopher is not daunted by it. For him the human mind is like a torch in a deep and complex cavern: slowly but surely it will illuminate every crevice. To us, however, many eighteenth-century thinkers seemed to take shadows for rocks, and to accept at once the many strange images that the flickering light did not reveal, but create. The closer we look at the great protagonists of a rational approach to humanity, the more we find a great deal of oddity, much prejudice and a penchant for the irrational – the first image quickly dissolves. After all, Voltaire not only regarded religion as essential for the lower orders, but also dedicated a tragedy to the Pope as '*Chef de la Véritable religion*'. Indeed, Voltaire's attitude towards religion always had a streak of ambivalence.* Montesquieu, a committed Christian, was also a freemason, as indeed was Thomas Paine, who believed that the masons were descendants of the sun-worshipping Druids.

* René Pomeau, *La Religion de Voltaire* (Paris, 1956); Robert Shackleton, *Montesquieu* (Oxford, 1961).

Indeed the astonishing rise into social prominence and the acceptance of freemasonry in those very circles of aristocratic and middle class culture which were supposed to be the most fertile seedbeds for rationalist principles is sufficient comment in itself on the hunger for a structured universe beyond the observable in the age of reason, even amongst its most ardent protagonists. And looking beyond the family of philosophers, we must admit that most of the educated and all of the half-educated were far more gullible. Cagliostro had no difficulty in persuading the educated citizens of London that he possessed semi-magical powers and that he could make gold.* Casanova found the Venetian aristocracy as credulous and they swallowed his hocus-pocus wholesale. Indeed their dedication to astrology was almost Assyrian. The bogus philosophies of Lavater and Mesmer were received with uncritical admiration by many who should have known better. Swedenborg's career is a sad commentary on the strength of a rational attitude in Swedish, Dutch and English societies.† Indeed between the stars of first magnitude are vast spaces of darkness and even the stars themselves, on inspection, seem less steady and more flickering.

If the Cagliostros, Swedenborgs and Casanovas are dismissed as extravagant and eccentric examples of human chicanery, a response to neurotic disorders common to any age, there are still numerous enough examples of credulity and superstition in the most sophisticated and intellectual circles. One has only to recall the dark terrors which flooded Dr Johnson's mind or the whimsies that cluttered

* If Cagliostro was the whale amongst impostors, there were plenty of sharks content with smaller prey. Gustav Katterfelto, master of the Blaenical and Caprimantic Arts, was making a living lecturing in the English provinces in 1781. See F. Ribadeau Dumas, *Cagliostro* (New York, 1967); also John Money, *Public Opinion in the West Midlands, 1760–1793* (unpublished Ph.D. thesis, Cambridge University), pp. 48–50; also *Dictionary of National Biography, sub* Katterfelto.

† Annibale Bozzola, *Casanova Illuminata* (Modena, 1956); J. R. Rivers, *Casanova* (London, 1961); S. Toksvig, *Emmanuel Swedenborg, Scientist and Mystic* (London, 1949); C. O. Sigstedt, *The Swedenborg Epic* (New York, 1950).

the head of bat-brained Boswell. Indeed, if we turn to England, how few of her great intellectuals or writers of the eighteenth century accepted a dominant critical and materialist philosophy: Pope was a papist, Swift an Anglican and a hater of scientists, Newton himself was ardently religious if indefatigably unorthodox. Fielding might be a sardonic man of the world, but he was no more of a rationalist *philosophe* than Richardson. True, there was a small articulate body of deists, and in Locke and in Hume England possessed two of the most important of the world's philosophers, who tried to interpret human existence and human society in human terms. Although many paid lip-service to their philosophy, they had no equals and the philosophic idol of the second half of the century was Edmund Burke, whose beliefs were anything but critical and materialist.

If one views English intellectual society of the late eighteenth century and compares it with the late seventeenth and early eighteenth century, one can discern a steady drift away from the principles of criticism within the social and political establishment. The upholders of an empiricist approach – Joseph Priestley, Jeremy Bentham, Richard Price, Tom Paine and the rest – were almost all outside the ranks of conventional society, mainly dissenters, and therefore second class citizens. Compare the reception of Locke's ideas with those of Hume: one was immediately acclaimed, the other cold-shouldered. Indeed there is a remarkable contrast between the period starting roughly from 1680 to 1720 and that from 1760 to 1800. We find an empiricist attitude sinking down into the lower orders of society, to the *menu peuple*, and a growing distrust of it amongst the governing and socially dominant classes.

Again, if one looks closely at the world of government – administrators, politicians and the like – in the middle of the eighteenth century there is a drift away from experiment and intellectual approach and a readier acceptance of inherited institutions. Criticism and innovation give way to rationalization and preservation. In the 1690s Locke and Newton both advised the government on currency problems: Locke sat on the Board of Trade, Newton was Master of the Mint, Gregory King, the great statistician, was employed by the Treasury: Charles D'Avenant likewise.* There was a realistic attitude to the value of statistics for population as well as trade; methods of finance and taxation were debated energetically and there was a far greater intellectual openness towards methods of government and administration than was to appear again until the nineteenth century. The innovations of this age in the use of statistics, primitive as they might be, was not due to accident but to discussion and decision, the result of an empiricist approach to questions of financial administration. The key lay, of course, in the spread of knowledge of, and faith in, mathematics and their proven value in engineering, cartography and navigation: these were the channels through which empiricism could trickle.

Men in the Augustan age, that is between 1689 and 1715, were not only deeply preoccupied with the methods of government, but also with its efficiency: reform and innovation came from within the governing groups and often, in finance at least, from above. The Bank of England was neither stumbled on nor derived from tradition; it was a conscious intellectual act, realistically and sensibly planned; stimulated surely by the Bank of Amsterdam, but nevertheless a reflection of intellect at work in government. Likewise the funding of the National Debt and the creation of the Sinking Fund. Never since has a British government shown such intellectual flexibility and ingenuity with regard to taxation. Nor was this accidental. It was the result, as seen in the person of that great administrator and innovator, Samuel Pepys, of the permeation of governing circles by a sense of scientific principle, and, in consequence, a weakening of tradition. Old methods of taxation had become no more sacrosanct than divine hereditary right.

If one compares the membership of the Royal Society in

* One may compare the acceptance of such intellectuals with the reception accorded to the group, Priestley, Price, etc., whom the Earl of Shelburne patronized in the reign of George III.

1680 with that in 1730, there is an obvious decline in men of affairs with strong scientific interests. There is an increase in dilettantes and country gentlemen interested in curiosities. Indeed, it is not without significance that whereas in the late seventeenth century many leaders of the nation were members of the Royal Society, in the mid eighteenth these were to be found more often in the Society of Dilettanti. Science did not die, indeed it continued to flourish, but in different circles, and rarely with the encouragement of the higher ranks of government, where there was a growing and strengthening conservatism, and increased veneration for what existed.* This change can be illustrated in yet another way. Few, if any, innovations in government were made between 1720 and 1780. Perhaps the changing situation is best exemplified by the fact that Sir Robert Walpole possessed a portrait of John Locke, which hung in a place of distinction at Houghton, but none of Locke's works were to be found in his library and, as far as I know, he never read a word of the greatest Whig philosopher. In a world of political stability, intellectual inquiry into the nature of politics and rational criticism of institutions is unlikely to be encouraged. After 1720 it was to be found only in important circles of opposition, amongst the dissenters and, above all, across the border in Edinburgh and Glasgow. In 1701 Captain Savery, the inventor of the first usable steam engine, was presented to William III. No one, as far as I know, suggested presenting James Watt to George III: by then the mechanical arts were less fashionable.† A similar change of attitude can be

* See Sir Henry Lyons, *The Royal Society, 1660–1940* (Cambridge, 1944), p. 162. 'Those who joined the non-scientific group of the Society during this period [i.e. 1741–78] showed no enthusiasm for the advancement of the Society's aims.' According to Lyons (ibid., p. 341), the proportion of scientific Fellows in the Royal Society declined from 33 per cent in 1740 to 28·6 per cent in 1800. And, as Lyons stresses, the Society was far less active during these years than it had been in the earlier part of the century. A further fact of importance is that science had become less metropolitan and less based on the universities.

† James Watt did not become a Fellow of the Royal Society until 1785 when there was, under the stimulus of Joseph Priestley and Erasmus Darwin, a renewed interest in 'technological invention'.

seen in the Royal Society, whose Fellows had been greatly interested in Savery and Newcomen's inventions at their birth. When contrasted with the Augustan Age in England (1688–1715), the first twenty years of the reign of George III are remarkable for the change in their intellectual climate.

Undoubtedly the reason for this was the widespread acceptance of Newtonianism broadly interpreted. Newton had illustrated the orderly nature of the universe, that it behaved in accordance with principles which could be rationally observed and rationally demonstrated. The step from Newton to rational theology was easily made.* Everything that existed had its place in the divine plan, which sooner or later would be revealed to the perceptive intellect. Such an attitude fitted the early eighteenth-century theologian, scientist and poet like a glove.

> All Nature is but Art, unknown to thee;
> All Chance, Direction, which thou canst not see;
> All Discord, Harmony, not understood;
> All partial Evil, universal Good:
> And, spite of Pride, in erring Reason's spite,
> One truth is clear, 'Whatever is, is right.'†

This did not mean that Pope was unaware of the corruption and evil of men; his satires are ample proof of the clarity of his social vision. However, he felt, as did most intellectual circles of his time, that beneath these surface blemishes, the mere corruptions of fallible men, lay the perfections of the supremely rational Godhead. This reflects, curiously enough, a growing political attitude: men in politics felt that beneath the corruptions of day-to-day politics there was a perfectly balanced constitution, suited to man's social condition. This new intellectual stability, a world of justification rather than explanation, chimed with the ever-growing,

---

* Expressed with the utmost clarity by the age's finest poet:

> 'Nature and Nature's laws lay hid in night:
> God said, *Let Newton be!* And all was light.'

† Alexander Pope, *Essay on Man*, ed. Maynard Mack (London, 1950), pp. 50–51.

ever-strengthening political stability of the Augustan Age. Society, politics, thought, even religion and science, were moving in the same direction.

Naturally this led to a hardening of tradition, a growing indifference to scientific speculation and increased dilettantism, and a far greater capacity amongst the educated élites for swallowing hocus-pocus. Perhaps the contrast between the philosophers who were regarded by each age as the outstanding masters makes the point sufficiently strongly. Locke, in spite of his religious beliefs, will always remain one of the pillars of rationalist thought: a philosopher, like Bacon, who wished to explore the realities of nature, including man himself. Edmund Burke, personally a much more complex man, capable of political realism, is nevertheless in the final analysis the philosopher of anti-intellectualism, a man who made a mystique of tradition. He was aware of the threat that empiricism, or even the rational principles used in the vulgar, non-philosophic sense, could be to the institutions which he valued: and he sensed that, once it was grasped by an educated electorate, the class structure which he knew would be in peril. A critical approach to political institutions and established authority made as uneasy bedfellows in eighteenth-century England as they did in France or in Prussia. Frederick the Great might take delight in Voltaire – both of them could enjoy a joke about orthodox religion or fulminate against superstition – but Frederick was quite conscious of the boundaries of rationalist inquiry and action based upon it.

Perhaps, therefore, one should argue with George Boas that the complexity of arguments and beliefs is always so great in any age that to label it is dangerous.* And certainly I think that too much stress on the existence of the *philosophes*, or even on the emergence of the Enlightenment itself, has its dangers. It leads to an underestimation of the strength of the reaction to the attitude of Bayle, Diderot, d'Alembert and the rest of the 'family' in the second half

* George Boas, 'In Search of the Age of Reason', in *Aspects of the Eighteenth Century*, ed. Earl R. Wasserman (Baltimore, 1965), pp. 1–19.

of the century: it also leads to an underestimation of the growing forces of occultism and credulity: and to the social transference that was taking place in 'enlightened' attitudes. This is particularly marked in English society where the social and political establishments were far less concerned with intellectual activity than they had been. In fact they had begun to fear it. Just as faith in reason starts earlier in England, amongst men of power, so does flight from it begin earlier too. By taking the whole of the eighteenth century as a single period we make our problems more complex.

Indeed if we wish to judge whether or not the eighteenth century in Western Europe deserves the label of the Age of Reason, we need to look beyond the intellectual and social establishment to what was happening in a larger segment of society. As Peter Gay has demonstrated, the principal object of attack by the leaders of the Enlightenment had been the Christian Churches and the Christian myths.* And this was both a symptom and a cause of the growing secularization of society which is so marked an aspect of England of the late seventeenth and of France of the late eighteenth centuries. In some ways Bayle and the rest are reflections of social attitudes as well as innovators or encouragers of new ones. There was a great and momentous change in the social role of religion between 1660 and 1760 which was, perhaps, of greater importance than the attacks of individual philosophers on religion itself in creating the more sceptical attitude of the eighteenth century. This is particularly marked in England, but it is not confined to Protestant countries. The rot that began to weaken the timbers of Christian ideology, Protestant or Catholic, was not confined to the laity alone.

Calvin, Luther, St Thomas and St Augustine had all regarded this world as a world of sin to be struggled through. Of course, there were plenty of men and women in all Christian-dominated ages who let their instincts have full play and who enjoyed deeply the pleasures of being alive,

* Peter Gay, *The Enlightenment*, 2 vols. (New York, 1966), p. 69.

but the moral atmosphere in which they moved was gloomily oppressive, God and Devil haunted, pervaded by a sense of man's wickedness and the vanity of all things. And Bunyan's *Pilgrim's Progress*, the most popular book of seventeenth-century England, was redolent with the same feeling. The world was evil and vain: suffering or retribution the lot of man. This had been drummed into men and women, Catholic and Protestant, century after century.

From 1660 onwards this religious chord was sounded less frequently in English pulpits as latitudinarianism acquired approbation and gathered force. Bishop Tillotson, whose sermons were exceedingly popular both with other preachers and the public, stressed over and over again that God's commands were not grievous, that religion was a matter of right behaviour: benevolence, charity, was required of men as well as conscientious work, prudence, thrift and regular habits.* The world, he told his congregations, was a happy place to be in, the world's goods proper for men to enjoy, modestly of course, but there was nothing evil in riches, places or profits. Indeed, as he said, a good Christian could be certain of a *place* in Heaven. As the Marquis of Halifax told his daughter, 'religion was a cheerful thing'. And so Hell and the Devil, the terror of God's wrath, gave way to a complacent Confucianism, in which a rational attitude to the Trinity, to miracles, to the divinity of Christ, could flourish without fear of the rack or the stake. This process was at work just as vigorously fifty years later in France. As Abbé Molinier told his flock, 'Deliberately, on principle, systematically, nothing supernatural must be believed; the mere mention of a miracle must provoke mocking amongst worldly people, and they must feel sorry for people like ourselves, who believe in miracles when they are obvious.'†

* For a discussion of the ways in which religion became more concerned with social discipline in the seventeenth century, see Christopher Hill, *Society and Puritanism in Pre-Revolutionary England* (London, 1964). Also Richard B. Schlatter, *The Social Ideas of Religious Leaders, 1660–1688* (Oxford, 1940).

† Quoted in Bernard Groethuysen, *The Bourgeois: Catholicism vs. Capitalism in Eighteenth-Century France* (New York, 1968), p. 20.

Nor was this merely a bitter diatribe against metropolitan fashion: Groethuysen has traced the same sentiments, growing ever stronger as the century progressed, in the sermons of provincial priests. And in spite of outbreaks of hysterical mysticism, the continuing strength of Jansenism in France or the success of Methodism in England, no one can deny that, socially speaking, the area of religion contracted sharply in eighteenth-century Europe. It no longer permeated men's minds as it had done prior to 1688. It enabled a rational attitude to such matters as witchcraft or possession by devils to be so socially acceptable as to be scarcely worth an argument. It also enabled secular attitudes to spread and acquire dynamic social force.

This secularization of society can be demonstrated in other ways. The bulk of seventeenth-century publishing had been religious: true, a considerable amount of history and a not despicable amount of travel literature had also found their way into print, and of course the classics had been extensively reprinted, but the quantity of theology, sermons and devotional books published was prodigious. The difference, however, with the eighteenth century is very marked: sermons are still plentiful, but the appearance of imaginative literature, of the moral essay *à la Spectator*, the vast increase in instructive manuals, the growth of magazines and newspapers, the phenomenal increase in ephemeral political literature, the steady increase in non-religious books of every kind, changes the balance. Literature is no longer dominated either by religion or the Church. It is intensively and actively secular: concerned with morality, maybe, but less and less with revealed religion. This, of course, is not to deny the very large segment of book publishing that was still dominated by religious and devotional literature, but the change in proportion is obvious. Religion not only invaded less of men's lives, but also took up fewer shelves in their libraries.

The culture of the middle class, of the educated artisan, shopkeeper or skilled worker, was both more diverse and more secular, more concerned with knowledge and information and social and political comment, than that of their grandfathers had been.* If we turn to one of the most neglected aspects of eighteenth-century social history – education – we find a similar situation. The curiosity, the thirst for knowledge and for rational explanation which had motivated the founders of the Royal Society, and the strong belief that empirical knowledge would unlock the secrets of the universe, had begun to seep down through society. The scientific revolution of the seventeenth century had largely been a gentlemen's affair, or of those clergymen, academics and administrators who were associated with the world of gentlemen. Nevertheless those involved in it had necessarily maintained contacts with skilled craftsmen, primarily instrument makers.† Although in no way preoccupied with the application of scientific knowledge, they were highly conscious of its usefulness.

Even so, public lectures on scientific subjects were few, mainly confined to London, Oxford and Cambridge, but very early in the eighteenth century this began to change, and change rapidly. There was a strong revival in London after a powerful committee led by Sir Thomas Rawlinson had petitioned the Lord Mayor in 1706 for the resumption of the Gresham Lectures, moribund since the Fire of London. Restarted, they lasted until 1768 when, perhaps significantly,

---

* G. A. Cranfield, *The Development of the Provincial Newspaper, 1700–1760* (Oxford, 1962), pp. 93–116; R. M. Wiles, 'Middle-Class Literacy in Eighteenth Century England: Fresh Evidence', in *Studies in the Eighteenth Century* (Canberra, 1969), pp. 49–65; Henry L. Snyder, 'The Circulation of Newspapers in the Reign of Queen Anne', *Transactions of the Bibliographical Society, The Library* (1968), pp. 206–35. Newspapers contained very little religious matter and they reached wider audiences than any other printed matter, except perhaps broadsheets and ballads. R. Altick, *The English Common Reader: A Social History of the Mass Reading Public* (Chicago, 1957).

† 'All sorts of Mathematical Instruments in Silver, Brass or Wood are made and sold by John Worgan under St Dunstan's Church in Fleet St where any Nobleman, Gentleman or Merchant may hear of fit persons to collect rents, or keep books, or teach the Mathematics.' Advertisement in Hatton's *Merchants Magazine* (I am indebted for this reference to my pupil, Dr Colin Brooks).

the premises in which they were given were sold to the Excise Office. In addition, both Whiston and Desaguliers were lecturing by 1720 on mechanics, hydrostatics, pneumatics and optics to large audiences of merchants, craftsmen and clerks.* Desaguliers' great success encouraged others and for the rest of the century London was never without its public lectures on scientific subjects or its scientific academies designed not for children but for adults who wished to explore the physical world by the new scientific methods. Not surprisingly these lectures were bitterly opposed by High Church divines who saw, naturally and rightly, a danger to revealed religion in the spread of scientific rationalism. But London was not the only city to provide such education. A Mathematical Society was founded in Manchester in 1718 and introduced public lectures in mathematics the following year. James Jurin may have been lecturing on experimental philosophy in Newcastle-on-Tyne even as early as 1715. By the middle of the century there were few towns of importance that did not have their courses of lectures on science.† By the last third of the century there were evening classes both in London and the provincial towns designed entirely for adult mechanics and craftsmen. And, of course, lectures dealing with the material world rapidly shaded into discussions of related problems of man's position in the universe, the criticism of society, the

---

* See F. Sherwood Taylor, 'Science Teaching at the End of the Eighteenth Century' in *Natural Philosophy Through the Eighteenth Century and Allied Topics*, ed. Allan Ferguson, *Philosophical Magazine* Commemoration Number (London, 1948), pp. 150–52. John Keil was lecturing at Oxford 'by experiments in a mathematical manner' in 1700.

† N. Hans, *New Trends in Eighteenth Century Education* (London, 1951), pp. 136–52; A. E. Musson and Eric Robinson, 'Science and Industry in the late Eighteenth Century', *Ec. Hist. Rev.*, 2nd Series, xiii (1960–61), pp. 222–44. By the middle of the century there were many itinerant lecturers who could make a living by lecturing on science. 'Some of them were nationally famous in their day; others were rather more local figures, but their importance in the general pattern of scientific education has not been generally recognized.' ibid., p. 231. John Banks stated in 1795 that he had been giving lectures for twenty years. The study of public lecturing in eighteenth-century England has still to be undertaken.

truths of revealed as opposed to natural religion. The High Church party was quite right to view with anxiety the growth of public lectures: popular education led to questioning accepted beliefs in religion and politics. What began as scientific curiosity often ended in political and moral speculation.

There was a growing market in knowledge, the first rumblings of that cultural explosion which we think, quite wrongly, peculiarly our own. The demand for knowledge – not merely of science, but knowledge of every kind – began to acquire its momentum in the late seventeenth century. This is the era of encyclopaedias, not merely of the great French compilation, but a series of humble ones, from John Harris's splendid *Lexicon Technicum*, first published in 1709, to the small specialized dictionaries, gazetteers and textbooks.* And this, too, is the era of the part book, by which means men and women who could only afford a penny or twopence a week or month could acquire the knowledge for which they thirsted.† And, of course, it is the great age of circulating libraries and book clubs, though they were not all, of course, radical, rational and scientific, or even educational. In all libraries serious works hugely outnumbered fiction, and towards the end of the century there was an obvious connection between dissenters, liberals and libraries. At Birmingham eighteen out of nineteen members of the committee who ran the library were dissenters, led by Joseph Priestley; the originators of the London Library were men with a strong liberal bias, supporters of America and

* For example, Benjamin Martin's *Bibliotheca Technologica* (1739); Augustus de Morgan, *Arithmetical Books from the Invention of Printing to the Present Time* (London, 1847). Forty-one titles are listed as having been printed in London between 1650 and 1700: many of these ran into several editions, and a goodly number were directed specifically to tradesmen and artisans. See John Collins, *An Introduction to Merchants' Accompts* (1675) and John Mayne, *Socius Mercatoris: or the Merchant's Companion* (1674). Edward Hatton's *Merchants Magazine: the Assessors and Collectors Companion* went through six impressions between 1699 and 1712.

† R. M. Wiles, *Serial Publication in England before 1750* (Cambridge, 1957).

16

sympathetic to the early aspirations of the French revolution. Coleridge, when a young revolutionary, did much of his reading in the Bristol public library.* By the end of the century the thirst for knowledge was often to be found in combination with a critical and realistic attitude to politics and religion. And one may say, I think, that an attitude of increasing empiricism had by this time begun to permeate the lower strata of English society. Certainly governing circles thought so; they were horrified that miners were reading Thomas Paine.† But the most effective protagonists of the powers of critical reasoning were those on the fringe of political and social power.

Take Josiah Wedgwood, a man of little or no formal education. By the time he had reached maturity he had as absolute a faith in the efficacy of reason as a hot-gospeller in the literal truth of the Bible. Everything, he proclaimed, will yield to experiment, and he possessed an absolute mania for measuring, weighing, observing, recording and experimenting. Nor did he limit his consideration of the rational to his activities as a potter and entrepreneur. He thought both religion and politics should be subject to a like process. This led him to be a unitarian in the former and a radical in the latter – a warm supporter of the American colonists, a firm believer in universal suffrage and a level-headed sympathizer with the French revolution. Nor was Wedgwood a unique phenomenon, at least in his ideas – his gifts are another matter.‡ The creators of the industrial revolution, irrespective of their religious and political views, which naturally

* Paul Kaufman, 'The Community Library: A Chapter in English Social History', *Transactions of the American Philosophical Society*, vol. 57, pt 7 (Philadelphia, 1967). See also John Money, op. cit., pp. 226–37, for a valuable and detailed discussion of West Midland libraries from 1760 to 1793.

† M. G. Jones, *Hannah More* (Cambridge, 1952), p. 133. Also James T. Boulton, *The Language of Politics in the Age of Wilkes and Burke* (London, 1963), p. 138.

‡ His views, trenchantly expressed, may be found in his letters, *The Selected Letters of Josiah Wedgwood*, ed. Ann Finer and George Savage (London, 1965).

varied a great deal – Matthew Boulton was, for example, a firm supporter of George III and James Watt a conservative – possessed a far more conscious attitude to the positive benefits of useful knowledge and technological experiment than any body of manufacturers had hitherto possessed. They did not stumble on their inventions by chance. And their economic success strengthened their ideological attitude.*

The prospect of change in institutions of government might frighten the establishment – and the social and political establishment of late Hanoverian England was a very complex organism with long tap roots in local society both rural and urban – but it did not scare those excluded from it. And one should remember that a sense of exclusion could be as acute in Wolverhampton as in Westminster. The establishment was caught in a dilemma. The economic profits of innovation became steadily more obvious. Expansion was profitable, desirable: all liked wealth. But the quickening commercial and industrial life was creating opportunity for many who would have had no obvious opening in traditional society. For these people without traditional status the route upwards seemed to lead through the acquisition of useful knowledge. The demand for education became as insatiable as it was dangerous. It was a dilemma that has faced all traditional societies caught in the grip of industrialism, and a dilemma that was to shift from class to class as industrial society grew.

Of course, one must not overstress the relationship between a desire for education and knowledge and the development of a critical attitude to the problems of human destiny and social organization. After all, the education-hungry citizens of Birmingham flocked to hear the pseudo-scientist, Gustav Katterfelto, with his mixture of bogus magic and esoteric nonsense. Like their betters, they succumbed to bogus

* Robert E. Schofield, *The Lunar Society of Birmingham* (Oxford, 1963); A. E. Musson and Eric Robinson, *Science and Technology in the Industrial Revolution* (Manchester, 1969), p. 8. This book contains a wealth of valuable material on provincial societies, scientists and industrialists.

knowledge very easily – perhaps this, however, is merely a reflection of the strength of their faith in it. The important factor is that the pursuit of useful knowledge had acquired great momentum in urban society, particularly amongst the skilled mechanics and craftsmen as well as the factory owners. This demand for knowledge was supplied by a new and elaborate complex of cultural activities: booksellers in the provinces in 1600 were rare, in 1750 plentiful. No town of any importance was without circulating libraries, subscription book clubs or museums. Debating societies were to be found in every town of any commercial or industrial significance and their debates ranged over every type of religious, political, moral, economic, social and even scientific question.* In the large towns, as at Birmingham, societies were formed to attack the illiteracy and lack of education of the young skilled worker and the same aim was pursued by most of the early Sunday schools.† There would have been a very general acceptance of the motto that a printer in Birmingham stuck on to one of his political pamphlets: 'Ignorance is the Curse of God: Knowledge the wings wherewith we fly to Heaven.'‡

In this attitude there was a great deal of naïveté and there was to be much disillusion. Nevertheless it was widespread, and during the last three decades of the eighteenth century optimistically believed by most important sections of English society. The position, therefore, at the end of the eighteenth century was this: amongst those classes of men (and women) who had little share in social and political power, yet increasing economic opportunity, there was a growing belief in the powers of education and empiricism. Amongst the governing classes, however, apart from one or two notable exceptions, there had developed a growing distrust of critical attitudes, a growing sense of the necessity to protect

* The role of the debating society in helping to crystallize social attitudes amongst the artisan élites has been too little explored. The best survey is in John Money, op. cit., pp. 206–26, and Appendix II. Liverpool had a most active debating society whose meetings were reported in Cowburne's *Liverpool Chronicle* for 1768–9.

† Money, op. cit., pp. 252–3.   ‡ ibid., p. 248.

and to justify traditional institutions: and there was far less preoccupation amongst the élite both with science and with Baconian philosophy than there had been a hundred years previously. In the ruling class there was an increasing fear that the spread of education would lead to increased social dissent. Soame Jenyns was not alone in the theory that the poor should be kept in their ignorant bliss: Hannah More and the evangelicals shared it passionately.* Indeed the dangers of education had been realized for centuries, but now the dilemma was more acute. The need for educated men and women was growing faster and faster, and furthermore, because education was a saleable economic asset, the demand strengthened where the injustice of institutions pinched most grievously, amongst men who had little or no political power to redress them. To Burke and his colleagues the ancient constitution might possess the beauty of a Gothic cathedral, redolent of the slow accretions of time. Organic growth might mean a great deal to the Marquis of Rockingham, but little to the skilled mechanic avid for a place in the sun.

Increasingly rationalization rather than empiricism gained adherents amongst the governing classes, while faith in reason was to be found amongst the intellectual élite of the dissenters and their supporters and converts from flourishing provincial towns – Manchester, Newcastle, Birmingham, Bristol and even Norwich. These provincial centres were developing a new consciousness of themselves, of both their economic power and their social problems. They felt tradition to be inimical to their interests. It is in such places that we find knots of men of influence who supported Wilkes, opposed George III's American policy, sympathized with parliamentary reform, advocated the abolition of slavery

---

* M. G. Jones, op. cit., p. 152. 'My plan,' Hannah More wrote, 'for instructing the poor is very limited and strict. They learn of week days such coarse works as may fit them for servants. I allow of no writing. . . . Principles, not opinions, is what I labour to give them.' For Soame Jenyns and the poor's 'ignorant bliss' see *A Free Enquiry into the Nature and Origin of Evil* (1757).

and read with approval Voltaire as well as Priestley, and believed that they based all of their opinions on knowledge combined with rational principles.

Here, indeed, was soil in which critical attitudes could grow, gradually reclaiming the acres of ignorance and superstition. So startling were the results of science and technology, or as men of the eighteenth century preferred to put it, the arts and sciences (for they considered theory as art, mechanics as science), that one might have expected a quick victory and the growth of a society in Britain addicted to education, knowledge, experiment and the scientific attitude. It was not to be.

We still await that world. The forces of tradition were too strong: the threats of a rational attitude too grievous. The critical approach to reality by its very nature is radical. That is why faith in it tends always to sink deeper in society as that society grows in wealth. But as it sinks deeper, it is often unfortunately lost sight of on the surface. In late eighteenth-century England, political radicalism acquired two very uneasy allies, the Americans who fought for and won their independence and the French Jacobins who, following England's example of a former century, decapitated their king. What was worse, the French revolution began to apply reason to social institutions. Hence it was France, and those satellite countries which had responded to the revolutionary ideas, that acquired a far more realistic code of law and a sounder educational system than England.

For England's governing class rallied ever more strongly about their traditional institutions: they began to develop a curiously schizophrenic attitude to science, which gave rise to some of the greatest intellectual tensions of the Victorian age. Of its necessity there could be no question, of its truth in an immediate sense there could be no doubt, of its value for manufacture there could not be two opinions, but its implications for religion, morality and social structure bred nightmares. This situation was made more traumatic because England acquired an empire whose rationale was hard to justify except by irrational beliefs or bogus moral assertions. The class needed to man it was best prepared by traditional education: the classics and dogmatic Christianity. Science played little or no part in public school education and the society which had begun industrialization turned a cold shoulder to the intellectual disciplines and techniques upon which its economic greatness was founded.* But, of course, this was true of but a part of society: rationalism, secularism, a passionate belief in knowledge combined with a distrust of tradition and myth was still at work, but at a different level. But that is another and a long and complex story. The rift that we noticed happening in the middle of the eighteenth century gets deeper and wider and is still with us.

Although one can point to a number of astonishingly gifted men in eighteenth-century England whose attitude to human affairs – sceptical, Baconian, materialist – was very much in tune with the Enlightenment, with, say, the attitude of Diderot and the Encyclopaedists, they were comparatively rare. They were, for reasons that still need to be sought, more common in Scotland. Nor were they readily accepted in England. Hume was regarded as a heretic and somewhat dangerous: Gibbon's style was admired more than his ideas. Bentham was regarded as a crank and lesser luminaries, such as Priestley, as little better than agitators. The great English idols of the late eighteenth century were Burke, Blackstone and Dr Johnson. Nor must we assume that an empirical attitude totally dominated the new manufacturing classes. After all, Wesley, who was basically anti-intellectual, in spite of an amateur interest in electricity and physics, had the greatest triumphs in the new developing regions.

Some men had never had much difficulty in keeping the rational and the irrational in the same head. There is a clash of ideas and of attitudes at all levels of society: there

* Thomas Arnold, the 'reforming' headmaster of Rugby, was personally interested in science and its achievements, but he thought that its teaching could play no role of significance in the education of a Christian gentleman: for that the Bible and the classics were essential.

were plenty of irrational, conservative working men, enough in Birmingham to burn down Priestley's house. Their very act, however, argues the social spread of rational attitudes. A hundred years previously there would have been no house of a Priestley worth burning down and no rationalists to jeer at. In his notable essay of 1965, George Boas reminded us how slight were the grounds for calling the eighteenth century the Age of Reason.

However one defines the Age of Reason, however revolutionary and anti-authoritarian one estimates its spirit to have been, it should be noted that neither the Roman Catholic nor the Anglican nor the Lutheran communions ceased their ministrations in 1750. Moreover, in England, men like Burke and Johnson and Goldsmith, as much earlier Pope and Addison, continued to believe in the religion and philosophy of their forefathers. In spite of Voltaire the Church was not crushed, and as soon as Napoleon became Emperor, the short-lived educational programme of the *Idéologues* was ended. If rationalism in the sense of analysis of ideas was the platform of the French Enlightenment, it proved a very shabby one indeed. At most it survived for about ten years.*

This, however, is only half true. The impression arises through keeping one's eyes too fixedly on the peaks of culture or considering as typical those men whom subsequent generations have come to regard as symbolic of their time. One should remember that both Paine and Priestley were far more widely read than Johnson, Goldsmith or, probably, Burke. And that London society or Parisian society were not the only milieux where ideas were debated or exchanged. One needs to study the social permeation of ideas. And if one looks at the centres of intellectual life in the English provinces – at Manchester or Liverpool or Newcastle-on-Tyne or Birmingham or Leeds – one discovers a different picture. We do not find Diderots or Humes, neither do we find Johnsons. What we do find are knots of enlightened men with a passionate regard for empirical knowledge, secular in their intellectual attitudes, although

* George Boas, op. cit., p. 18.

often they are also muddled, uncertain and tentative. We must not expect consistency, nor be surprised when we find rational and irrational attitudes combined in the same man, but the tone of empiricist society in contrast with a society of taste is easy enough to discern.

We need a closer study of these provincial élites – such towns as Antwerp, Lyons, Marseilles, Nantes, Milan and many others.* It is there where we shall find the ideas unleashed by Locke and Newton on the one hand, Bayle and the Encyclopaedists on the other, being as naturally accepted as the empirical attitudes of the scientific revolution of which they were the true heirs. As a belief in empirical criticism weakened in the governing classes, it strengthened amongst those who traded and manufactured. Too much attention, it seems to me, is paid to the monopoly of ideas amongst the intellectual giants, too little to their social acceptance. Ideas acquire dynamism when they become social attitudes and this was happening in England. Reason was no longer the propaganda of a family of philosophers, it had become the weapon of a social class.

1971

* For an excellent study of one of these élites, as well as Schofield's *Lunar Society* cited above, see Eric Robinson, 'The Derby Philosophical Society' in *Annals of Science* (1953), ix, pp. 359–67.

2

Bedlam

Although human societies are capable of infinite variety in customs, morals, social organization and disposal of wealth and power, all breed individuals who are so aberrant – mad, if you wish – that they cannot be absorbed into the accepted patterns of living. And it was these – the idiots, the madmen, the mentally deficient – who, with the crippled at birth, created, perhaps, man's oldest social problem. Such wild aberrations from the norm not only needed to be explained, which was rarely difficult, but also to be treated. The easiest explanation was that such human deformities – idiots, dwarfs, cripples, and at some times and in some places even twins – were manifestations of evil, the devil's work, and so best destroyed as soon as born. And, of course, no matter how absurd the reasoning, the biological effect was good – wild mutations were prevented from breeding. In general the more primitive the society, the more likely it was that draconian measures would be used against creatures who would be a social burden from birth. They would need to be nursed and fed and protected, an extravagance that poor food gatherers, hunters and peasants could not afford.

Certainly, exposure of the physically and obviously mentally deformed has been widely practised, and still is, if in a more sophisticated guise. Until very recent times, twins were killed at once by tribes living along the banks of the lower Niger in West Africa, and even in our own societies hideous monstrosities that can and do occur are not encouraged to live, even in the best equipped hospitals. And yet, even palaeolithic man could be tender. A skeleton has been discovered at Shanidar in the Zagros mountains of a man of forty, with a severely deformed shoulder and arm, so badly deformed that he could never have been much use as a hunter or as a provider of food. But he lived for his time a very long life. Someone explained his weakness away: compassion, love or possibly ingenious ratiocination triumphed over terror and the burden of deformity. Of course, many abnormalities are not obvious at birth. Mongolism in children is not easily discoverable in the first few weeks of life: schizophrenia, hysteria, hallucinations manifest themselves quite often in adolescence. In early childhood the babbling of the idiots and the sane is not far apart. And often men and women live in two worlds, the sane and the insane, flitting like bats in and out of darkness. And the menopause was no kinder to women in earlier societies, if they reached it, than it is today. This and widowhood, combined with loneliness and poverty, drove many an old village woman to the borderlands of sanity. And those borderlands possessed their own magnetism in earlier ages. In the West, as in many continents and in many societies, they were peopled by devils: mysteries could be learnt there; mysteries that led through to power over men and beasts, over the wind and the weather. Magic and madness were near allied.

So all human societies, no matter how small, were sooner or later confronted with a profound problem – what to do with the mad, whether permanently insane or intermittently so: how did one ward off the powers that possessed them?

The response was diverse: as diverse as human beings could make it. In some Siberian and Amerindian tribes, the hysteric or the epileptic was reverenced as the mouthpiece of the gods, to be cherished in awe. Frequently in medieval Europe and even later, the simple-minded were regarded as possessing a kind of innocence, the innocence indeed of children, hence close to God. Sometimes if they were very lucky and perhaps capable of exploiting their position, they might become the plaything of a noble household, along with a dwarf or a two-headed calf, to amuse the children or provide bucolic comedy for the master of the household. Such idiots were lucky; most suffered a harsher fate. Until very recent times, villages had their ogres locked up in attics, chained in cellars, filthy, half-starved, treated worse than animals. A few were tolerated, allowed to wander at large, the object of derision, to be pelted and tormented by half-frightened boys. More unnerving still to the village were the mad old women and men, potential witches and wizards, who might release the forces of evil: bring disease to cattle, blight to crops and sterility to women. But because their power could control evil too – out-hex the hexes – they were needed. Although the mad old might be tolerated, at times an orgy of hysteria would sweep them to the gallows or the fire, along with a bevy of totally sane but victimized men, women and children: victims, as at Salem, of the unbalanced hysterics. For century after century madness added a dimension of fear and terror and drama, as well as cruelty and comedy, to village life, but most communities lived with it face to face, day after day. The drooling of the idiot and the fierce cries of the chained madmen were everyday experiences throughout the world, century after century. From earliest childhood everyone was aware of chronic insanity.

In towns, especially large towns, the problem was more difficult. There was a less close family relationship than in villages; and far more isolated individuals drifted into London or Paris or Milan, totally alone and without friends. Disease decimated towns: plagues blew up like tornados and laid the urban population waste: many a sole survivor of a family had to fend as best he might, and death did not always take those least fitted to survive.

So the problem of the insane at times became much more of a communal and less of a family responsibility. True, in the great cities the majority of the mad were kept in the family which produced them – their own private horror. The burden of the rest during the Middle Ages fell, of course, on the Church, and particularly on the monasteries. Just as they felt a responsibility for the sick and old, so they did for the witless, and indeed, in England, they were encouraged to do so by the Crown and by the patriarchs of the City of London. The capital was ringed with monastic hospitals many of which contained a miracle-working relic, some specific to a disease, and some remarkable for their efficacy. Indeed one cure for the mad was to truss them up by an altar and leave them in the church overnight. This, like whipping, frequently administered, or ducking in water, acted as a shock treatment, and if records may be believed occasionally worked wonders. But, then as now, the incurable remained incurable: and when Britain's most famous hospital for the insane, Bedlam (i.e. Our Lady of Bethlehem), emerges into the full light of history in 1403, the grim facts speak for themselves. A Royal Commission investigated the defalcations of Peter Taverner, the hospital's porter. Among his thefts are listed:

2 pairs of stocks,
4 pairs of iron manacles,
5 other chains of iron,
6 chains of iron with locks,

strange gear for a monastery dedicated to the worship of Our Lady, but essential, for already Bedlam was the leading repository for the luckier of London's lunatics. Lucky, because even if chained to a post in a small cell, they were fed and their personal wants attended to: in the rough, brutal medieval world at least they had what so many were denied, the basic essentials of life – a roof and food. Even though, as the centuries passed, Bedlam grew into one of the largest and most magnificent of hospitals, it was never large enough. The majority of the mad never had the luck to get there. They remained the responsibility of their families, who kept them as best they might or, if poor, friendless, and rejected, the fools either fended for themselves or ended up in the workhouse. As the Home Secretary wrote in 1807:

There is hardly a parish in which may not be found some unfortunate creature chained in the cellar or garret of a workhouse, fastened to the leg of a table, tied to a post in an outhouse, or perhaps shut up in an uninhabited ruin; or sometimes he would be

28

left to ramble half naked or starved through the streets or highways, teased by the scoff and jest of all that is vulgar, ignorant
and unfeeling.

And that was after two centuries of growing humanity
towards the insane!

This growth was slow, as it ever is where prejudice and
deep fear battle with compassion. Yet compassion was never
absent. Much of it was casual, semi-superstitious – the gift of
a coin, a small personal sacrifice to ward off evil, to pay, as
it were, for one's own luck. Even in the fourteenth century,
citizens of London had wandered out beyond Bishopsgate
on Sundays and feast days to look with curiosity and fear at
the lunatics in the hospitals of Bethlehem, Spitalfields and
Bridewell. And many were moved to leave small donations
to help relieve the sufferings they had witnessed: one or two
were more deeply stirred or, with personal experience of the
horrors of madness, bequeathed all that they possessed. By
1550 Bedlam had become an established institution, re-
nowned throughout the world.

With the growth of vagabondage in the sixteenth century,
when chronic inflation and population growth drove many
poor men to desperate measures, 'Tom o' Bedlam' became
a common imposture. In torn clothing, often daubed with
blood, these pretenders would scare villagers with their mad
antics until bought off with food and drink. They preyed
on the unwary in towns and villages as well as in London.
They soon passed into folklore and into literature. In the age
of Shakespeare and Jonson 'Tom o' Bedlam' was one of the
most popular of songs. Later it was said to have been set to
music by Purcell.

> From forth my sad and darksome cell,
> And from the deep abyss of hell
> Poor Tom is come to view the world again
> To see if he can ease distempered brain.
> Fear and despair possess his soul
> Hark how the angry furies howl.

By Shakespeare's day Bethlehem had weathered the
Reformation. The monks, including the exorcists who had

29

done their best to relieve those obviously possessed by devils, had been pensioned off. The holy relics, often so efficacious at least temporarily, were destroyed, the altars hacked to pieces; but the buildings and endowments remained. Indeed the endowments grew, and Bethlehem gradually became what it had perhaps not been before, a hospital devoted entirely to the insane. Within a hundred years it had become not only one of the great show places of London, but a must for all foreign travellers. Every day its rooms and corridors were filled with curious spectators: on 'Sundays and holidays the crowds became prodigious'. And so there came into being a spectacle which to modern tastes seems as repellent, as macabre, as ghoulish as the eighteenth century's fascination with public executions and public torture. Those who visited Bedlam were not the riff-raff of society but, often, the sophisticated and well-educated middle class, the same class of people who in Paris fought to get tickets to watch Damiens torn apart by horses, after being broken on the wheel, for attempting to assassinate Louis XV. By the middle of the eighteenth century Bedlam was established as one of the sights of Europe. In 1794 William Hutton, a struggling and poverty-stricken bookseller from Birmingham, felt that his penny spent on visiting Bedlam had, indeed, been well spent. It was the only entertainment that he allowed himself.

It was not only the drama, the horror, the comic and the macabre that drew English visitors in their thousands and foreigners in their hundreds. Bedlam was also one of the architectural splendours of London. In Charles II's reign it had moved from its old medieval site to a new one in Moorfields, a little further to the west. Here a building had been planned for the specific purpose of housing lunatics, the very first of its kind. The design had been given to one of England's most famous scientists, Robert Hooke, the secretary of the newly founded Royal Society and a close friend of Sir Christopher Wren, whom it is thought may have suggested the elevation with its markedly French features. Be that as it may, the design was elegantly functional, with wings for male and female inmates, cells with iron grilles for the ferociously mad, large galleries for the gentle insane, in which they were free to walk and talk with the visitors, and big high-walled courtyards for exercise. All foreign visitors were amazed by its orderliness, its efficiency and its cleanliness. Indeed no city in Europe could boast so well-designed a lunatic asylum.

Also the host of visitors which may strike us as macabre possessed considerable value, both for the inmates and the governors themselves. Everyone had to pay at least a penny to get in: of course, collecting boxes abounded, and frequently the generosity of visitors was stimulated by the misery which they witnessed within. Again, physicians of the day maintained that the company of visitors, the conversation, even the laughter and merriment and the noise which was often provided to entertain them, invigorated the spirits of the inmates and helped to relieve their condition. In a sense there was in this spectacle a rough, coarse humanity that worked both ways. True, the visitors often laughed themselves silly at the antics of the man who thought he was the Great Cham of China, or hugely enjoyed the religious ravings of a self-appointed saint. This to us is gross and argues a deplorable insensitivity, but the total isolation of the insane into padded cells and strait-jackets, with visits restricted to a minimum and confined only to close friends and relations, which was to come in the nineteenth and twentieth centuries also shows considerable insensitivity. By pushing away horror, the need for compassion disappears too: if we save ourselves knowledge of the terrors of madness, by so doing, we perhaps diminish our own humanity.

The tastes of men and women throughout Europe in the eighteenth century were stronger. They lived closer to the realities of life – to poverty, to disease, to violence, to madness and to death. And, even to the most sensitive and humane of men, Bedlam was a part of life's terrible realities. Furthermore, it usually held within its cells some men of eminence, whose condition seemed to give added point to the moralities and beliefs of the age. For example, Oliver Cromwell's porter, Daniel, a religious maniac, proved a great attraction for many years after the Restoration and his condition was used to demonstrate the follies of excessive puritanism. A sprinkling of well-born men and women, noblemen and gentry, illustrated the vanity of worldly riches. The small clutch of scholars from Oxford and Cambridge pointed the dangers of excessive study, whilst rip-roaring, red-faced, drunken Nathaniel Lee, bad poet yet successful playwright, underlined the folly of the bohemian life. Indeed Bedlam could be and was used to illustrate that homely, middle-class morality in which most citizens of London believed.

It is not surprising, therefore, that Bedlam inspired William Hogarth, the compassionate moralist, whose pictures when engraved sold in their thousands. Amongst his most successful were the series called 'The Rake's Progress' – the story of the young heir, Thomas Rakewell, who through folly and dissipation is swindled and robbed by the rapacious crooks of London until in the last picture he is shown being manacled in Bedlam, vacant-eyed, wild with scarcely suppressed violence. Hogarth did not invent. He must have visited Bedlam time and time again, for many of the well-known incurable lunatics adorn his canvas: the idiot who thought he was the Pope, the crazed astronomer, and in the locked cells two of the great sights of Bedlam – one maniac who insisted on living like Nebuchadnezzar with the beasts of the field and the other who lived in an uncontrollable religious frenzy. This picture is one of Hogarth's greatest. It is austere, totally lacking in sentimentality: the mad are obviously totally mad, nothing relieves their insanity, all the absurdities are there, down to the musician wearing a paper hat made out of a score. The cruel reality lingers in every line and the result is harrowing. Few could contemplate Hogarth's picture without feeling compassion, or without feeling both a sense of luck and of danger. Here are men and women like ourselves, here we may be too.

Hogarth was well aware that he had painted a masterpiece and he held back the engraving of it until the day after the Copyright Bill, for which he had fought, became law. He proved wise, for he made a small fortune from this series and it was not long before the engraving plates were so worn that they had to be recut. Indeed it proved so popular, particularly the Bedlam scene, that pirated versions were soon on sale, along with savage caricatures of Hogarth as an inmate of Bedlam.

The deep note of pathos that is struck in Hogarth's pictures is indicative of a growing mood amongst the more thoughtful and sensitive men and women of the eighteenth century who were concerned about the brutalities, super-stitions and coarseness of an earlier age. True, they went to Bedlam as to a menagerie, but they were pained, not amused, by what they saw. They grew to hate the carnival atmosphere, the coarse jokes played on the inmates, the obscenities that were provoked with the mad females. 'I think it,' said Harley, the hero of Henry Mackenzie's best-selling novel, *The Man of Feeling*, 'an inhuman practice to expose the greatest misery with which our nature is afflicted to every idle visitant who can afford a trifling perquisite to the keeper; especially as it is a distress which the humane must see with a painful reflection that it is not in their power to alleviate it.'

That double stress on humanity and humane behaviour is in tune with the best spirits of the age, with the rising tide of enlightenment which touched the problems of insanity, crime and punishment as well as education, philosophy and politics. A generation earlier the magazine *The World* had protested against the inhumanity of spectators who made a sport of the inmates, and the tide of protest grew so strong that visitors were allowed to see female patients only under the strictest conditions. In 1770 admittance to Bedlam was restricted to ticket holders, who had to be accompanied by a keeper. Certainly this reduced the holiday atmosphere and kept out the apprentices and their girls, who had previously paid a penny for their sport, but the well-dressed middle class who were prepared to pay could still indulge their macabre tastes. However, it was the beginning of a deep change in social attitude to madness, an indication that the tide had begun to flow towards greater compassion and better treatment.

After the exorcist had quit with the Reformation, medical practitioners, incompetent, clumsy and baffled, took their place. They offered little at first in the way of cure except restraint, whipping and shock, and the usual paraphernalia of low diets, bleedings and violent emetics. There still lingered the belief that derangement and possession were close allied and that only God could heal the sufferings He had allowed to come about. But as the decades turned into centuries, science and humanity won their slow, tenuous victories. After 1660 the aristocracy and upper middle classes in England became increasingly affluent. They could afford to ease the burden of family horror by sending off its mad member to private asylums, which by Daniel Defoe's day had proliferated around London. Wisely he pressed for their public inspection, but another century was to pass before that was achieved. And so naturally they varied. Often they were far more inhumane than Bedlam with its stream of visitors could ever be. Sometimes the mad were brutalized and starved to death: heirs and heiresses were kept incarcerated after they had recovered their reason, even if they had ever lost it (this happens less often in real life than in romantic fiction, but there are authenticated stories). Some asylums, however, were kept by highly intelligent, fully qualified doctors bred in the traditions of Bacon, Harvey and the Royal Society. It was one of these, the Rev. Dr Willis, who was called in to treat George III.* Willis kept a private asylum in Lincolnshire which was a mixture of traditional obscurantism and enlightenment.

Blow was returned for blow; the strait-jacket was rapidly applied if needed, and the usual bleedings, blisters and low diets resorted to, but the insane were not confined. They lived two by two in cottages with a keeper. They were

---

* It is now being argued that George III was suffering from porphyria, a disease of the kidneys whose symptoms are similar to manic depression, but whether this was true or not, to his wife, his Court and his ministers George III appeared mad, and he was treated as such.

encouraged to take a great deal of exercise in the open air. Willis did his best to provide cheerful, almost gay surroundings: indeed he maintained that bodily health combined with cheerfulness worked his cures, and his method certainly led to George III's recovery in 1789, when a recovery seemed impossible. Perhaps George III would have recovered in any case, but certainly Willis's successful treatment gave an enormous fillip to the humane treatment of lunatics. Gradually, as the eighteenth century turned into the nineteenth, in England, France and Italy little knots of dedicated men began a public crusade on behalf of the mad. In Paris in 1795 Dr Pinel ordered all chains to be taken off the insane at the Salpêtrière, France's Bedlam. A few decades later Gibbon Wakefield and Lord Shaftesbury made a *cause célèbre* out of old Norris, the famous madman of Bedlam, who had been chained up for decades. Nor did they forget the village idiots, the workhouse horrors, and the senile old. They pressed for proper asylums, and if at first these proved little better than hygienic prisons, it was an advance on the old brutality and neglect. Yet, like 'workhouse', the very word 'asylum' struck terror into the hearts of the nineteenth-century working class, with its visions of padded cells and strait-jackets. Nothing has been harder for society to accept than the fact that mental illness is just an illness, a sickness of the brain, and as devoid of moral implication as disease of the heart or liver.

The mad were better cared for later in the nineteenth century in the great new hospital built for Bedlam in South London; no one could deny that. The manacles went, the whippings were abolished, the jeering crowds vanished. And yet there was loss. The insane were deprived of contact with normal life; the high-spirited jostling, the noise, the music, the sense of a real world about them had been of great benefit for those who lived in the twilight world between sanity and madness. The great grim asylums possessed their own inhumanity and in recent times there has been a fresh attempt to bring the mad back into contact with normal living and family life. However, no one would

35

wish a return to a world in which Bedlam was a model of modernity.

We often underestimate the great changes which began in the eighteenth century. Too often the eighteenth-century enlightenment is dismissed as superficial, yet it marks the decisive turning point in the growth of European civility – that age that saw the spread of humane feeling – to women, to children, to criminals and to the insane. The grossness and brutality of early ages may have taken a long time to die: indeed much is still with us, but in many aspects of life growing civility has been maintained. Few would now find merriment in the antics of a madman, and it is rare, thank God, for a village idiot to be baited like a bear. The vile, crude world of yokels that Bosch and Brueghel painted for us has faded into oblivion, and so, too, has Hogarth's Bedlam. And when, as we so often do, we despise our own world, belittle our own achievements, ignore the world's growing civility, it is as well to be reminded of such things.

1969

3

Henry Fielding and the Rise of the Novel

The most astonishing aspect of the English novel, and the European novel as well, is how young a thing it is, a bare two centuries old, a seedling, so to speak, in the ancient garden of literature. At the time of its birth, its very medium, prose, occupied a rather low estate. For in spite of the success of Cervantes' great epic, *Don Quixote*, few great writers in the sixteenth and seventeenth centuries used it, outside the theatre. The proper vehicle for the highest expression of human feeling remained verse – verse, too, that was not only hedged about by its own elaborate rules of prosody but also strictly limited in its diction: many words of common usage were regarded as alien to good poetry as a botched rhyme or mishandled caesura. Within this narrow literary compass, great genius had found little difficulty in expressing itself Shakespeare, Milton, Dryden, Corneille, Racine, Camoëns had given the world works of enduring quality. And comedy and satire – in Lope de Vega, in Molière, in Congreve – found a satisfactory outlet in prose drama.

Prose, of course, was used for some imaginative literature – especially for political or religious allegory such as Bunyan's *Pilgrim's Progress* – as well as for the romantic literature that was needed to fill the lonely hours and lonelier imaginations of many women. But such books did not receive much critical attention at the time and most are now forgotten. Apart from Bunyan's work, only a few romances, like the works of Mrs Aphra Behn – a curious mixture of platitudinous morality, wild adventure, and blatant eroticism –

37

have crept into the histories of literature; but most of these prose works, allegories or romances, are so lacking in merit that their existence is only known to bibliophiles.

Within a brief space of fifty years, 1700 to 1750, a dramatic literary revolution took place in England, one that was to influence the world's literature profoundly. Through Defoe, Swift, Richardson and, above all, Henry Fielding, prose, through the medium of the novel, came to be regarded as a proper vehicle for the expression of the *full* imaginative treatment of man's entire moral and emotional life: comedy, satire, tragedy could be expressed realistically, through the description of the lives and adventures of men and women whom the readers could recognize as similar to themselves. The kings and princes, the ancient Romans, distant Greeks and improbable Persians of seventeenth-century literature gave way to apprentices, serving maids, squires, doctors, lawyers, parsons, everyday people doing everyday jobs. Their adventures were usually odd, but their reactions, their emotional responses, belonged to the recognized world of eighteenth-century middle-class England.

The greatest innovator of this new realistic fiction was Daniel Defoe, spy, crook, journalist, tradesman: and father of the English novel. His quest for realism often led him to use actual records, and it is still difficult to disentangle fact from fiction in many of his novels. Defoe possessed a wonderful sense of the telling incident, a flexible prose of marvellous clarity, and a natural story-teller's control of narrative. But his imagination was prosaic: and the factual surface of life mattered more to him than emotional response to it. His interest in psychological conflict or the divided personality was non-existent, and his innovations might easily have ended with himself. Swift's *Gulliver's Travels* shows how much of Defoe's technique could be adapted for satire and, also, how easily Defoe's work might have ended in little else.

But the hunger of the reading public for realistic, or semi-realistic, fiction, which had been revealed by Defoe's success, still remained. It was educated to a more sophisticated diet by Samuel Richardson, a seemingly commonplace little man who made a modest living as a bookseller.

Richardson possessed none of Defoe's qualities. His experience of life was narrow, his interests limited and his style dull and verbose: but his imagination was capable of projection into lives totally different from his own. He chose a technique – a novel in the form of letters between two correspondents – that would have taxed the genius of the most sophisticated craftsmen in fiction, and a theme – the attack on the chastity of an unmarried girl – that had been made tedious by generations of writers of ephemeral romantic literature. His success, therefore, was as staggering as the originality that he revealed. His novel, *Pamela*, established itself, in spite of absurdities and the flat-footed boredom of much of Richardson's moralizing, as a great work of art, a contribution to literature of the greatest importance. The reason for this could be found in Richardson's careful investigation of the psychology of his characters, their hesitations, anxieties, illusions and self-doubts, all done with the utmost realism. In his book, characters no longer illustrated a principle, a humour, or a type, but were unique individuals, deeply concerned with the problems of morality that their age set for them. And it was both to add a sense of immediacy to these, as well as to intensify the appearance of reality, that Richardson made his heroine a servant girl. Indeed to suggest that such a girl might not only defend her chastity but also convert her pursuer to her own moral values gave a startlingly original twist to his theme. It entranced Richardson's middle-class audience.

The bookseller's moralizing, however, struck his satirical, aristocratic contemporary, Henry Fielding, as ludicrous and absurd. Full of contempt, he produced a parody called *Shamela*, and so launched himself on a course as a novelist that was to make him greater than either Defoe or Richardson. Lacking Defoe's almost brutal sense of external reality, and certainly devoid of Richardson's sensitive intuition of inner life, Fielding was nevertheless a more gifted novelist than either, showing greater technical range and, perhaps, a deeper sense of humanity, if not of specific human beings. His great books, *Tom Jones, Joseph Andrews, Amelia* and *Jonathan Wild,* drew deeply on his own wide experience of the vicious, tumultuous and savage life of eighteenth-century England.

Henry Fielding's great-grandfather was an earl. One grandfather was an archdeacon, the other a judge, and his father a soldier who in the fullness of time became a general. By ancestry, therefore, Fielding would seem to belong, unlike Defoe or Richardson, to the highest circles of eighteenth-century English society. In fact, he lived a hand-to-mouth, often debt-ridden existence. He was friendly with few of the great, but drawn to men like William Hogarth, the painter, whose savage satires on tawdriness, cruelty and poverty portrayed a world that Fielding knew at first hand.

Success played hide-and-seek with Fielding and affluence came but slowly, so slowly that Death was already lurking in the wings by the time Fielding had really prospered. His was a difficult life, and more often than not a sad one; yet it was made endurable and significant by the huge appetite, the wonderful gusto, the irrepressible humanity that he brought to living. He loved human beings, particularly the odd, the gullible, the transparent man of good intentions. He knew enough of the baseness of men to guard his spirit with an ironic shield, but his irony never crushed his instinctive wonder nor turned his hope to despair.

He was born on 22 April 1707, the eldest son of Edmund Fielding, a soldier of fortune, active in Marlborough's wars. Sarah, his mother, was the daughter of Sir Henry Gould, the judge. Something of an heiress, his mother inherited a small estate which her father carefully entailed on his grand-children, to the exclusion of their feckless father. By the time Henry was eleven his mother was dead and his father, who had already dissipated what money he had by gambling, soon married again, this time an Italian and a Roman Catholic. He quarrelled violently with Lady Gould, who started proceedings against him, partly to get the little estate out of his clutches and partly to shield the children from the

Roman Catholicism of their stepmother. The father lost, and Henry, who had been packed off to Eton, was brought up with his sisters by his grandmother, partly in Somerset and partly in London.

His father went on living his rackety life, running through two more wives but climbing slowly up the military ladder, and always spending any money that he could lay his hands on. Nevertheless, Fielding remained attached to his father, although he was thoughtless, unreliable, and probably an inveterate gambler. Such a father probably strengthened Fielding's craving for the simple, good life, lived in a tranquil countryside, but at the same time he introduced him to the wild, dissolute, intensely provocative life of London that always held Fielding in its grip; thereby creating that dichotomy between illusion and reality that is one of the most attractive features of his novels.

He left Eton at eighteen, neither proceeding to the university nor going on the Grand Tour. Aristocratic origins he might have, but near-poverty was his lot. He tried to alleviate it by carrying off a fifteen-year-old heiress, Sarah Andrew, but her trustee thwarted his attempt, and Fielding only succeeded in making a nuisance of himself. London proved to be his destiny: neither his nature nor his abilities would permit him to settle down as a country gentleman of small estate, even had he possessed the means to buy one.

London in the 1720s was a rip-roaring place: a vivid contrast between extravagant luxury and grinding poverty – the London of Hogarth's 'Rake's Progress', 'Marriage à la Mode', 'Beer Street' and 'Gin Lane' – tough, brutal, savage, yet full of colour and life; luxurious and magnificent for the rich, harsh and disease-ridden for the poor. It was a world in which the crafty, the sly and the hypocritical could get away with deceit and double-dealing, where the good-natured, honest man could easily be overborne, where morality was at a discount. The law was slow and expensive and witnesses not difficult to suborn. The vices and follies of mankind were written large across the metropolis. The great and powerful could exercise, usually unrebuked, petty tyranny, and the good man had to find satisfaction not in public acclaim but in private knowledge of his ethical behaviour. Towering over this riotous, rich, rough, ruthless society was 'the Great Man', as Sir Robert Walpole, the king's minister, was known. He ran politics, the Court, and Parliament. Few men had ever acquired so much power as he or roused up such a vigorous or so gifted a literary opposition. Swift, Pope, Gay had all tried to get favours from Sir Robert; all had failed. So they poured out their hatred in some of the most brilliant satires England has known. *Gulliver's Travels, The Dunciad, The Beggar's Opera*, were all aimed at 'the Great Man'. In ballads, pamphlets, burlesques and plays, Walpole was mercilessly lampooned, to the delight of Londoners, who enjoyed this novel paper war with the gusto it deserved.

It was an exciting literary world that young Fielding entered in 1729. He had spent eighteen months at Leyden University studying literature and he felt fully equipped to take London by storm. In the next nine years, Fielding wrote twenty-six plays – enough for the lifetime of a modern dramatist, but in the eighteenth century the theatre catered for a small audience and within a few performances everyone who was likely to wish to see the play had done so. In consequence, dramatists needed to work hard and fast to get a living. Fielding produced, almost at command, anything that could be acted – comedies, farces, ballad-operas, burlesques and dramatic satires; he avoided only tragedy. George Bernard Shaw, in one of his more extraordinary *ex cathedra* judgements, maintained that this work of Fielding's made him England's most considerable dramatist, Shakespeare alone excepted, between the Middle Ages and the end of the nineteenth century.

For the few who have read Fielding's plays, this will seem less bewildering than for those who have not. Everything that Fielding wrote sparkled with intellectual energy and verbal irony of the kind that Shaw admired: 'I tell thee, caitiff, gaols in all countries are only habitations for the poor, not for men of quality' (*Don Quixote in England*), or

'Marriage, like self-murder, requires an immediate resolution' (*The Wedding Day*). His plays were almost entirely political or social, bitter about the Court and Parliament or equally savage in the exposure of the vice and folly and debauchery of contemporary London life. *Beyond the Fringe* or *The Establishment* are tepid stuff compared with Fielding's razor-edged satire. He was totally careless of the laws of libel, indifferent to any charge of obscenity, and gave full rein to a genuine, pessimistic hatred of the political corruption that ulcerated English life, as in *A Rehearsal of Kings* in which Walpole appears thinly disguised as 'Macplunderkan, King of Rognomania'.

At that time, during Sir Robert Walpole's administration, many sensible and intelligent men believed that the high ideals of liberty, for which their fathers and grandfathers had fought and died in the seventeenth century, were being destroyed by self-seeking politicians, interested only in the riches that power could bring. With the steady growth of a literate public such bitter satire as Fielding and his fellow authors produced found a warm and responsive audience. The theatres were crowded, his plays were rapturously received, and he could live the wild life that his father had taught him to enjoy. His dark, saturnine, ironic face was often to be seen in the *bagnios* of Covent Garden or the boxes at Ranelagh.

Yet when fame and fortune seemed to be at his feet, Walpole acted. In 1737, prompted almost entirely by the violence of Fielding's satire, an Act of Parliament was passed that required all plays to have the permission of the Lord Chamberlain before they were performed on the English stage. For Fielding, it meant ruin, for he knew that he would be banned. Satire was his trade; irony his genius. His career disappeared overnight.

Fielding, however, was now a married man with children to feed, and he faced a bleak future. So he played safe, turned away from literature and became a lawyer, using what little capital he had acquired to secure professional qualifications. He had no success. He toured the Western

Circuit as a barrister, but briefs were few and meanly paid. His bitterness and resentment towards Walpole grew in intensity. He edited, in order to eke out a threadbare existence, as well as to vent his spleen, the major opposition newspaper, *The Champion*. But straightforward political diatribe cramped his imagination. He proved competent, for he was too good with words not to be, but he was neither better nor worse than a score of political journalists. Fielding had lost his way. Fortunately his fury at the lush sentimentality and hypocritical piety of *Pamela* became so intense that he had to vent it in print. His ironic satire *Shamela*, a book which he never acknowledged, had great success. Almost immediately he began a longer skit which grew into a full-sized book, and one that established Fielding as one of the founding fathers of the English novel.

Joseph Andrews, a footman, was Pamela's brother and, like her, his chastity, lovingly cherished, was endangered by his lascivious, middle-aged employer, Lady Boothby – a ludicrous situation that is made serious and revealing by the insight that Fielding displays into the feelings of a rich, highly placed woman, tormented by her lusts. Realizing his powers as he rapidly scribbled thousands of words, Fielding developed *Joseph Andrews* beyond satire into a comic epic, deliberately modelled on Cervantes' *Don Quixote*: extraordinary incidents, strange coincidences, remarkable adventures stud Joseph's journey from London to the village of his youth. His companion, the English Quixote, is Parson Adams, one of the great creations of English fiction – and one that other writers adopted as assiduously as other painters copied the pose of Titian's 'Venus'.

Adams is the lovable, gullible, eccentric ass with a golden heart and unbreakable endurance. He is poor, bullied, set upon by Fate. Absent-minded, crazed with unrealizable hopes and drugged with improbable ambitions, he is tossed from misfortune to misfortune, yet he is never soured, never rancorous, never evil-minded. He will fight but never bully; denounce but never rail; act but never deceive. The result is a character larger than life, yet as actual as a living man.

Adams might easily have become incredible, but Fielding was careful to domesticate his epic by the use of realistic details. He drew on his carefully observed knowledge of the drifting riff-raff of the eighteenth-century English highways to give verisimilitude to Adams's adventures. Bad barrister Fielding might be, but his imagination had never been more alert than when he hacked his way along the dreary miles of the Western Circuit.

Joseph Andrews combined the realistic detail of a Defoe with some of the psychological subtlety of a Richardson, but it also possessed a quality which neither Defoe nor Richardson possessed – a warm, an irrepressible joy in human beings, an irresistible sense of the delight of instinctive life. Astonishing high spirits, mixed with ironic compassion, breed in this book a feeling of delight. The coldness of Defoe and the sensitive myopic probing of Richardson are replaced by an almost riotous appetite for life in all its forms. Yet this boisterous book was written in a few weeks against a background of poverty and despair: Fielding's daughter, aged six, was mortally ill, his wife on the verge of death, his pockets empty, his prospects miserable, and his own health insecure.

London received his book with acclaim. A few critics, the poets Thomas Gray and William Shenstone, were a little cool, but the public snapped up the first edition. Spurred by his success, Fielding set about his old rival, Sir Robert Walpole, who, ironically enough, had tottered to his fall from power in the same month that Fielding achieved his remarkable success as a novelist, in February 1742 – a nice irony that Fielding appreciated. He took a real character, Jonathan Wild, the notorious fence who had been exposed and hanged before one of London's largest crowds in 1725, and he used Wild's life as an allegory of Sir Robert Walpole's ministry. The setting is Hogarthian in its realistic horror. Fielding knew London's underworld as well as the painter whose close friend and admirer he was. The pimps, bawds, thieves, blackmailers, corrupt justices and professional witnesses of London's underworld are presented in *Jonathan Wild*

45

with the same savage realism that Defoe might have given them.

Although Wild gets his deserts, this book's most haunting quality is the sense of man's brutality to man; the lurking disaster that awaits all good men: that no life, not even a life as virtuous as Heartfree's, the foil to Wild, can escape pain, misery, degradation. Even in circumstances as revolting as the tribulations of Heartfree, Fielding, however, maintains that some men can remain the epitome of goodness. Goodness fascinated Fielding. It did most eighteenth-century writers: *The Vicar of Wakefield* by Oliver Goldsmith is a novel concerned with little else. Indeed the goodness of men preoccupied an eighteenth-century novelist as much as the loneliness of the individual does a modern writer. In many ways it is the constant theme of Fielding's books, as much a part of his last two masterpieces *Tom Jones* and *Amelia*, as of the books just described, and it is as well to understand why.

The humanity that Fielding knew lived in a brutal, depraved, drink-sodden, debauched jungle. As a barrister, he had spent months with the human flotsam and jetsam that washed in and out of the courts of justice. When in 1749 Fielding at last received a crumb of patronage for his years of political propaganda, it was the post of stipendiary magistrate at Bow Street, London; and day after day he had to sit in court, dealing with the riff-raff of the most vicious quarter of London. Fielding knew all too well the human vultures who preyed on the weak, the stupid, the gullible and the feckless. His daily experience was of the dregs of human society. His knowledge of human corruption was, perhaps, wider, if not deeper, than that of any novelist who has lived.

In this world, Fielding quickly realized, the ruthless, the tough, the men of power and money, could all too easily win: they could bribe, kidnap, even kill, and more often than not get away with it. Justices of the Peace could be bought, witnesses suborned, the poor browbeaten and the humble stamped on. A vicious rich man of authority could break the lives of his innocent victims. 'If a poor fellow robs a man of fashion of five shillings, to gaol with him. But the man of fashion may plunder a thousand poor, and stay in his own house' (*Don Quixote in England*). Life in eighteenth-century England was very uncertain; the whirligig of Fate turned faster than ever and its effects could be cataclysmic. Neither society nor the law offered much protection. Arson and robbery, as well as kidnappings, duels and murders, grew to monstrous proportions, so monstrous that Fielding felt compelled to direct public attention to this vast increase in crime in his excellent pamphlet, *An Enquiry into the late Increase of Robbers* (1751).

Yet, in the midst of this despair, Fielding came across a few, rare human beings whose goodness proved indestructible, who bore the outrageous blows of fortune with stoical fortitude, who retained, in the midst of violence and vice, an unsullied innocence. No matter how ill the world treated them, they remained good in its deepest human sense – charitable, forgiving, compassionate, honest – not gloomy and foreboding, like Job, but buoyant and resilient with hope. As Parson Adams says, 'Whilst my conscience is pure, I shall never fear what man can do to me.' Such beings were rare, but they fascinated Fielding quite as much as the world of vice and cruelty through which they made their pilgrimage.

These natural innocents, however, were not the only human personalities to capture Fielding's sympathy and imagination in the violent world of eighteenth-century England. They were the rare and wonderful creatures who fortified his faith in human nature. Parson Adams, Squire Allworthy, Mr Heartfree – such men existed in Fielding's world and Fielding felt nothing but admiration for their characters, but his appetite for life was too strong, his sympathies too broad, to reject the rest of mankind. In *Jonathan Wild* Fielding painted the portrait of a human monster who moved through the jungle of London's underworld with the certainty of a leopard: killing without compunction, raping where he could not seduce, missing no chance of a swindle or a theft, even picking the Ordinary of Newgate's pocket as he was about to swing into eternity.

47

Wild wallows in his evil, yet with such gusto, such wolfish appetite for life, that he becomes almost forgivable, almost heroic. Fielding could never resist gusto. He was a very sick man by the time he came to be a novelist and this, no doubt, gave him a heightened sense of the value of instinctive life, its richness and its satisfactions. Certainly these two pre-occupations – his obsession with goodness and his delight in gusto – are the emotional driving forces in his masterpiece, *Tom Jones*.

The History of Tom Jones, the greatest of all English picaresque novels, was published in 1749. Fielding got £600 for the copyright and there is a tradition that because it sold so well, the publisher added later another £100. It brought Fielding immediate fame and the admiration of generations of novelists and critics, Coleridge, Scott, Thackeray and many others. Every talent that Fielding possessed is displayed here at its maximum capacity. The narrative is complex yet every incident is vital to the story; not a scene could be cut out without marring the plot. Although coincidences abound, and Chance zigzags through the lives of the characters like an erratic comet, nevertheless Fielding's exceptional care with precisely observed detail and realistic dialogue renders the picaresque adventures of Tom Jones completely plausible. Jones himself, with his gaiety, high animal spirits, and transparent good nature, never runs away with the book, for the other characters, from the major to the minor, are equally vivid; as distinct and as actual as the living people we know. Indeed the veracity of Fielding's character drawing in *Tom Jones* led Hazlitt to write, 'As a painter of real life he was the equal of Hogarth and only a little inferior to Shakespeare', and Byron called him 'the Prose Homer of Human Nature'.

Yet none of these eulogies does Fielding full justice. One of the great subtleties of Fielding's character studies is the way he depicts his characters being moulded by their social circumstances as well as by their innate desires. Squire Western, Blifil, Lady Bellaston, are unique individuals, in the fundamental structure of their personalities timeless as all great characters in fiction should be, yet the nuances of their temperaments, the growth of their basic natures, have been developed by the conditions of eighteenth-century life. Fielding always, and most deliberately, called his novels *histories*; imagination lay only in the plot – incidents and character, circumstances and personalities were drawn with all the accuracy and judgement that Fielding could muster from his own experience of life. And the result is a panorama of Georgian England that is a social document as well as a work of fiction.

But *Tom Jones* had to be written rapidly, in those rare hours of leisure that Fielding's drudgery as a political hack afforded him. His elevation to the bench at Bow Street, a mere month before the publication of *Tom Jones*, added immensely to his burdens. He became the chief magistrate of the most crime-ridden quarter of London. Already he was a sick man, and contrary to what the high spirits of Tom Jones might lead one to believe, a very sad one. Children had died; so, too, his wife after a few years of marriage; his second wife, a servant girl, did not eradicate the grief he felt for the loss of the first, compassionately fond of her though he was. A sense of tragedy had always haunted Fielding; poverty, injustice, human misery settled like locusts on his warm and generous spirit, eating away his hopes, his love of life, and darkening his vision.

He worked hard and long on questions of poverty and crime. He pressed the government for reforms, he instituted the Bow Street Runners, the first rudimentary police force that London knew. He was tireless in his struggle with the terrible human conditions that his duties constantly brought to his notice. Little availed. Fielding became ever more harrowed by a sense of life's injustice – good men were battered by misfortune, yet bad men prospered; the innocent were violated, and the corrupters received public honours; society itself conspired to help the sly, the corrupt, the superficial and the cynical. Few achieved that simple happiness which Fielding felt ought to be man's true reward – a decent competence, a loving wife, the respect of

49

neighbours. Simple as it might be, he knew that for most it must prove illusory.

Fielding's last novel, *Amelia,* reflects the decline of his spirits. Here he lays bare the viciousness and the hypocrisy of his age. The savagery of the law and the inhumanity of gaolers, which he knew as well as any man, he depicts mercilessly. When he wrote this book, Fielding was exhausted and drawing near to death: he pillaged his old books for characters to save himself the labour of new invention. And at times, too, the magistrate gets the better of the novelist, and incidents are introduced in order to educate laymen in their rights and powers at law. Lacking the animal zest and high spirits of his earlier books, *Amelia* has become the least read of all Fielding's novels, yet it contains what is, perhaps, the most accurate account of low life in eighteenth-century London. In many ways it is one of the most honest social documents produced in the age of Johnson.

In less than three years Fielding was dead. By the spring of 1754, a combination of jaundice, asthma and dropsy had so wrecked his health that he was advised to try the blander air of Portugal. Within a few weeks of his arrival in Lisbon, he collapsed. He died as he had lived, writing. Nothing but death could stop his pen. The novels upon which his immortality rests are but a tiny fraction of his work. He wrote millions of words in journals, newspapers, pamphlets; every month of every year brought some sharp comment from Fielding on the world about him. Like so many great creative artists, his restless imagination needed constant outlets, and he produced a torrent of allegories, parables, incidents and stories to plead for that simple morality which runs like a golden thread through Fielding's work – charity, compassion, gentleness – 'nothing carrying with it', he wrote, 'more pure and savoury delight than beneficence'. Yet about Fielding there was a touch of Harlequin; high spirits, strong humour, animal delight, were always allied to a knowledge of the evil that lurks within and to a high consciousness of the rarity of man's humanity to man.

Henry Fielding also possessed, as few great writers have,

a confident masculinity. He was a virile writer, though not in the sentimental false hair-on-his-chest manner of a Hemingway nor with the neurotic insistence of a Lawrence. Fielding experienced no sense of insecurity; he was completely confident of his manhood. Although this may have limited his sensitivity and blunted, perhaps, his intuitive insight into the complexities of human nature, it gave him a balanced, and better still, a confident, judgement of men and women. His natural toughness of fibre led him to display his characters through action and incident rather than in emotional conflict with each other. Fielding painted character through events, not through analysis of feelings, and in so doing strengthened the structure of the novel.

Under Richardson's influence there had been more than a danger that the new realistic novel might lose itself in an analytical morass, as intuition after intuition was explored with feminine delicacy. Fielding, however, introduced into the modern novel the narrative of action which had been one of the most powerful attractions of the epic. And this, apart from the purely technical device of using a journey as a theme, is almost all that he did take from traditional romance or epic. His influence on the novel was revolutionary. His detail is as realistic, as rooted in the social life of his time, as Defoe's: but he was never content to remain merely a reporter of what he saw. Fielding believed passionately in human rights and was not afraid to say so. He is the first great novelist of social criticism, the precursor of Dickens, and the maker of a tradition that has only grown feeble in modern times. Active in society, he possessed and used the right to condemn it. Unpreoccupied with his own nature, he kept his pity for others.

1964

4

The Spectator*

It is easy to forget the turbulence of seventeenth-century society, not only its civil wars, plots, executions, but also the casual violence which was so deeply embedded in its social life. The duels of Lord Mohun are notorious, the Mohawks – a more violent aristocratic version of skinheads – get less publicity, but oblivion has descended on the casual assaults of Charles II's aristocracy who beat, wounded, and occasionally killed, with impunity those members of the lower orders at whom they took offence. When high with drink or temper, they were licensed murderers. Gentlemen were little better: they might kick, horsewhip and beat their servants, children or tenantry; and so long as they avoided permanent injury, the consequences of their acts were trivial or non-existent. And middle-class folk could be, *en masse* at least, as violent as their betters. In 1705, at Coventry, the Tories with their cudgels set about the Whigs, felled a score, and knocked out the mayor's teeth. Nor should one be taken in by the formal courtesies of social intercourse. Augustan elegance was only skin deep – manners from the Court to the cottage were coarse.

By our standards, they were to remain earthy for most of the eighteenth century, yet compared with what had gone before, they softened. Rustic habits and manners became mildly comic, and old-fashioned was used to describe not only the paraphernalia of life – houses, furniture, clothes – but also types of human temperament: Sir Roger de Coverley, Squire Western and the like. To be smart, to be

* *The Spectator*, ed. Donald F. Bond (Oxford, 1966).

elegant, to be in fashion was to be metropolitan, not rustic. In the late seventeenth and early eighteenth centuries a new society of power and authority was forming in London, quite separate from Court life, although in association with it. Steadily its confidence grew in its attitudes to religion, politics and manners. During these years an Establishment was formed in London and Addison and Steele in the *Spectator* helped to clarify its responses to the world in which it found itself. And because they fulfilled this task so admirably, for their sense of the Establishment's *persona* was as brilliant as the clarity of their prose, the *Spectator* remained a widely read English classic for two hundred years. So long as the Establishment continued to grow and absorb emergent professions, financiers and industrialists, the *Spectator* had a social purpose to perform, and indeed remained a textbook of social morality.

Its first task was, of course, to mock at the barbarities of those rustic, turbulent, quasi-feudal relationships which still littered English life as comic, old-fashioned or reprehensible. No one is sterner against duelling than Addison or Steele, none so superbly ironic about antic ways of life; true, there is much kindliness, perhaps even a little compassion in the portrait of Sir Roger de Coverley, yet their kindliness is as devastating as their irony. One cannot be kind to a powerful, antipathetic and dangerous social force, and it is remarkable that these two Whig writers should have been so certain of the ineffectiveness of the Tory squires who, when they were publishing the *Spectator*, were still dominant in Parliament. It bespeaks an inner confidence, a conviction that Whiggery and the future were already allies, as indeed they were.

Of course, this self-confident mockery was immensely effective. No previous paper had enjoyed half the success of the *Spectator*. It was published daily and read avidly by thousands. Of course, its major public was in London, and if its subscribers are a true indication of the nature of its readership, then its appeal was strongest with the politicians, civil servants, bankers, merchants, the men and women associated with government. Since the revolution of 1688, government had increasingly separated itself from the Court, and this ever-growing class required a clarification of its social and moral attitudes. Hence the *Spectator*'s success went deeper than politics. Of course, it spread far beyond this group of readers. Success made it fashionable, and the gentry and their wives, isolated in the country, looked forward eagerly for its arrival, willing to laugh at their neighbours if ignore themselves.

In the very first number Addison and Steele had stressed their intention of avoiding party politics, but this was the usual lip-service to impartiality made by all journalists. Both of them were deeply committed Whigs and one has only to compare the sound sense of Sir Andrew Freeport to the mild absurdities of Sir Roger to realize that their intention was to further their party views by ridicule. But as Addison developed the character of Sir Roger, his ridicule struck a more telling note, and one which went deeper than the party necessities. By mockery of Sir Roger and all that he stood for, he helped to create a sense of inwardness, a sense of belonging to a vastly superior world of moral and social excellence. To laugh at Sir Roger was to be cultured. What had begun as a political satire ended as a social catalyst. And this, of course, gives the *Spectator* its stature in the history of English letters. In the seventeenth century literary culture was largely dominated by the Court. Swift, Addison, Steele, Pope and the other Augustans made the middle class the arbiters of taste: and in that transition the *Spectator* played a leading part. Historical importance does not, however, necessarily confer literary excellence, and this new, splendidly edited edition in which all the *Spectators* are printed as they first appeared in their daily dress, gives a welcome opportunity for reassessment.

Apart from the de Coverley papers, and one or two other essays, it is as dreary if as smooth as an ocean of tapioca pudding.

Foppish and fantastick Ornaments are only Indications of Vice, not criminal in themselves. Extinguish Variety in the Mind and you naturally retrench the little superfluities of Garniture and Equipage. The Blossoms will fall of themselves, when the Root that nourishes them is destroyed.

And so on, and so on. Such sententious platitudes stretch over page after page. Although the prose runs as sweetly as toothpaste, the matter is awful in its banality. Take the seven pages on wit written by Addison and Steele in May 1711; there is not an idea of the slightest originality. Although the expression is uniformly felicitous, the matter might have been composed by a sixth-form master for slightly backward pupils. And rather like a schoolmaster Addison inserts a little knowledge in the pulp — a quotation from Hobbes and Locke, a little information about Classical authors, a reference to Aristotle, etc. – a few neatly chosen morsels of learning, that could be swallowed with ease by the most self-distrusting readers. One has only to compare this with Gombrich's recent discussion of Freud's concept of wit to see how far the intelligent general reader has travelled in two hundred and fifty years.

But the real boredom lies, for the present age, in the *Spectator*'s all-pervading, arch, cosy morality, a tea-table morality which is less of the heart than of manners. The good life is the life of good breeding, of kindly charity, of modesty, of the golden mean. In short, it was a morality for those who had arrived and could look forward to a *place* in Heaven. Passion, conflict, frustration, wild hope or wild despair have no part in it: the respectable life can only deplore excess. Yet for an emerging class such precepts helped to provide social cohesion, to give the air of truth to attitudes to which it was necessary to pay lip-service, if nothing more. After all, the affluent in a sea of poverty have to present a becoming modesty, a seemly charity, and a delicate distaste for excess. These essays of the *Spectator* were admirable moralities to read aloud to the unmarried daughter and well-disciplined son. This, at least, was how the middle-class life should be lived, even if it rarely was so in practice. Put against any deeply personal diary or collection of letters of the eighteenth century the *Spectator*'s moralities begin to take on the air of hollow sham, as hypocritical as anything that the age of Victoria produced.

Even so, the achievement was formidable. Few writers have won immortality in ephemeral literature of this kind, or established modes of literary expression. After all, this was a daily paper, often written rapidly off the cuff, and the standard of *sheer* literacy remains remarkably high. Distasteful as much of its moralizing now seems, it remains remarkably readable. And it is doubtful if bourgeois moralizing could ever have been done with more elegance or grace. But now it is dead prose: useful for the social historian; still, perhaps, of nostalgic charm to the few remaining pockets of gentility; but its language is the language of a society that has vanished.

Nothing has taken its place, every attempt to give our emerging world a code of literary manners has failed. In our present age there is no acceptance of a common attitude to social morality or manners, or of what makes for good breeding. We still lack a voice which will express the morality which we want and the future will accept. Today most of the effective political nation has two moralities, one private, the other public, one which it believes, the other which it distrusts. The genius of the *Spectator* lay in its ability to give public validity to personal and private morality; in a world of competitive individualism this carried with it the force of truth. To speak so convincingly for a class and an age is remarkably rare and although, apart from the de Coverley papers, no longer very readable, the *Spectator* will always remain one of the most valuable of historical documents, and in this edition by Professor Bond it receives a treatment worthy of its quality. The annotation is scholarly and unobtrusive; the judgements always sound.

1966

5

The Royal Porcelain Craze

'A porcelain factory,' said Karl Eugen, Duke of Württemberg, 'is an indispensable accompaniment of splendour and magnificence,' and he thought that no prince of his rank should be without one, a sentiment that was echoed throughout Germany in the 1750s. Four electors – Mainz, The Palatinate, Bavaria and Brandenburg – possessed flourishing factories, in output if not in profit, at Höchst, Frankenthal, Nymphenburg and Berlin. The prince-bishop Heinrich von Bibra succeeded at Fulda, even though his brother ecclesiastics at Treves and Cologne failed; elsewhere dukes, princes, bishops, *landgraves* and *margraves* were all in china, right down to the tiny principalities of Nassau-Saarbrücken and Pfalz-Zweibrücken. Most lost money, and all were overshadowed by factories supported by kings; but prestige demanded them.

The factories of kings, of course, were larger, more costly, more magnificent. The most famous of all, which belonged to Augustus the Physically Strong (his prowess derived from the boudoir, not the battlefield), Elector of Saxony and King of Poland, was established at Meissen in 1710. So famous were its wares, which for a time were unique, that it made a profit. This state of affairs did not last, because Louis XV of France sponsored a manufacture of china in Vincennes that put beauty before cost, even before the lives of its workmen, and for whose products the King himself was prepared to act as a salesman. No more magnificent and extravagantly expensive china has ever been produced in Europe than that made in France, but it had keen competition from the granddaughters of Augustus. When married off to their monarchs, they expected to have a porcelain factory near at hand; so the King of Naples set one up in Capo-di-Monte for Maria Amalia, and when they inherited Spain, they shifted it, along with their jewels and pets, to Buen Retiro, near Madrid. And Maria Anna, wife of the Elector of Bavaria, had her own factory at Nymphenburg, which was to produce some of the finest china figures of the eighteenth century. Only the English monarchy kept cautiously aloof and so avoided the appalling costs that drove Bow into bankruptcy, Longton Hall and Chelsea into closing, and Derby and Worcester close to ruin. George II, in whose reign most of these factories began, does not seem to have bothered to order either a dinner service or a suite of vases. The British royal family acted very much in character: they enjoyed their parsimony.

As with monarchs, so with their subjects; the craze bit deep. Aristocrats ordered fabulous services running to hundreds of pieces; young English noblemen on the Grand Tour ransacked the fashionable Parisian china shops. They had pieces mounted in gold and silver and ormolu; they boxed their china picnic sets, even their knives and forks, in elaborate tooled leather cases lined with satin. By 1750 all Europe was in the grip of china-fever. No mania for material objects had ever been so widespread, so general to the rich of all nations; even the world beyond Europe was soon caught up in the obsession: Russians, Turks, Moguls, the Emperor of China himself, wanted the porcelain of Europe.

Only once before, and curiously enough in staid, bourgeois Holland, had there been so wild a craze. In the early seventeenth century the Dutch had gone mad about tulips; bulbs soared to astronomical prices, rare specimens fetching the modern equivalent of a good Renoir. But tulip mania rose and fell with the suddenness of a hectic fever, whereas the craze for porcelain burst like a thunderstorm that had been rumbling for days in the distant hills.

The making of porcelain began in China in the ninth

century – which is why its alternative and more common name has always been china. It was harder and more vitreous than other forms of pottery. It could be made thinner, moulded into more delicate shapes, and given a more brilliant glaze. Its secret lay in the special clay from which it was made – kaolin.

A few pieces of china had crept into Europe in the late Middle Ages, but they were inconceivably rare and little appreciated. In the early Renaissance they became somewhat more common. Some of the brilliant blue-and-white Ming porcelain reached Italy, and it could be a piece of this superlative china that is depicted in Bellini's 'Feast of the Gods'. The first clouds of the coming storm began to gather shortly after the Spanish discoveries of the New World had reached across the Pacific to the Philippines. Along with Inca gold and the bright feathered garments of the Aztecs, the Spaniards sent crates of brilliant Ming china in their great galleons going to Europe. Usually this was the common but very handsome blue-and-white ware that China exported to the East. Common in China, it was rare in Europe, rare and beautiful and desirable, fit for monarchs and noblemen but well beyond bourgeois dreams. The Dutch, precariously poised in Japan in the early seventeenth century, imported more, but not enough to meet the demand, and when they lost their foothold, the supply became uncertain for a time. But the demand grew insatiable.

The Dutch at Delft made some splendid imitations in pottery, but pottery was not porcelain: it lacked the glittering whiteness, the sharpness, the splendid enamel glaze; also it chipped easily. The obsession for true china was becoming a mania. The holds of the great East Indiamen were crammed with it: one ship alone unloaded 146,748 pieces in 1700. Yet this was a mere sop. The market knew no bounds as the obsession to possess china seized the rich. Naturally men dreamed of making it, for a fortune awaited anyone who could rival the Chinese. Jesuits, keenly alert to Europe's need, penetrated into Ching-tê-chên, the great manufacturing centre for exports, and sent back a report on how it was made, but mixed up the names of the clays – which did not matter so very much, since no one knew what the names meant anyway.

Throughout Europe at this time there were alchemists seeking vainly to transmute base metal into gold. One of these, Johann Friedrich Böttger, was persuaded that porcelain, if he could make it, would be worth as much as gold, perhaps more. He joined forces with a scientist of repute, Walther von Tschirnhaus. Luck favoured them, for they found the most important of all the ingredients for porcelain – kaolin – near Meissen in Saxony, close to Dresden. By 1710 they had produced a hard china, indeed one so hard that it could be cut and polished like a jewel. The quest was over, and the storm burst. The factory was established under the patronage of Augustus the Physically Strong at Meissen, and its wares were soon intoxicating Europe.

Of all the monumentally self-indulgent kings and princelings of the eighteenth century, Augustus, hereditary Elector of Saxony and elected King of Poland, was the most fabulous. He was a short, square-shouldered, thick-necked bull of a man with a vast, powerful face. Immensely strong, he could crush iron horseshoes in one hand, jingling a bag of gold in the other, a feat that he often performed to impress the ladies; obvious and vulgar though it may have been, the trick paid excellent dividends, for towards the end of his life there were three hundred and fifty-five official bastards on the government books. A man of such formidable appetite could scarcely be delicate in the choice of food for its appeasement, and it might have been easy to write off Augustus as a tough stud-animal but for his obsession with china, which led him not only to patronize Böttger but also to create by his sympathetic interest much of the style of early Meissen.

Augustus, more pleased with his china than with his children, decided to create a porcelain palace, with rooms lined with porcelain as a setting for enormous vases, huge figures of animals and birds and life-sized statues of the Apostles – all in china. Almost certainly he had heard of the great porcelain tower at Nanking and wished to rival it. In order to cope with this challenge three first-class modellers were employed, the most distinguished of whom was Johann Joachim Kaendler. Some huge animals and birds, not entirely successful, and a vast quantity of Ali Baba-like vases of considerable merit were produced; but the value of the experiment was that it enabled Kaendler, a man of real artistic genius who was to prove himself to be the Bernini of porcelain, to explore the range and plasticity of the material. He discovered an individualistic style of modelling and the scale that was appropriate to his medium. Like many men of strong imagination, Kaendler's output was very large. He produced hundreds of models – peasants, miners, Tyrolean dancers, groups of lovers, animals (almost a zoo of them) – but he returned time and time again to the tragicomic figure of Harlequin and the other characters of the *commedia dell' arte,* whose hold on the imagination of Europe at this time was like that of Charlie Chaplin in our own. It was Kaendler more than any other modeller who seized on the artistic possibilities of china and established the porcelain figure as one of the minor decorative arts of the West. He has rarely been equalled.

These were the great creative years of Meissen, for besides Kaendler, there was J. G. Höroldt, who began to paint naturalistic harbour scenes in silhouette, and Adam von Löwenfinck, possibly the most original of all china decorators, who developed a weird personal vision of Cathay in which fabulous animals gambolled with strange Chinese figures – Chinamen that existed only in the European imagination. The final achievement of this crucial period was the discovery of a magnificent range of ground colours, lavender, yellow, sea green and puce; these were used with the decorative panels for the great vases that adorned Augustus's Japanese palace.

Much of the early production at Meissen reached a high level of taste, but there were times when imagination ran out and the plasticity of the material took control. Then strange monstrosities were born, like the absurd teapots modelled in the form of a cockerel being ridden by a China-man, or a monkey suckling its young; such excruciating lapses in taste occur again and again in the German factories but rarely in the French.

The triumph of Augustus's factory was the envy and delight of Europe: orders poured in from Edinburgh, Moscow, Stockholm and Cadiz. Meissen china, usually called Dresden in England and *Saxe* in France, became the rage, and no aristocratic drawing room was complete without a vase, a figure, or a dish; the fabulously rich began to eat off it, drink from it, wash in it, even spit in it. The market boomed, and jealous eyes grew beady: spies, *agents-provocateurs*, blackmailers and seducers began to lurk about Meissen; in our own day only top-level nuclear physicists have been prone to such temptations as were offered to the 'arcanists' of Meissen. These men who knew the secrets of porcelain making proved human. As early as 1719 a run-away Meissen workman, Samuel Stölzel, had sold his secrets to Claudius du Paquier in Vienna. Paquier produced a glaze inferior to that of Meissen – it is so greenish-toned that some historians refuse to believe that it is based on the Meissen formula and regard it as a separate creation – but he decorated his pieces with such panache that they now command staggering prices. After Stölzel's defection, security was redoubled at Meissen, and all arcanists were carefully watched and rigorously disciplined. No further leakage of secrets took place.

Indeed, Meissen, and to a far lesser extent Vienna, had a monopoly of the market – their only rivals Oriental imports – until the 1750s, when, as in a cheap novelette, a wicked arcanist, Jakob Ringler, secured the friendship of Paquier's daughter, persuaded her to betray the factory's secrets, then bolted. He tried to set up a factory at Künersberg, failed, and moved to Höchst, where he succeeded. Realizing he was in possession of a gold mine, he moved on to Stras-bourg and sold the secrets to the great ceramist Paul-Antoine Hannong (who was afterwards banished by Louis XV and took the hard-paste formula to Frankenthal).

In the meantime, with the bit now between his teeth, Ringler moved on to Bavaria (Nymphenburg), then to Württemberg (Ellwangen and Schrezheim), and finally settled down at Ludwigsburg, where he remained manager for the rest of the century. Like some virus, he had spread porcelain factories throughout Germany; his associates completed what he had started, and by 1760 there was scarcely a *waldgrave* who had not got a porcelain factory under his patronage – and usually subsidized by his peasants.

This rage for a factory was not due to Augustus the Physically Strong, nor even to the beauty of Meissen; it was due to the fact that Louis XV, the arbiter of Europe's taste, had given the royal imprimatur to porcelain. Indeed, Louis had done more than this. He did not think it beneath his dignity to conduct personally an annual sale of his factory's products. At the end of each year, spread out on trestles in the splendid galleries of Versailles, were rows of plates, cups and saucers, soup tureens, *pots de chambres*, vases, eye baths, watering cans, ewers and basins from his factory at Sèvres. The courtiers had to buy: the monarch acted as auctioneer. Nothing better indicates the reverence, the idolatry, that the European aristocracy lavished on china than that the Most Christian King, who could not socially meet a bourgeois, should have been willing to act as its huckster.

What he sold, however, was not the hard-paste porcelain from China or Meissen. It was more curious, more beautiful, much more expensive – not only in materials but in men who succumbed to the deadly diseases of silicosis and lead poisoning that its manufacture engendered. It was nearer to glass than Meissen was, the soft paste holding the clay in suspension. The softness of texture, however, absorbed colours more successfully than Meissen. Often it achieved quite dazzling whiteness, and the glaze possessed an unmatchable brilliance. It easily went wrong in the firing, warping and cracking and breaking up in the kilns, yet the factory and the King insisted on perfection; in consequence the wastage was fantastic. It was, therefore, as it has remained, the most expensive porcelain ever produced in

Europe. Known first as Vincennes, it was called Sèvres after the factory was moved to a royal château in 1756.

Of course the French had been trying to make porcelain for a long time. The proper clay, kaolin, eluded them for the best part of a century, but they had stumbled on soft paste, first at Rouen, then at Saint-Cloud near Paris. But the paste was poor, the designs imitative. In the collector's eye they have a certain charm, but the products were primitive, in a sense amateurish. Under the protection of two great aristocrats, the Prince de Condé and the Duc de Villeroi, Chantilly and Mennecy did better. Many of their products have both charm and technical excellence, but they did not rival Meissen; indeed they never reached beyond the quality of a minor German factory.

That the French did in the end secure a factory that surpassed Meissen was due to Louis XV and his exquisite, sensitive mistress, Madame de Pompadour; cool, extravagant, far better at the decorative than the amorous arts, she dictated French taste. The manufacture of soft paste of high quality had already begun when Madame de Pompadour's interest was first aroused, but it was failing through lack of funds. The management was changed, royal funds soon flowed; the royal cipher, interlaced L's, were allowed to be stamped on the ware to proclaim Louis XV's interest. Great artists, including François Boucher, were persuaded to design for Vincennes, and the royal goldsmith was commanded to put all his technical knowledge at the factory's disposal. All other factories were forbidden to use gold. These draconian measures produced immediate and startling success.

In 1747 Vincennes was producing rather indifferent imitations of Chantilly and occasionally even attempting an exact copy of Meissen. By 1750 it had found a style sophisticated, rich, and attuned to its material in a way that has scarcely been equalled. No factory ever achieved such beauty of colour, and that includes those in China and Japan.

Vincennes took Europe by storm. The purity of its whiteness surpassed the famous *blanc de chine* of Fukien. Its glaze possessed a brilliance equal to that of Meissen, but its real triumph lay in the extraordinary way the body absorbed and held colour, giving a softness and a depth that Meissen could never equal. And to proclaim its royal protection, Vincennes now used gold in superb profusion. Cups and saucers, even spittoons and chamberpots, were festooned with it. But Vincennes was fragile, very hard to make; the process was slow and expensive. Moreover, Vincennes, or Sèvres, possessed certain limitations – limitations that the collector has turned to great advantage. The clay, unlike that of Meissen, did not lend itself to large figures or groups of figures. They were attempted and made for some years in a brilliant white glaze – some of the most perfect objects ever made in china – but the wastage was so prodigious that often only two or three copies of these exceptionally beautiful objects were successfully made. Fewer survive, and competition for them is savage. As soon as the technicians succeeded in producing figures in an unglazed china, called biscuit, they stopped making the white glaze figures. This biscuit which makes the china look much more like marble or stone, became immensely popular, and François Boucher designed a number of models that were afterwards executed by Étienne Falconet. Though the Victorians collected biscuit with passion, modern taste turned away from it; only in the past two years has the tide turned once more, and the prices of biscuit have begun to soar.

But the glory of Sèvres lay in its useful wares – in its chocolate cups, its teapots, its toilet basins, butter dishes, soup tureens and needle cases; indeed, every simple object that could be made in china was, even absurd little watering cans, so that a marquise might sprinkle a rose growing in a Sèvres pot. Never have men and women eaten from, or for that matter spat into, such exquisite china. Madame de Pompadour ordered an entire conservatory of china flowers. It cost nearly a million livres. Emperors, kings and princes ordered colossal services, running to hundreds of pieces. Catherine the Great's service cost more than three hundred thousand livres (in modern money, about £375,000). Even

Ch'ien Lung, the Chinese Emperor, deigned to accept from Louis XV a vast service, together with some remarkable vases to act as centrepieces. Rarely have objects of utility been either so expensive or so beautiful.

The ground colours surpassed all but the rarest of Meissen shades, lavender and puce. They possessed, moreover, a softness, a richness, a lustre, that the Meissen lacked. The colours at first were simple deep blues splashed thickly and absorbed unevenly so that the result possessed the texture and highlights of velvet. The same effect was achieved a little later with apple green; but more sumptuous, and more expensive still, was turquoise, or *bleu céleste*; rarer and extravagantly difficult to achieve in pure colour was yellow, the light daffodil yellow. But rarest of all was pink, made only for a few years and associated with Madame de Pompadour. Pink proved almost impossible to make – it so easily strayed into orange or purple, thus creating an unpleasingly harsh ground. The consequence was a dearth of pink. When it was successful, a colour was produced that no other factory could rival. There was never enough, and collectors have sought it and paid wild prices for it. Today a pair of pink icecups fit only for midgets will cost with luck £1,000 at an auction and may be three times as much in a shop – if they can be found. A very large piece will command twenty to forty thousand pounds. And yellow, turquoise and green are not far behind.

Coloured pieces were usually inset with painted decorative panels that ran on a few popular themes. Birds, sometimes copied from beautifully printed plates of exotic birds of South America, often just imagined, festooned cups, plates, dishes, vases of all kinds. Two painters, Aloncle and Evans, excelled at toucans, parrots, orioles and birds of paradise, which were shown preening themselves or swooping improbably through the air. Flowers, of course, were the most common theme of all, developing from the rather slavishly copied botanical specimens that the artists at Meissen favoured to splendid sprays of garden flowers scattered in stylized abandon across the surface of a plate or cup. But perhaps the most successful theme of decoration was children, drawn usually from sketches by Boucher – sometimes clothed, often naked. They sprawled on clouds, bottoms up, a wicked glint in the eye, playing the most improbable instruments; or, clothed like miniature adults, they chased birds, pushed wheelbarrows, watered flowers, bowled hoops – but always with a charm, a lightness, a gaiety, that removed them at once from the heavy and rather puddingy imitations that the Meissen factory was forced to make.

In brilliance of colour, in splendour of decoration, in lavishness of gold, and in almost intolerable expense, Sèvres out-distanced all of its rivals and in the 1750s and sixties dominated the taste of Europe. The great French cabinet-makers not only used it for table tops but also inserted plaques in the friezes of tables, secretaires, consoles, and corner cupboards and at times produced articles that seemed at first sight to consist of nothing but china set in ormolu.

But Sèvres, except for those in biscuit, could not make figures – the porcelain was too soft for the sharp, certain edges that figures required, and the factory never attempted to rival Meissen. However, the lesser German factories did, and many of them had their chance when the Seven Years War hindered production at Meissen. Few matched the achievement of Kaendler, but Simon Feilner was successful at Frankenthal (a set of his Italian comedy figures was sold at auction a few years ago for £18,750). Only one modeller – Franz Anton Bustelli – surpassed Kaendler and Feilner. Bustelli, a Swiss from Locarno, has claims to be the only creative genius, apart from Kaendler, who has worked in china, the only one to realize completely both the possibilities and the limitations of the material and at the same time stamp it with his own unmistakable and remarkable style. His vapid, pinheaded creatures of astonishing elegance, which he made simply with swiftly moving converging planes, linger in the memory as few other porcelain figures do. They lack the strength, the vigour, the humanity, of Kaendler at his best, but these very qualities of Kaendler's drive out of one's mind the fact that his pieces are of china;

whereas with Bustelli one is always conscious of the fragility of the materials. About Bustelli there is a touch of Mozart – the elegance, the harmony, a hint of the tragedy that time holds for all men. Their success may be measured by the fact that since the day they were made they have never been out of fashion. They have been for nearly two centuries the prized possessions of museums and collectors. Now, like the Impressionists, only millionaires can really afford them.

Bustelli came at the time when the great period of porcelain making was drawing to a close. The wonder and excitement of the new material grew stale with use: the severe standards of neoclassicism checked the exuberance of the rich, rioting, rococo style, which might have been invented for the wilder fantasies of porcelain. Also Josiah Wedgwood moved in: not only could he mass-produce but also his creation of jasperware was exceptionally well adapted to the neoclassic style with its formalized friezes of Muses or Grecian dancers. All too soon the modellers and painters of Sèvres were slavishly copying his models. With Wedgwood's technique pottery was thought to rival china in beauty, at half or a quarter of the expense. The result was that the mantelpieces, the occasional tables and the dining rooms of the middle classes rivalled those in the mansions of the aristocracy.

The cult of porcelain persisted; indeed it has never died, but it has never achieved the ingenuity, the excitement, or the sheer exuberance of its early period. The circumstances of its development were curiously appropriate; at that time the fashionable world was enthralled by China – its mystery, its sophistication, its philosophy, as well as its crafts. Indeed writers and artists combined to create a vision of Cathay that first enticed, then seduced, the Western world. The triumph of porcelain manufacture occurred when Europe, particularly France, had reached a standard of excellence in the decorative arts achieved in no other time or place except in Mandarin China. The European aristocrats of the eighteenth century were closely tied together, certain of their taste, and possessed an attitude towards the patronage of the arts that arose not only from their education but also from the very idea of themselves as gentlemen. That the cup that touched their lips should be an object of exquisite beauty aroused no thoughts of effeminacy, or even of connoisseurship or dilettantism; it was merely fitting, its expense a matter of pride. It would be useless to deny the self-indulgence, the indifference to poverty and to the pain and suffering of their fellow men, of the society that gave birth to porcelain, but as time passes, works of art disentangle themselves from their age and live serenely for other times and other men.

1968

6

British Attitudes to the American Revolution

On 20 May 1779 the Earl of Pembroke was in despair. He felt a deep sense of shame that was impossible to hide. As he wrote to his son, Lord Herbert, who was making the Grand Tour in Italy: 'I wish I were a Laplander, or anything but a Briton.' Lord Pembroke was, of course, as his ancestors had been, Lord Lieutenant of Wiltshire. He was still a colonel in a most distinguished regiment, the Royals, although now too old to serve. At the accession of George III he had been made a Lord of the Bedchamber, a post that he had lost not through any political indiscretion but because of an amorous scandal. Indeed the result of that scandal, a son whom Pembroke somewhat infelicitously named Reebkomp (an anagram, of course, of Pembroke), was serving in the army in America. It was his letters as well as George III's policy that made Lord Pembroke a prey to fury and to such misery.

A month later, he explained at greater length to his son the reasons for his dissatisfaction.

Our ministry, taken *en gros*, are certainly such as no wise nor honest man can trust, and in whom the country can conceive no hopes; men who proved themselves incapable, whose characteristic is indolence, and whose system is unwise, who are overpowered by misfortune because they are leagued with absurdity, whose obstinacy is not to be softened by advice, and whose eyes are not to be opened by experience.

As a soldier Pembroke was distressed by the defeats sustained by the British forces in America – hence his shame – but his anger with the government welled from deeper springs than this. In his quick-tempered, completely uninhibited letters to his son, he does not disguise his contempt for the members of George III's Parliament. He considered it an utterly corrupt institution, and he wondered that the people did not nail up the doors of both Houses and set fire to them. He scoffed at the idea of a parliamentary union with Ireland. They will want, he forecast, to go America's way and not join up with 'our rotten institutions'. In all cities, he told his son, there was the utmost discontent, particularly amongst manufacturers. His sympathy was with them.

Indeed the political state of England in 1779 was a sorry mess, and for nearly two decades every ministry had proved itself totally incapable of dealing with the American question. During the 1760s, harshness alternated with weakness, repression was followed by conciliation as one Whig ministry rapidly followed another. The House of Commons was composed of small Whig factions struggling for power, and George III's faith in Lord North derived from the fact that North in 1769 had brought to an end the confusion of a decade and created a stable ministry, solidly Whig at the core, but supported by many Tories and independents. Of course, North had not been able to secure the support of all the Whig groups, and the important group, led by the Marquis of Rockingham, whose formidable spokesman was Edmund Burke, stayed outside the government as did Lord Chatham (William Pitt) and his supporters. Not until rebellion flared up was North's American policy much more consistent than his predecessor's. As rebellion turned to war and the war itself grew long and difficult, many of North's erstwhile supporters began to have doubts of the wisdom of his policy. Criticism grew in volume. And criticism mattered. Public opinion was important in a crisis, even in the oligarchical structure of British politics. Since the accession of George III in 1760 the feeling that a Parliament of landowners, dominated by the aristocracy, was becoming out of touch with the true needs of the nation had steadily strengthened. Criticism of the parliamentary system as well as of North's American policy had become widespread. There had developed an ever-increasing band of radicals whose radicalism was social, legal, religious, though not, of course, economic. They believed in a wider democratic franchise, toleration of religious belief and the rationalization of law and administration. They were irritated by anachronism: that little girls and boys should be hanged for theft or that a duchess should draw a fat salary as a housekeeper for a non-existent palace infuriated them. These views were particularly powerful amongst the radical intellectuals and publicists, Joseph Priestley, Richard Price, Tom Paine and Junius, that savage critic of George III who still retains his anonymity. Their books and pamphlets were read as eagerly in the provinces as in London, and they had helped to make the American question a dominant issue, not only for members of Parliament, or even for parliamentary electors, but for all who could read. They appealed particularly to that mass of Englishmen who were politically dispossessed by the quaint franchises of the unreformed House of Commons, and who, therefore, felt a natural kinship with the Americans in revolt. Their attitude to America was based on their hopes for their own society, and they felt a community of interest with the rebelling colonists both in ideas and in political aspirations. Historians have underestimated the extent of British sympathy for America which flourished in the 1760s and early seventies, just as they have overlooked the reasons for its decay once rebellion turned to war.

First it is necessary to look more closely at those who sympathized, the manner of men they were. This radical sympathy for America is nowhere reflected so sharply as in Sylas Neville's *Diary*. Like Lord Pembroke's papers, the *Diary* is a comparatively recent discovery, and one that has certainly passed almost unnoticed by the political historians of George III's reign. For those who believe that radical public opinion mattered little in the eighteenth century, it is an uncomfortable document.

Neville kept his diary from 1767 to 1788, during his early manhood. He was born in 1741 and died in 1840, just a few months short of his century. His diary is remarkable for the bitterness with which he refers to George III and his ministers. Here are a few of his sentiments culled from 1767:

No person is a true friend of liberty that is not a Republican.

The evils of which monarchy is productive should deter any wise nation from submitting to that accursed government.

The Gazette says 10,000 people a year go from the North of Ireland to America and 40,000 in all. May they flourish and set up in due time a glorious free government in that country which may serve as a retreat to those Free men who may survive the final ruin of liberty in this country; an event which I am afraid is at no great distance.

Such comments would have done credit to a Boston radical, but these were not peculiar to Neville and his friends: strong, blunt sentiments such as these found their echoes elsewhere. William Turner of Wakefield in Yorkshire urged his son to emigrate:

Through the folly and wickedness of the present, you of the rising generation have indeed a dark prospect before you. . . . Your best way will be to gather as fast as you can a good stock of the arts and sciences of this country; and if you find the night of despotism and wretchedness overwhelm this hemisphere, follow the course of the sun to that country where freedom has already fixed her standard and is erecting her throne; where the sciences and arts, wealth and power will soon gather round her; and assist and strengthen the empire there.

Neville was also in touch with many like-minded men and women; some were well-known London radicals such as Mrs Catherine Macaulay the historian, Caleb Fleming, the unitarian minister of Pinners Hall, and Thomas Hollis whose lavish patronage of liberal ideas helped to keep republican sentiment alive in the middle decades of the eighteenth century.* These ardent radical intellectuals certainly fortified Neville's attitude. Fortunately, however, radical intellectuals

---

* For a discussion of the influence of these dissenting radicals see Caroline Robbins, *The Eighteenth-Century Commonwealth Man* (Harvard, 1959), pp. 320–77, an invaluable book on an obscure and difficult subject that still needs further detailed study.

were not the only characters in Neville's diary to share his sentiments. People who but for him would have merged into the nameless millions of history echo his republican sentiments as well as his hatred for George III's government – Kearsey, Bacon and Mrs Winnick and their friends who entertained him with tea and radical politics. Obviously in the sixties there were little knots of republicans and radicals scattered throughout London and its suburbs.

Even more impressive, however, are the chance conversations that Neville had, or overheard, which indicate the width of public criticism and the frequency with which it was expressed. Viewing the Raphael cartoons at Hampton Court, Neville heard a man tell his wife that they would soon belong to the people of England, and at Terry's Coffee House in August 1767 he got into conversation with a stranger who said that he 'wished N. America may become free and independent, that it may be an asylum to those Englishmen who have spirit and virtue enough to leave their country, when it submits to domestic or foreign Tyranny'.

I find it hard to believe that Neville's experience was singular and untypical or that the sympathetic sentiments which he seems to have encountered so often were at all exceptional. After all when he moved from London to one of the most brutish and least enlightened parts of Norfolk – Scratsby near Great Yarmouth – he had little difficulty in finding kindred spirits to dine with him on calf's head on 30 January in honour of the execution of Charles I, or to share this treasonable toast: 'May the example of this day be followed on all like occasions.' From this it might seem that sympathy for America and tenacious adherence to liberal and radical sentiments reached down to the grass roots and was not merely a cause for opposition politicians, dissenting intellectuals and self-interested merchants, as recent American and British historians have stoutly maintained.* Fortunately, Neville's diary is not the only new

---

* J. C. Miller, *Origins of the American Revolution* (London, 1945), p. 145. 'Although it must be recognized at the outset that some factions of the Whigs such as John Wilkes, John Horne Tooke, Joseph Priestley,

source that illuminates the strength and intensity of pro-American feeling amongst those classes of society that wielded next to no formal political power and whose voice received little notice at the centre of affairs.

At Birmingham, then a rapidly growing manufacturing town, a group of professional men, manufacturers and dilettantes had come together for the purpose of discussion and mutual improvement. They had been fascinated by the ideas of the Enlightenment, as indeed had many similar intellectual élites from Philadelphia to Marseilles.* The importance of such groups – and particularly the British ones that are to be found in most large provincial towns – is that they represent people not outside the mainstream of economic and social development but right in the heart of it. This is certainly true of the West Midlands group, largely based in Birmingham. Their names are well known: James Watt, the inventor; Matthew Boulton, the manufacturer; Erasmus Darwin – grandfather of Charles – poet, philosopher, doctor; Joseph Priestley, chemist and publicist; Dr Small, the tutor of Jefferson; Thomas Day and Richard Edgeworth, both educationalists and both weirdly eccentric; and, perhaps the most interesting of the rest, Josiah Wedgwood, the potter.

Wedgwood, a man of vast intellectual appetite and broad human sympathy, makes a strong contrast to Neville. Everything that Wedgwood did succeeded, and he rose from obscurity to international renown. He was happily married, blessed with brilliant children, prosperous, secure, the admired and admiring friend of many distinguished men in

---

Richard Price and Catherine Macaulay, adopted a liberal, conciliatory position in the dispute between Great Britain and the colonies, it cannot be claimed – as has so often been done – that they represented English public opinion.' Also Eric Robson, *The American Revolution in its Political and Military Aspects, 1763–83* (London, 1955), pp. 36, 80.

* Groups which, I might add in passing, are badly in need of more detailed research, and one can only wish that many European cities had received the same scholarly attention that Carl and Jessica Bridenbaugh have given to Philadelphia.

all walks of eighteenth-century life. He certainly cannot be dismissed as a social misfit, as an unkind critic might dismiss Neville, nor can he be lumped with Price, Cartwright, Priestley, Mrs Macaulay and the rest as a disgruntled radical intellectual. He was a supremely successful man of affairs. He and his friends would have been thoroughly at home in the purposeful, expanding world of Franklin's Philadelphia. They would have shared its eupeptic self-confidence in its expanding commerce, and discovered the same ideas about politics and government, science, education and the arts as their own, amongst its intellectual leadership. As with Philadelphia's élite so with the Lunar Society; its members felt the future in their bones. They were ready for a new world, freer from tradition, closer to the rational principles upon which they modelled their industry and commerce. After all, reason and its application, they believed, had brought their success in life. Of course, as in Philadelphia, not all translated their intellectual liberalism into radical politics. Matthew Boulton supported Lord North although his friends teased him endlessly on that score; Thomas Day, a dedicated follower of the philosophy of Jean-Jacques Rousseau, found it difficult to support the Americans so long as they maintained slavery. In general, however, the members of the Lunar Society felt as Wedgwood did.

Wedgwood's views on the American problem were conveyed in his letters to Richard Bentley, his partner, whose judgement in politics as well as in the arts, sciences and social intercourse he revered.* Wedgwood and Bentley were, of course, wholehearted supporters of the American cause. They thought coercive measures wicked, preposterous, and doomed to disaster. Wedgwood sent for Dr Price's *Observations on Civil Liberty*. He wrote back enthusiastically: 'I thank you for Dr Price's most excellent Pamphlet: those who are

---

* See N. McKendrick, *Transactions of the Royal Historical Society*, 1963. I am deeply indebted to Mr McKendrick for the transcripts of the Wedgwood MSS here quoted. He will himself deal much more extensively with Wedgwood's political attitudes in his forthcoming book on Wedgwood.

neither converted, nor frightened into a better way of thinking by reading his excellent and alarming book may be given up as hardened sinners, beyond the reach of conviction.'* And he asked for more copies so that he could distribute them in the right places. Later Bentley sent him Paine's *Common Sense* and many other pro-American pamphlets to fortify, if fortification were needed, his strong sympathies for America and to help in Wedgwood's work of conversion of others. Wedgwood willingly subscribed £20 towards alleviating the miseries of American prisoners captured by the British. 'Gratitude to their country men for their humanity to G[eneral] Burgoine and his army is no small motive for my mite.'†

Wedgwood and Bentley's views chimed not only with those of their immediate friends but were echoed in the correspondence of other industrialists. Even Elizabeth Strutt, a mere girl of sixteen, weighed down with grief by her mother's sudden death, felt compelled to write to her father: 'I read the determination of the American Congress yesterday and I am sorry to see what distress they are brought to. How sensibly they write, with what courage and what coolness. What havoc and bloodshed can a few ambitious men create amongst whole nations' (c. August 1775).‡ Doubtless, being a dutiful girl, she knew that such sentiments would please her father, Jedediah, one of the greatest figures in the industrial revolution: his great cotton mills at Belper in Derbyshire are still among the largest in Europe. In Bristol, Manchester, Birmingham and Leeds, indeed wherever the middle-class manufacturers were to be found, sympathy for the American attitude abounded.

Of course, it is not surprising that many of the leaders of the industrial revolution should have been so strongly pro-American: they too wanted a social revolution, an end to the

---

* *Barlaston MSS*, J.W. to B., 24 February 1776.

† ibid., 22 December 1777.

‡ R. J. Fitton and A. P. Wadsworth, *The Strutts and the Arkwrights, 1758–80* (Manchester, 1958), p. 159.

77

system of oligarchy and patronage which created not only a sense of keen injustice but also real practical obstacles to their industrial activities. Whatever they wanted – a canal, improved roads, efficient lighting or paving of streets, more education, better law and order, or a new water supply – they had to struggle to get it for themselves, and not only struggle but pay. Neither local nor central government in Britain provided initially the slightest aid; and it is no wonder that the whole oligarchical, unrepresentative structure of eighteenth-century English society should become as much anathema to *them* as it was to Sam Adams. What is surprising is that these social élites, which were beginning to wield so much economic power, proved in the end to be so weak an ally for the American cause.

This was only partially due to the nature of the British political system which put all effective power into the hands of the landowning classes, for many of the industrialists had contacts with politicians, particularly those Whigs, led by the Marquis of Rockingham, who were in opposition to Lord North. The widespread sympathy for America failed to be effective for a more profound reason: the change in the nature of the conflict itself.

In the 1760s, even in the early seventies, friendly support for America could be indulged with a clear conscience. The policy of successive ministries lacked consistency; many acts, particularly the Stamp Act, seemed to be as inimical to British commercial interests as American; both British and American merchants appeared to be the victims of these arbitrary acts, so resentment could be shared in common. But American resentment hardened, developed a programme, and became a revolt, violent, bloody, bitter, that, as Chatham had foreseen, turned itself into a European war. Doubts began to cloud sympathy and many consciences became uneasy. It required political and moral convictions of a thoroughly radical kind to support unquestioningly the right of the Americans to obtain their independence by any means whatsoever, *once rebellion had started to transform itself into war.*

Indeed this is sharply reflected in Wedgwood's correspondence. On 6 February 1775 he wrote to Bentley:

> Doctor Roe had been at Manchester about a week before – exceeding hot & violent against the Americans, Dr Percival told me he quite frothed at the mouth, and was so excessively rapid in his declamations, and exclamations, that nobody could put in a word 'till his story was told, & then away he flew to another House repeating the same Rigmorow over again. . . . And away he flew to promote the same good work at Leeds, Hallifax &c – & I find . . . from these Towns, that his labor has not been in vain. . . . Many were surpris'd to find him so amazingly alter'd in his sentiments, but nevertheless his harangues, & even those simple queries have had a very considerable effect amongst many, Dissenters & others.
>
> I do not know how it happens, but a general infatuation seems to have gone forth, & the poor Americans are deemed Rebels, now the Minister has declared them so, by a very great majority wherever I go.

Although Roe might have swung over many moderates in one of the most radical areas in Britain, the sympathy for America remained both extensive and vociferous. At a meeting at Stafford to adopt a Loyal Address in support of the policy of George III towards America, Mr Wooldridge produced a counter-petition and proposed it so vigorously that, according to Wedgwood, 'the gentlemen were cut down and could not answer it'; nevertheless most of them signed the Loyal Address. It is true that Wooldridge and his friends, not to be outdone, advertised their counter-petition in the local press and signatures were canvassed in Birmingham, Lichfield, Walsall and Hanley. Yet Wooldridge's and not Roe's proved to be the losing game.

The contrast between the effectiveness of merchant radicals in America and merchant radicals in England became quickly apparent. War strengthened the former, weakened the latter. The taking of New York by the British army brought the mob out into the streets. 'Our people at Newcastle', wrote Wedgwood, 'went wild with joy', and he was relieved that those stalwarts who refused to illuminate their houses to celebrate the victory were not attacked.* Elsewhere, too, the mob roared their delight at a British triumph. War had inflamed the natural xenophobia of the semi-literate, as indeed it did in America, but whereas in America mob support, the hopeless anger and despair of the dispossessed, strengthened radical and revolutionary attitudes to government and society, in England the reverse process took place. British mobs became increasingly patriotic, for the Americans could so easily be blamed for the economic tribulations which the working classes had to endure. When Wedgwood as early as 1774 came across an armed mob of four hundred working men who had been out machine-breaking, they blamed the loss of their livelihood on the decline of trade, due to the American troubles.

This, of course, was scarcely half-true, but it was good grist for the patriot's mill. And once war began it changed many minds. Indeed nothing illustrates this better than the case of Bristol, where the earlier opposition to the American policy of Lord North's government was gradually overwhelmed; in 1775 the mayor, corporation and clergy sent in a Loyal Address to George III and in 1777 so did the Merchant Adventurers, expressing support of North's policy.

Also many Bristol merchants, who like Richard Champion worked for the American cause (short of independence) and supported wholeheartedly Burke and the Rockingham Whigs, feared an open alliance with the radicals when the real test of war came. 'The Leaders,' he wrote of the radicals,

are in themselves so little adequate to the task they have assumed, and conduct themselves with such a wildness of popularity, and so little attention to common sense, that with respect to the great point in view, the removal of the dangerous Faction at Court, which threatens destruction to the Liberties of the whole Empire, it can have no effect.†

---

* *Barlaston MSS*, J.W. to R.W. Mr Holland of Bolton, Lancs. (n.d.), c. November 1776.

† G. H. Guttridge (ed.), *The American Correspondence of a Bristol Merchant, 1766–76* (Berkeley, California, 1934), p. 2.

Champion's attitude to radicalism, of course, was similar to that of many New England merchants who, frightened of radicalism, became loyalists as the revolution developed. In America events, however, strengthened the radicals who secured the almost total support of the working classes and sufficient of the merchants to forge a common policy of action if not of ideas.*

Events reversed this process in England. Many British merchants feared not only the victories of the radicals but also that American independence would lead to a ruin of trade; and their fear was enormously strengthened when Congress entered into an alliance with France. Indeed the effect of this alliance on the British attitude towards the revolution has been consistently under-stressed. And here again, the distinction between what happened in America and in Britain is of exceptional importance. In America, radicals were able to exploit patriotic sentiment and so wrest the leadership from the more doubtful and conservative northern merchants or southern planters. Loyalists, supporters of conciliation, could be regarded as traitors, and treated as such.† The radical detestation of aristocracy could be clothed in hatred for British officials and royal servants. The xenophobic moods of the American mob could be used to threaten violence against all who suggested compromise. By such means the radical theories of natural rights, of the equality of men, the belief that all men had a right not only to life, liberty and the pursuit of happiness but also to overturn and abolish governments which did not grant them, became essentially American: here radical attitudes and patriotism were united by the call of war.

In England war *divided* radicalism and patriotism, and tainted the support of America with sedition. Tom Paine became not a hero but an anathema, the symbol of a violent, radical traitor. No one had been more constant in his sympathy towards America than Wedgwood; but war

* Philip Davidson, *Propaganda and the American Revolution, 1763–1783* (Chapel Hill, North Carolina, 1941), pp. 43–4.
† ibid., pp. 139–52.

brought him doubts. In the summer of 1779 the extension of the war had so denuded Britain of regular troops that the government encouraged its supporters to raise subscriptions or regiments or both in their counties. On 7 August 1779 Wedgwood attended a meeting of the Lord Lieutenant, Sheriff and gentlemen of Staffordshire: 'The meeting was thin but respectable in number,' Wedgwood reported,

and its proceedings enlightened only by a trenchant speech by Mr Eld, a man of eighty who, after complimenting the soldiers on their bravery, went on to say,

'In the times of our prosperity & exultation we, the gentlemen of this county, thought ourselves of consequence enough to address the throne, &, with offers of our lives & fortunes, call'd upon our sovereign to pursue the coersive measures already begun in America. In these days of our humiliation & despondency, which shd be a time for learning wisdom, I wish we cd now think ourselves of importance enough to address his majesty once more, & humbly beseech him to grant such terms to his late subjects in America *as freemen may accept.* I have heard of none such being hitherto offer'd to them. Submission without terms – Unconditional submission! are offers for slaves, & those who accept them must be such. I hope & trust we are none of us in love with slavery.' Mr Eld broke off rather abruptly, & without speaking to the specific business of the day, as I wish'd him to have done. He said ma[n]y good things, & said them well, & with great energy for an old man of 80.*

Wedgwood wished Eld to say more because he was troubled. He read all the arguments that he could about not subscribing, yet they did not carry conviction with him. They broke down because in the last resort they conflicted with his patriotism.

I am not at present fully convinced by them, that it is better to fall a prey to a foreign enemy rather than defend ourselves under the present ministry. Methinks I would defend the land of my nativity, my family and friends against a foreign foe, where conquest and slavery were inseparable, under any leaders – the best I could get for the moment, and wait for better times to displace an obnoxious minister, and settle domestic affairs, rather than

* *Barlaston MSS*, J.W. to B., 7 August 1779.

rigidly say, I'll be saved in my own way and by people of my own choice, or perish and perish my country with me. If subscribing would certainly rivet the present ministry in their places, and non-subscribing would as certainly throw them over, the nation at large being in no hazard at the same time from a foreign foe, I should not hesitate a moment what to do, but none of these propositions seem clear to me.*

Here we see how 'hazard from a foreign foe' was circumscribing Wedgwood's radical attitude. Radicalism was becoming unpatriotic; what in America gave radicalism its opportunities, in England inhibited them.

The upsurge of patriotic sentiment that Wedgwood experienced was typical of many men of similar views. Even Major Cartwright, one of the most dedicated supporters of the American revolution, who, indeed, sacrificed his military career and chance of marriage by his refusal to serve against the Americans, nevertheless took to organizing and drilling the militia in Nottinghamshire in case invasion by the French became a reality. Although such radical leaders as Cartwright continued to demand not only independence for America, but also linked it with the need for the reform of Parliament and an extension of the franchise, their support in Britain contracted rather than expanded once the country was involved in a large-scale war.

This also proved true of radicalism's best organized and strongest supporters, the freemen of the City of London. In the middle seventies they left Lord North's government in no doubt of their sympathy for the American revolution. In 1773 they chose two Americans, Stephen Sayre of Long Island and William Lee of Virginia, as sheriffs; in 1774 they insisted on their parliamentary candidates signing pledges to support a bill which would have given America the right to elect its own Parliament and tax itself. Naturally the Coercive Acts were denounced; even as late as 1778 they refused to give public support to the war. Yet even amongst men as tough-minded as these, there is a marked decline in their pro-American activity after 1776. The war constricted

* ibid.

~~their sympathy and restrained them from an all-out attack~~
on the institutions by which they were being governed.

In spite of the widespread radical sympathy that had existed for ten years or more, little had been done to channel it into an effective political party capable of action. It was this lack of organizational structure that permitted patriotic sentiment to corrode radical fervour and inhibit action. Yet the impotence of the radicals, particularly between 1774 and 1776, must not be exaggerated. They had captured more or less effective control of the Corporation of the City of London, and they even had one or two representatives in Parliament. And it should be remembered that in many ways the City Corporation was the most powerful single institution in Great Britain after Parliament. Although war certainly weakened the radicals' attitude and their influence, their ineffectiveness cannot be entirely explained either by the upsurge of patriotism or the incompetence of their political organization; a contributory cause, and an important one, arose from their total inability to carry any major Whig politician with them.

Lord Brougham, a radical himself and a politician with long parliamentary experience, wrote early in the nineteenth century, 'Is any man so blind as seriously to believe that, had Mr Burke and Mr Fox been ministers of George III, they would have resigned rather than try to put down the Americans?'* And it should be remembered that Charles James Fox spoke in favour of the Declaratory Act as late as 1778. The Whigs brought neither consistent action nor consistent policy to the American situation. In 1774 when radical agitation was at its strongest, the Whig leaders in opposition to the government showed the utmost reluctance to concentrate their energies on the problem of America.† The Duke of Richmond said he was sick of politics and Edmund Burke had to convince the Marquis of Rockingham

* Lord Brougham, *Historical Sketches of Statesmen who flourished in the time of George III* (London, 1839), I, pp. 303–4.

† G. H. Guttridge, *English Whiggism and the American Revolution* (Berkeley, California, 1942), pp. 76–7.

of 'the necessity of proceeding regularly, and with your whole force; and that this affair of America is to be taken up as business'.

Here was no realization of the profound social causes at work both in America and Britain; no sense of the future, nor of the need to reform political institutions as well as change ministries. The American problem was a useful weapon for Rockingham with which to attack North's administration, but he and his friends did not welcome the wider political and social implications of the American revolt. And yet without some effective leadership in Parliament, radicalism was hamstrung. Dissatisfaction with the oligarchical and aristocratic structure of British political and social life was widespread, but the frustration was neither deep enough nor savage enough to create an organization bent on forcing change.

Lacking political leadership in Parliament, smeared with anti-patriotism, the widespread radical sentiments of the late sixties and early seventies failed, except in the City of London itself, to become a powerful factor in the American revolution.

In the end neither the attitude of politicians nor radicals, not even the voice of merchants or industrialists, and least of all the pressure of the mob, proved significant. It was the disillusion of Lord Pembroke and his kind that brought about North's fall. The acceptance by Britain of America's independence was secured by those country gentlemen who had decided every major political issue in Great Britain since the Reformation. The country interest, the independent members who sat in Parliament as Knights of the Shire, who never spoke in debates and usually voted with the government, finally rebelled, for the very same reason that they had given their initial support to George III and Lord North – taxation. Self-interest, the need to lighten their own taxes, to relieve themselves of the costly burden of defending America, had combined with their traditional respect for the Crown and the sovereignty of Parliament to make them tolerant of the ramshackle confusion, the endless contradiction of what passed for American policy in the sixties and seventies. What broke their spirit was defeat at Yorktown and, more especially, the cost of defeat. They could not face the prospect of a protracted war of uncertain outcome.

Lord Pembroke's cry that he wished that he was a Laplander or anything but a Briton was the true patriot's cry, wrung from him by his deep sense of shame at his nation's failure. And basically this was the attitude of the country gentlemen. Indeed patriotic sentiment deeply influenced all British attitudes to the American revolution – perhaps more than any other factor. It was only to be expected that sympathy towards America should be rarest amongst those who were content with the fabric of British society – the aristocrats, gentry, government officers, admirals, generals, lawyers and ecclesiastics, and that it should be strongest amongst those new men – the industrial and aggressive commercial classes – to whom the future belonged. The extent of that sympathy was much wider, the identity of their interests with America much closer, than has been generally believed. Radical sentiment was very widespread in the late sixties and early seventies but its ineffectiveness became ever more apparent once the American revolution had become a European war: by that fact a terrible dilemma was created for the radicals and this, as much as anything, weakened resolve and helped to inhibit action – in such marked and vivid contrast with the developments of radicalism in America itself.

And this proved to be more than a transitory handicap to the development of radicalism in Britain, for although radicalism, especially in its demands for parliamentary reform, began to climb back to respectability under the aegis of William Pitt and William Wilberforce, the revolutionary wars with France reimposed, even more markedly, the stigma of disloyalty upon it. Demands for political and social equality became seditious: the ancient institutions – monarchy, aristocracy, landed gentry – were sanctified by patriotic gore. And this sanctification took place when the archaic institutions by which Britain was governed – an extraordinary hotchpotch of feudal custom, medieval charted rights and Tudor legislation – were becoming even more inadequate to meet the needs of the rising tide of industrialism. So when reform came in the nineteenth century, it was piecemeal, *ad hoc*, never radical in any fundamental sense: and Britain never enjoyed, as did America and France, the purging joys of a social and political revolution. In consequence a radical attitude to political institutions and social organization was in England always tainted with disloyalty. And, perhaps, it should be stressed once again that eighteenth- and early nineteenth-century British radicalism demanded no more than political and social equality, no more, in fact, than Americans were guaranteed by their Constitution. Such ideas, however, were no longer regarded as British; they were alien, Jacobin, Yankee or French.

Of course traditional institutions were strengthened by other factors apart from the alienation that took place between radicalism and patriotism at the time of the American and French revolutions; the possession of empire, particularly in India, fortified aristocratic and patriotic attitudes as well as the monarchy. Nevertheless the American revolution was almost as much a watershed in the development of British society as of American, for it rendered feeble a widespread middle-class intellectual radicalism that was beginning to take root in many of the socially and commercially aggressive sections of British society. Its failure to develop and grow; its relegation to political insignificance; its exclusion from the heart of British society, was to taint its middle-class radicalism with oddity, eccentricity, social neurosis, and so justify the continuing anti-intellectualism of the British Establishment. And the corollary was to link patriotism with George III, with monarchy no matter how stupid, with aristocracy no matter how incompetent. As a future of social equality and equal opportunity opened for America, Britain became more firmly saddled with its feudal past.

1964

7

*The Great Revolution**

The French revolution, mother of monsters – Robespierre, Marat, Fouquet, Napoleon; or a gorgon of iniquities, destructive of religion, of tradition, of the slowly accreted virtues of human society; or a breeder of evil that even in this century has spawned tyrants such as Hitler and Stalin; or was it rather the awkward, blood-stained dawn of all that is best in the modern world? Does the passionate hatred of injustice, of tyranny in all its forms, racial, colonial, religious, stem from these few dramatic years in Paris, when the age-old laws of subordination were irrevocably broken? Is it possible to eradicate all the subtle propaganda from the dashing Scarlet Pimpernels and heroic Sidney Cartons to the subtler denigrations of a Madelin or an Aulard? Can we ever forget the picture of the Terror in which fine-drawn aristo-crats met their death with stoic wit and unbearable dignity? Or readjust our ideas of Robespierre, Danton, Marat? Will Robespierre for ever remain in the historic consciousness of the West as the epitome of cold-hearted, passionless, in-tellectual revolutionaries who love ideas but hate men? Will Marat always seem to be as full of evil as of pus? And Danton lion-hearted but wrong-headed? Questions, indeed, that are far from rhetorical, for the French revolution has been too valuable a parable for the conservative forces in Western society for them to permit, without a struggle, novel and disinterested judgements.

For the conservatives the importance of the revolution lies

* R. R. Palmer, *The Age of Democratic Revolution*, vol. 2 (Princeton, 1964).

in its failure. In their hands it becomes a demonstration of the appalling folly of intellectuals prepared to use violence to achieve their ideals. The attempt to create a new society, to break with deeply rooted traditions, led merely, so they say, to wanton bloodshed, to corruption, to the triumph of sordid adventurers, and finally to aggressive tyranny. In their hands this becomes the pattern not for one, but for all, revolutions. Atheistical and rational societies, they hope, will get the short shrift that they deserve from historical destiny. But they go further than this. They argue that the revolution bred in the French a contagious folly and their addiction to the idea and practice of revolution brought about the insecurity and the instability of nineteenth-century Europe as the virus spread east and south. And they particularly castigate the idea, first adumbrated in the French revolution, that a band of dedicated intellectuals might capture and mould the forces of society to their own purpose. For this they feel has brought the present world, through its success in Russia and China, to the brink of ruin. How much wiser, they feel, would Europe and the world have been to have followed the methods of Britain and the precepts of Edmund Burke: to have put their trust in the slow, organic growth of society, for each nation to have found, cautiously and empirically, those institutions of government and social forms that were best suited to its nature and conformable to its history. True liberalism, they suggest, is to be found in the history of England and America and not in the over-excitable, over-intellectual history of France. The revolutionary nature of America's struggle with Britain is elided, becomes essentially conservative, reformatory, an affirmation of state and corporate rights, of freehold and liberty: indeed the restoration of those essentially British virtues which England had momentarily betrayed at the behest of a stupid king and corrupt government. Nor is this all; the heroic defiance by Britain of revolutionary and Napoleonic tyranny saved more than liberty, more than freedom, it also preserved the Christian foundations of Western society, American as well as European. For the revolution was directed not only against kings, and nobles, but also against God and the Church, Protestant as well as Catholic.

Such attitudes are unconsciously present in most of us and are to be found, at times blatantly, at others subtly, in scholarly as well as popular histories of the French revolution, certainly of those that form the basis of our education. Professor Palmer has attempted to provide an antidote in a book that is as remarkable for the coolness of its judgement as the width of its scholarship. Unfortunately Professor Palmer is so level-headed that he becomes flat-footed. The Himalayan grandeurs of the revolution are reduced by his remorseless prose to the monotony of a steppe. Perhaps he has deliberately turned his back on all forms of literary craftsmanship in order to strengthen the impact on the reader of his deliberate, purposeful, common-sense, scholarly based judgements. If so, it is a pity. Professor Palmer is equipped as few other professional historians are to produce an outstanding work of synthesis, and one which could have played a vitally important role in the historiography of the French revolution. There is an overwhelming need to make the work of continental scholars available to an English reading public and thereby to readjust our attitude towards the French revolution, which is so misunderstood both in America and in England. Professor Palmer has missed a golden opportunity.

Few professors, let alone students or schoolteachers, will plod through the monotonous swamps of this splurging book, which at times reads like a string of ill-digested review articles, at others like a précis for the classroom of the works of outstanding European scholars – Soboul, Godechot, Cobb, Zagli, etc., etc. The construction of the book, too, leaves much to be desired. The theme, the French revolution and Europe, presents great difficulties and probably no treatment would be entirely satisfactory. Also, it is part of Professor Palmer's purpose to deal with the revolutionary movements in Hungary, in Holland, or in Naples, etc., in their own context and not view them from a Parisian standpoint, nor in terms of the European war, nor indeed in the light of the famous, such as Napoleon or Nelson. The revolutionary movement is his preoccupation, no matter how distant or remote (even Bahia gets a mention). The result is a lack of balance and a failure of coherence. It is strange, for example, that the revolutionary movement in Austro–Hungary should have been given as much space as the Terror in Paris. Yet, in spite of these strictures, which to some may seem too severe, this is the most important book on the Europe of the French revolution published in English for more than a generation.

It marks the turn of the tide, demonstrating as it does the hollowness of the current conservative interpretation of the revolution, and it will discredit for the future all sloppy generalizations about Jacobins, demagogues and revolutionary mobs. First, however, to Professor Palmer's credentials. Work on the French revolution is voluminous and multi-lingual and since the war output has been intensified. Professor Palmer has mastered this in five languages and where not linguistically equipped has gone to great trouble to secure personal translations and précis of important works. His knowledge of printed sources is exceptionally thorough, ancient as well as modern, and his judgement of what is good and reliable seems unerring. He accepts a great deal of the work of the young radical historians of France, particularly A. Soboul, who is a Marxist, but never uncritically. Rightly Palmer cannot conceive of understanding the French revolution except in terms of class conflict. He would allow situations, ideas, or even sheer blind chance greater significance than Soboul and he is less ready to see the Communist content of Babouvism or the effectiveness of revolutionary élites, but he accepts Soboul's analysis of the nature of the *sans-culottes* and the Jacobins, as indeed all scholars must.

Indeed here is the basic question that Palmer constantly asks and constantly answers. Who were the revolutionaries, not only in Paris, but also in Milan, Budapest, Warsaw, Frankfurt, Basel, Rome, Naples, Geneva, or anywhere else that gave birth to revolutionaries or supporters of the revolution? Were they cranks, misfits, screwballs, secret society addicts, charlatans, or near lunatics such as Cagliostro or

Poderatz, or sensible, well-integrated citizens with positive social ideals and reasonable political aims? Throughout his detailed analysis, Palmer discovers the same basic result, which varies naturally according to the different social circumstances of Eastern, Western or Southern Europe, but remains in essence the same. The revolutionaries, the Jacobins, were most frequently doctors, lawyers, professional men of all kinds, interlaced with bankers, merchants, bureaucrats, university professors, and occasional clerics; in places they were joined by members of the lower nobility; sometimes where national issues were acute, as in Poland or the Hapsburg empire, members of the aristocracy also threw in their lot with the revolutionary forces. In the main, however, it was a solid middle-class movement that derived its major support not from the landless peasantry or the urban proletariat but from skilled craftsmen, shopkeepers, small backyard manufacturers, clerks, schoolmasters, and some minor clergy – from, indeed, the petty bourgeoisie who stood to gain most from a state freed from traditional privilege, feudal obligations, and oligarchical graft. And the ideals for which the revolutionaries fought, and frequently died, were those which the twentieth century has come to regard as belonging to the party for humanity – for that party which feels that all men, high born or low born, shall be equal before the law, that there shall be no distinction of race, creed or colour, that education should be public, discussion and comment free, and that the laws of nations should be based on reason. Such men based their faith neither in tradition nor in Providence but in man and his capacities. And perhaps it is as well to remind American readers that the Jacobins wherever found, whether in the ruthless Committee of Public Safety or in the Senate of the Cisalpine Republic, had more beliefs in common with Sam Adams or Benjamin Franklin than they had in difference.

For English readers it is even more salutary to stress that their long war against France was a war not only in defence and in extension of their vast commercial empire but also in support of the ramshackle monarchies and aristocracies of feudal Europe; that they fought not for liberty but for privilege, not for equality but for human subordination. The limit to what the British could tolerate is shown by their action in Corsica when it became a part of the British dominions. They set up a landowners' democracy on the English model and when their efforts failed offered the island to Catherine of Russia. Perhaps there is no better comment on the British position than that displayed by Nelson himself. After the defeat of the Neapolitan revolution he wrote to his subordinate Foote, 'Your news of the hanging of thirteen Jacobins gave us great pleasure; and the three priests I hope [will] dangle on the tree best adapted to the weight of their sins.' Better the Bourbons than the bourgeoisie. That is why so many forward-looking, intelligent, generous-hearted Englishmen bitterly opposed the war against revolutionary France as they had that against revolutionary America – a fact ignored by some but forgotten by most British historians.

Because there is an attitude of mind and heart that needs correcting, it is a pity that this wise book is not better presented. We live with history, it informs all our reactions to the world about us, and we need an understanding of the French revolution in order to comprehend our own problems, hatreds and jealousies. The distorted myths with which we have been fed have confounded and baffled the aims of the Enlightenment and the nature of liberalism to our own loss. This last one hundred and fifty years the bogey of revolution has too frequently led the United States and Britain to support murderous regimes of outmoded privilege in Latin America, in the Caribbean, in Africa, and in the Far East, and to their own cost and loss. The middle classes of the Western world have been taught to hate their own revolutionary origins. If only Garrett Mattingley had written this book, the bogeymen would be in danger. As it is, the tumbrils will still rattle over the stones, those dignified aristocrats, the epitome of human and Christian virtues, will still go nobly to their sacrifice amidst the bloodthirsty jeers and obscene revellings of the Parisian *canaille*. Someone soon, however, will write the book that will blow this garish nonsense away. For scholarship has done its task, and the world is both more understanding and more sympathetic to the causes for which the French revolutionary fought and died. When the book is written, it will owe an immeasurable debt to Professor Palmer, to his scholarship, to his stamina, and above all to the excellence of his judgement.

1964

8

*Edmund Burke and his Cult**

The world of political ideas is an odd world to move around in, and none odder than Russell Kirk's *Conservative Mind*,† in which Edmund Burke is revealed as the great prophet of Anglo-American conservatism. Throughout this book, the implication is that radicals are addicted to non-realistic, richly sentimental, over-optimistic abstractions, whereas conservatives are down-to-earth men, whose ideas are firmly anchored in a hard-headed appraisal of human nature and a deep sense of the history of mankind. Quaint, indeed, to think that 'equality' is more abstract than 'tradition', that 'moral essence' should mean more than 'human need', that reverence for the past should have a higher moral value than hope for the future. Above all, there is the monumental self-deception of the conservative that anti-rationalism is wisdom. Russell Kirk quotes Keith Feiling with solemn approval: 'Every Tory is a realist. He knows there are great forces in heaven and earth that man's philosophy cannot plumb or fathom. We do wrong to deny it, when we are told that we do not trust human reason: we do not and we may not.' Distrust of reason: here is the self-revealed core of conservative belief and so, as we might expect, a few sneering asides are made by Kirk about a 'world smudged with industrialism' and 'corrosive intellectual atomism'. And it comes as no surprise that at the end of his essay on Burke he should drool about 'the tidy half-timbered inn, the great oaks and the quiet lanes of Beaconsfield' and sneer at the villas, housing

* Carl B. Cone, *Burke and the Nature of Politics*, 2 vols. (Louisville, Kentucky, 1957, 1964). † London, 1954.

estates and light industry that have bitten deep into Buckinghamshire countryside since Burke's day. Here is Tory realism with a vengeance: like the half-timbered inn, it is largely phony. The rationalization of prejudice, the sanctification of the status quo, the attribution of historical inevitability and Divine Providence to inequality and human suffering certainly acquired its most persuasive apologist in Burke and so, perhaps, it is not surprising that he is rapidly becoming a cult.

As well as a cult, Burke is a serious historical figure. The mass of his papers and the variety of his correspondence, to say nothing of the devious nature of his life, have, however, made him a professional historical problem of the first magnitude. Professor Copeland has organized a team of dedicated Anglo-American editors, and the volumes of his correspondence are flowing from the press, beautifully and skilfully edited in the highest traditions of American scholarship. This type of task is so much more professionally and skilfully accomplished by American editors: and British scholars would never have achieved so definitive an edition if left to their own devices. After the correspondence, one can only hope that the papers will follow and then a critical edition of the published works, for after all Burke is one of the founders of European conservatism and no matter how silly and self-deceiving his views may be, they deserve, historically speaking, a proper treatment. They require understanding but not an idolatrous revival.

Many scholars will regard Carl Cone as being immensely venturesome in producing a long two-volume life of Burke before the essential work of editing is completed. Burke was, rightly from his own point of view, extremely sensitive about many of his activities, particularly those which involved money and his relatives. His namesake, William, whom he called cousin, was an adventurer devoid of any sense of financial morality, whose sole aim in life was to make a fortune by any means that came handy. Although a fortune eluded him, he bore his burden of personal debt (£20,000 alone to Lord Verney) with indifference, if not panache, and lived the life of eighteenth-century affluence. Burke was not only devoted to him but also involved in many of his dubious financial transactions. Burke's relations with his brother, Richard, almost as devious as William, remain equally obscure, and far more light on the more disreputable side of Burke's life may yet be forthcoming. It will not, however, alter the essential picture. The vast amount of detail about Burke's life and politics, already known, make this huge biography very well worth while. Delay would not have improved it. Again, like the edition of Burke's correspondence, this biography is typical of much sound American professional scholarship. There is little analysis, little judgement, but a steady, accurate, comprehensive narrative of Burke's life, interspersed with an excellent précis of what he said and wrote. As an account of Burke's life it will survive many generations. For an interpretation of Burke's character, however, it will have to be supplemented by the brilliant, brief biography which John Brooke contributed to the *History of Parliament*.

Brooke and Namier have been castigated for their treatment of Burke, for taking a low view of his character, for dismissing so many of his ideas as self-deceiving humbug, and for accusing him of creating the absurd mythology which has clouded so much of the history of George III's reign. Wrongly, it seems to me. Burke was not a simple man. His nature demanded action and constant justification for what he did, intended to do, and even hoped others might do. Rationalization was a deep psychological need, so his pursuit of power and fame required to be justified in moral and philosophic terms. Hence his concern lay rather with political attitudes than political action. He was led to those attitudes by the necessities of his own life – money, patronage, status. Yet no matter how self-seeking the motives, or self-righteous the implications, the views which Burke adumbrated must be judged as views, as ideas, as political attitudes. Although it helps us understand his character to juxtapose his ardent advocacy of the economical reform of the Royal Household with his avaricious demand when in office for places,

sinecures and pensions for his dependants, this does not in-
validate his arguments. There is no essential contradiction
between Burke as a great political philosopher and the
character of him drawn by Brooke.

There is a need to know his character and circumstances
to appraise the emotional force of his ideas and why they
have struck such a sympathetic echo in the unconscious
minds of generations of men: for, in many ways, Burke
persuades by rhetoric rather than by argument. As Namier
and Brooke have been quick to point out, Burke's exceptionally difficult family life deeply influenced his attitude to
authority and power. His mother was neurotic, possibly she
suffered from mental illness; his father was tyrannical. Re-
jecting his father's plans for his career, Burke arrived in
London with little but his wits to sustain him. Although a
gifted and ambitious man could move about eighteenth-
century English society with ease, he could never hope to
feel that deep sense of belonging that came naturally to those
born within it. An alien adventurer of remarkable literary
gifts, perceptive insight into human nature, powerful if
disturbed character, and a greedy ambition for affluence,
Burke needed patrons as he needed roots: he wanted to find
the security that as a child he had never known, and as a
man would always elude him.

This sensitivity to the needs of his own security was
generalized and projected with great subtlety by Burke not
only into political action but also into political thought.
Insecurities in all their varied forms riddle most human lives
creating needs for habits, rituals, shibboleths, even historical
tradition. And it was in this area that Burke's own personal
compulsions fused with the needs of mankind, and he
possessed the gifts of thought and language that could give
a sense of inevitable destiny to this urge for security. And yet,
of course, this alone could not have been responsible for his
vast reputation with ensuing generations. In Burke's world
insecurity was growing – the revolt of America, the stirrings
in Ireland, the onslaught of the French revolution, the turmoil in India, all threatened the security of eighteenth-

century society. But insecurity went deeper than this, and continued to grow: new forms of wealth in commerce and industry challenged the supremacy of those great landed families whom Burke liked to picture as the great oaks of England. Graver still were the growing threats of violence from the lower classes, interlaced with cries for liberty: and the ever urgent demands for reform and a wider democracy. In Burke's day the voice of the *sans-culotte* echoed round the seats of power and made their occupants nervous. To natural psychological insecurities which beset men were added, therefore, fears for wealth and authority. And as these insecurities grew with the developing social and industrial revolutions of the nineteenth and twentieth centuries, so grew the veneration for Burke. What for him had been largely a psychological need became a philosophy of anti-democratic greed.

Burke, throughout his life, operated in many dimensions, but two are of major importance – his contribution to the political structure of eighteenth-century England and his general political philosophy. The former is a bone of contention between scholars. What he tried to do, and his motives here are of no great importance, was to give a greater unity of principle and a firmer consistency in action to the Rockingham Whigs, to transform them in their own and in other people's estimation from a faction to a party. In the highly personalized politics of eighteenth-century England fragmentation of political groups took place with ease and frequency, making it so much easier for an active monarch, such as George III, to influence policy and decision. So Burke tried to weld the Rockingham Whigs into a party of known principles which would act consistently in opposition and enter office as a body on their own terms, which they finally achieved in 1782. Certainly this crusade of Burke's helped to revitalize politics and helped to create the sense that opposition should be based on political and intellectual alternatives to the government in office rather than mere factional warfare. Although much of Burke's own analysis of the contemporary political scene was biased and wrong, nevertheless he remains one of the most significant figures in the constitutional history of Britain in the late eighteenth century, and this aspect of Burke's career is exhaustively and admirably dealt with by Professor Cone.

However, Burke's major dimension lies in his role as the founder of modern conservatism – now the object of a special and dedicated lobby among American historians, who are steadily pushing Burkeian studies into political philosophy courses as a means of propaganda. Burke believed that wisdom was instinctive and religious rather than rational or intellectual. Time and Providence, the slow revelation of moral law and moral purpose, human wisdom gradually accreted over the centuries like a geological sediment, the poverty of reason compared with the Divine Plan which mysteriously binds past, present and future together, the idea that there is an order, sanctified by God and History, that keeps things (and men) fast in their place – these concepts litter Burke's works and speeches. Reason, or enlightenment, these are figments of dreams, delusions, fairy lights in the scarcely knowable mysteries of human society. These the wise man scoffs at. In phrases such as these, often rhetorized into paragraphs and pages of compelling eloquence, Burke gave an air of virtue, morality and godly wisdom to an attitude that was anti-intellectual, and dominated by the meaner and more aggressive aspects of human nature. It is extraordinary that such lucubrations should be regarded as having any intellectual value whatsoever – emotional value for those who need them, perhaps, but intellectually most of Burke's political philosophy is utter rubbish, and completely unhistorical.

There is no room to argue the case against Burkeian conservatism fully here but the nub of the matter would seem to lie in this. Why should a rationalist, intellectual approach to the problems of human organization seem either wicked or stupid or both, when such problems as man has solved – control of power, the diminution of diseases, etc., have been achieved by their application? Why should a reliance on intellect be regarded as foolishly optimistic or wildly idealistic and an addiction to tradition, ancestral wisdom, and the mysteries of Providence be the hallmark of sound judgement? Burke clothed in the eloquent language of religion and ethics the nakedness of private greed and public oppression. He himself was too complex, his needs too conflicting for his thoughts and actions to be synthesized in a few sentences, but certainly that has been his value for the generations of conservatives who have revered him. As an outsider who never got in, Burke often felt himself drawn to the oppressed, the wronged, the impotents of society: and alongside Burke the conservative there was also Burke the reformer who gets scant attention. As Professor Cone illustrates again and again Burke is often far more complex, far more fascinating in action than when his pen flows with piety and gets lost in the meaningless verbiage of political theology.

1965

9

*Slavery, Race and the Poor**

Often social change is imperceptible to those living in its midst. It is like water oozing through a dam – at first a faint dampness, a trickle, a spurt, the cracks multiply and either the dam crumbles or the pushing waters are sufficiently eased to create a new, if unstable, equilibrium. To the Black Panthers and other groups of activists the change in social attitudes in America towards the Negro is derisory, and when not derisory a conscience-easing fake. To white Anglo-Saxon Protestants, conscious or unconscious, or to ethnic groups living near to black ghettoes or in competition with blacks for jobs, the rushing of the waters is so deafening that they are driven towards panic and hysteria. To the uneasy liberal, the situation borders on the grotesque. He wants to be fair, to make retribution, and yet he cannot easily accept the new black contempt towards the white. He is also conscious, per-haps over-conscious, of the militant blacks' hatred of white democracy, and their growing insistence on authoritarian, almost totalitarian, attitudes within the black community.

The situation of the historian is equally acute. What has been the role of the Negro in American history? What have been the long-term results of slavery and deprivation of civil rights? Indeed what was the true nature of American slavery – was it the most evil type the world has known or no better and no worse than the rest of the New World experienced?

* Winthrop D. Jordan, *White over Black: American Attitudes towards the Negro, 1550–1812* (Chapel Hill, North Carolina, 1968); *Black History: A Reappraisal*, ed. Melvin Drimmer (New York, 1968); *American Negro Slavery: A Modern Reader*, ed. Allen Weinstein and Frank Otto Gatell (Oxford, 1968); Michael Banton, *Race Relations* (New York, 1968).

These problems have never been easy to answer, but in the context of the present time they are much more difficult, for now the question has to be posed – how far was racism itself responsible for the wretchedness of the Negro slave? Did it give a peculiarly vicious twist to slavery? Indeed what are the connections between racism and slavery? And of course this raises the question of the nature of slavery – unbridled racism combined with absolute, or near absolute, authority of the racist master was unlikely to lead to anything but social brutality, of treating the slave more as a chattel than as a person.

At the present time possibly the problem of racism and slavery is the most insistent, for obvious reasons. For the professional historian there are others equally difficult but intellectually perhaps more exciting. There is Stanley M. Elkin's brilliant and disturbing investigation of slavery and the Negro personality, examining the reasons for the development of the 'Sambo' response of the Negro slave to his environment which would help to explain the paucity of slave revolts in America. (No amount of black protest or black rewriting of history can overcome that fact. The American Negro slave protested less in his society than the free peasant class of Europe, or of England for that matter, and this needs explanation.) Less original, but more deeply and professionally argued, is Eugene Genovese's memorable book, *The Political Economy of Slavery* (1965), which attempts to relate all aspects of Southern life to its peculiar means of economic exploitation. Indeed Genovese analyses the social system, based on slavery, from its basic economic structure, through its institutionalization of power, to its self-justification and its sense of pride in itself. Slave society, Genovese has shown, was far more complex than most historians have allowed.

Apart from Elkins and Genovese many historians have recently made contributions of great value to the story of slavery and the South. Indeed the richness of historical writing is well brought out in the two anthologies under review. This type of book is stupidly despised by academicians with lunatic standards of scholarly endeavour, usually not for themselves, but for their pupils. Yet how could the modern undergraduate cope with the swelling bibliographies on any major theme without such assistance? Both *American Negro Slavery: A Modern Reader* by Allen Weinstein and Frank Otto Gatell and *Black History: A Reappraisal* provide an admirable selection of the best writers on the Negro question and will give the moderately diligent student an insight into the difficulties, arguments and material of the problem.

Here he can read in fascinating apposition the bland apologetics of Ulrich B. Phillips, the moral incisiveness of Kenneth Stampp, the sophisticated approaches of David Brion Davis or Winthrop Jordan, and the valuable and all too rare local studies of Edward W. Phifer, whose account of slavery in Burke County ought to have a myriad of imitators, since even the best analyses of slavery rely far too heavily on the great plantations of the Tidewater or the accounts of foreign travellers who kept to a well-worn track. Slaves, like the industrial proletariat, were exploited in myriad ways, and, like the proletariat too, in varying degrees of in-humanity. It is as important not to concentrate on the worst as not to forget it.

Yet in all this wonderful range of work on slavery, as exciting, as deeply original, as any going forward on any other aspect of American social history, there is one singular omission. There is no comparative study of slavery and poverty. By this I do not mean a study of the economic condition of slaves compared with free Negroes in the slums of southern cities such as New Orleans, which indeed has been examined by Richard C. Wade, but of the attitude of slave owners towards slaves compared with the attitude, not only of industrial, but of pre-industrial owners of wealth towards the poor, especially in Europe, from 1540 to 1750, for in a sense America had too few poor in the early centuries for any comparison to be meaningful.

New World slavery raises two profound problems. Why was it so easily accepted by all Western European nations at a time when slavery had ceased to be socially important for many generations in their own countries? And secondly why did abolitionists become socially and politically effective from the last third of the eighteenth century? The answers to these questions will obviously illuminate the whole nature of slavery. It is my conviction that these answers can only be found within the non-servile context of the exploitation of labour, and the ideology that goes with it. And this brings one to Winthrop D. Jordan's outstanding book, a volume to be placed alongside Stampp, Elkins, Davis and Genovese.

Jordan's thesis is straightforward. The Elizabethan Englishmen coming across primitive black men for the first time were repelled. To them black men were associated with beastliness; their inferiority made them the lowest link in the great Chain of Being. Blackness stimulated the Englishman's sense of guilt and horror. His Devil was, after all, black, and he always put a high price upon fairness of skin. The primitive societies of West Africa, with their strange and divergent customs, strengthened the Elizabethans' belief in the eternal, God-given inferiority of the Negro – a little higher, maybe, than the apes, but infinitely lower than the white Englishman. Negroes naturally were 'addicted unto Treason, Treacherie, Murther, Theft and Robberie' as well as idleness and lechery.

Hence the proper status of Negroes was slavery. Slavery fitted their natures whose outward sign was the blackness of their skin. And it was because they were black that it became easy to justify slavery and maintain it. This racism can be further illustrated by the treatment of free or freed Negroes, whose rights were subject to strict limitation; even the onus of proof that he was free rested with him, for society expected, owing to his colour, that he would necessarily be a slave. From the earliest days of slavery this element of racism – evident also in the detestation of miscegenation – was dominant and it became more and more powerful as Negroes grew in number and slavery became the dominant social system of the South. This, in essence, is Jordan's argument and it is based on a wealth of material which ranges from the sermons of sixteenth-century English bishops to obscure travellers' reports from Africa, court session records of the Slave States, newspaper files throughout the South, the lucubrations of philosophers in the eighteenth century, the voluminous correspondence of the Founding Fathers and a host of other sources. Indeed the range of Jordan's reading is prodigious.

That racism gave an added dimension to slavery cannot be doubted; but it is a most difficult question to decide on its extent. Jordan contends with a wealth of quotation from Elizabethan literature and from African travellers' tales that the sixteenth-century Englishman regarded the Negro as not only savage, heathen, biologically close to the ape, but also as theologically damned; for the Negro was descended from Ham, Noah's disinherited son, who was cursed by having black offspring. Since the Englishman's Devil was always portrayed as black, Negroes were associated with evil and linked ever more firmly to God's curse. Furthermore, they proved helpless against the 'angel-like' English, whose whiteness proclaimed them to be beloved of God: so, rightly, good was triumphing over evil.

These attitudes to the Negroes made the enslavement of them by the English both natural and ferocious. Unlike Catholic Europeans, the English had no interest in conversion and so long as the black remained a heathen savage in a Christian society the Negro slave could have no rights. Hence the slave possessed fewer human rights in English slave-holding societies than in others ancient or modern. From start to finish American slavery was racial: indeed Jordan calls it racial slavery. In one essential Jordan is correct. Negroes were considered born inferiors, born slaves if you will, to a degree that was not applied to many other groups of slaves. The Roman slave was treated just as brutally, at times far more brutally, than the Southern Negro. He certainly possessed no more rights. But, once freed, the world was open to him. He and his family could rise or fall like any other man in the Roman state, so long as he had either ability or money or both. Not so the Negro. The freed Negro entered a caste which was excluded from most of the benefits and all of the power in the society to which it belonged. And the basis of this exclusion was racial. This far one can go with Jordan.

But it could also be argued that racism went far beyond slavery, so that it cannot be viewed simply in terms of slavery. Racism was not, of course, confined to the Southern slave masters or to Southern slave society in the sixteenth and seventeenth centuries. It was just as rampant in the Portuguese empire. Franciscans in the seventeenth century in Goa attempted to prevent Portuguese born of pure white parents from entering their order on the grounds that having been suckled by Indian wet-nurses, their blood was contaminated for life.* This surely is racism as extravagant as any to be found in the Southern States. Again, Jordan makes a great deal of the deliberate exclusion of the Negro from the Anglican Church, but Catholic slave owners were no more eager for their blacks to be a part of their Church. As one Portuguese slave owner exclaimed indignantly, 'Should my Kaffirs receive communion? God forbid that I should ever allow them.'†' Indeed the literature of the sixteenth and seventeenth centuries is full of savagely expressed racism directed not only to the Negro but the Hindu, the Hottentot, the Welsh, Scots, Irish, French against English, English against the Dutch.

Nor was Negro slavery the only slavery justified on racist grounds, nor was the Englishman's attitude unique, as Jordan implies. If one glances at the reaction of the Chinese mandarins of the T'ang dynasty to the primitive peoples of Nam Viet (the tropical south) the response is the same; a combination of curiosity, superiority and utter loathing. 'Both conscience and law permitted the enslavement of these subject peoples all the more readily because of two persistent views of them,' writes Edward Schafer in *The Vermilion Bird*,‡ his remarkable study of the T'ang mandarins' involvement with the south, 'an older one, that they were not really human, and a younger one derived from the first, that they were not really civilized.' These arguments are frequently used about the Negro: yet the enslavement of the primitive people of Nam Viet never developed into the equivalent of Negro slavery, for the Chinese did not require slaves on such a scale.

* C. R. Boxer, *The Portuguese Seaborne Empire* (London, 1969).
† ibid.   ‡ Berkeley, California, 1967.

Racism does not create slavery. It is an excuse for it. Racism was a rampant feature of the centuries when slavery was being established in America and it was, therefore, easy to make it one of the justifications for the institution. But racism could be intense and not lead to slavery – and racism does not explain why the European nations found so little difficulty in adopting slavery in their colonies long after the institution had become insignificant in Europe's economic structure.

Although the institution had no economic relevance in contemporary Europe, the idea of slavery was both potent and entirely acceptable on stronger grounds than those of race. The English House of Commons did not even turn a hair at the suggestion that persistent English vagabonds should be enslaved by their fellow countrymen and they passed an Act in 1547 for this purpose: along, of course, with branding the victims with a large S. It failed and was repealed, but not on humanitarian grounds. No one wanted slaves – there was enough cheap labour without them, requiring no more food and less supervision. But the idea of white slavery was in no way repellent to the Tudors, or limited by them to savages and heathens. Indeed the condition of slavery had been accepted by the Church and by society from time out of mind; a part of that great law of subordination without which the whole edifice of society might crash to the ground. Without slave status, what would happen to bonded servants, to children sold as apprentices, to the indignant poor who had no rights in society except to labour? Slavery was only the most extreme of all servile conditions. Servant and slave were more than semantically linked.

The type of abuse that was hurled at the slave was hurled at the poor, particularly in English society, from which many Southern slave masters were drawn. Take these remarks of William Perkins, the popular puritan preacher of the early seventeenth century:

Rogues, beggars, vagabonds . . . commonly are of no civil society or corporation nor of any particular Church; and are as rotten legs and arms that drop from the body. . . . To wander up and down from year to year to this end, to seek and procure bodily maintenance is no calling, but the life of a beast.

or this from his colleague Sibbes: 'They are the refuse of mankind: as they are in condition so they are in disposition.'

These puritan divines were more charitable than many. The rogues and vagabonds were, of course, the wandering poor desperate for food. Their lot was bloody whippings, frequent branding and enforced labour. The early slave codes were very similar to the legislation designed to control the Elizabethan unemployed poor. Again, the poor, like slaves, were, it is now thought, neither expected to go to Church or be welcomed there. And as for cruelty, treatment of apprentices could be vicious, the floggings and brandings meted out to the 'dregs of society' of Elizabethan and Stuart England almost as savage as anything the Negro knew; perhaps at times more so, for the poor were no man's property, and hence valueless if sick, weak or contumacious.

Again, miscegenation: the taboos against marrying the poor were formidable – for a woman it usually meant total ostracism – yet, of course, the young servant women, like slave Negresses, could be and were fair game for their masters. And even the Sambo mentality can be found in the deliberately stupid country yokel or the Cockney clown of later centuries. And so, too, the belief, as with Negroes, that they were abandoned sexually, given both to promiscuity and over-indulgence. Slave, servant, worker were the objects of exploitation, the sources of labour, therefore wealth; hence we should not be surprised to find similar attitudes, similar social oppressions operating against the poor as against the slave. Slavery and poverty in these centuries are not different in kind but different in degree, and the disadvantage was not always the slave's for, as property, he might be treated with greater consideration in sickness or in old age than the wage-slave. Because America did not know poverty, rural or urban, as Europe did in those early formative years, historians tend to attribute to slavery conditions which spring from the intensive exploitation of labour, whether 'free' or servile.

I do not doubt that racism gave an added intensity, a further degree of hopelessness and degradation to slavery and the slave's lot, but it is important to see the similarities in the treatment of slaves and the poor: otherwise one cannot realize how natural slavery was to the majority of men who practised it or accepted it.

To underline this, if underlining be needed, slavery was often – not always but often – at its cruellest where intensive economic exploitation was at its highest, namely on the great plantations. The comparatively mild slavery of Cuba turned into a far more vicious and disciplined form with the rise of the large sugar plantations, as Michael Banton points out in his admirable *Race Relations*, a book which really deserves a far more extensive treatment than can be given it here. Just as a discussion of slavery without a consideration of the exploitation of other labourers tends to obscure fundamental issues, so too can racism and questions of civil rights obscure the deeper issues. No amount of civil rights can alleviate the Negro's lot, for much of the hatred of the black springs from the rich's fear of the poor and dispossessed. The basis of the problem is exploitation: the gross injustice which acquisitive society always inflicts on those who have nothing to offer but their body's labour. Hence the absence of an extended consideration of other labouring poor weakens to some extent the force of Jordan's book.

Once Jordan moves into the eighteenth century there is a greater sense of mastery, and he is particularly skilful in tracing the evasions of the Founding Fathers and the reasons why they could not face the question of abolition. Jordan analyses very subtly the conflict between the insistence on natural rights and the Lockeian concept of the holiness of property. The easiest escape was to defend natural rights negatively, and after the first flush of idealism, revolutionary America had little difficulty in pushing the question of slavery on to the sidelines. But this was as far as it could be pushed: for by 1800 white America's dilemma became both clearer and more devastating to its conscience. How could they keep the purity of white America free from Negro contamination?

How could they preserve all that they thought was best in American society, even the inviolability of family life, if they allowed Negroes to be emancipated? And yet their revolutionary cultural heritage, their growing sense that Destiny had placed the moral future of the world in their hands 'prohibited extreme, overt manifestations of aggression against them'. Here were the roots both of a crisis of conscience and of its solution. Slavery was destroyed, yet racism preserved. And how this was achieved has been little understood.

The story of abolition, the reasons why the whole of Europe in the last third of the eighteenth century began to acquire a strong distaste firstly for the slave trade and even for slavery itself, is a vast question which none of the great historians of slavery – Davis, Jordan, Stampp, Genovese, Elkins – have yet attempted. It is a highly complex issue. The important factor is not the conversion of Quakers to anti-slavery attitudes, nor the convictions of a few intellectuals; voices, some weak, some powerful, had always been raised against slavery. The real question is why did abolition acquire a strong social basis, why did it become a passionate political issue? Again, I believe that this cannot be understood in isolation from the working class and the different attitude which was developing towards it. The most fertile ground for conversion to anti-slavery agitation, besides the Quakers, was in England amongst the entrepreneurs of the industrial revolution: the manufacturing districts (as against the commercial) were inclined to produce the subscribers, the speakers and the supporters of the anti-slavery movement; not all, of course, but it was an area of marked sympathy.

From the middle of the eighteenth century, and indeed far earlier amongst the Quaker industrialists, one can find a changing attitude to the poor labouring man, the attitude that he turned into a better, more profitable tool if he were given incentives, that is if he were encouraged to feel that his work possessed opportunities for self-advancement and better conditions, no matter how rudimentary. Furthermore, the new industrial methods required more self-disciplined skilful, better educated, literate labourers. The more imaginative, speculative manufacturers, such as Josiah Wedgwood, Jedediah Strutt and Robert Owen, experimented with higher wages, bonus schemes, better housing, works canteens, children's schools and the like. Instead of labouring men, exploiters now wanted tools, and far more tools than the old craftsman methods of industrial organization permitted: also their new tools needed to be more specialized and more limited. Master craftsmen were not wanted. Tools or 'hands' were wanted, and they could be created from the labouring mass. Also a pool of labouring men, skilled, semi-skilled and unskilled, selling their labour on a free market, was invaluable for keeping down wages. In a world of violent business cycles, 'free' labour obviously had great advantages over unfree. Manufacturers' attitudes were rarely as crudely materialistic as this, any more than those of the slave owners. Many were devoted to their workers, helped them in harsh times and developed a patriarchal attitude, but this does not disguise the basic situation.

And so the whole attitude to exploitation began to change, very slowly but with gathering momentum, and the poor began to turn into the working class: but this working class, of course, was sharply differentiated within itself and, in a society that needed a mass basis of free wage-slaves, was treated often with a callousness which was no less evil than slavery and often justified by the same bogus quasi-scientific arguments that were used to justify racism: that the poor were biologically inferior. And, of course, racism did not die, indeed, given the right conditions, as with the influx of East European Jews into London's East End in the late nineteenth century, it intensified. And the same is true with Negroes in America.

The flourishing state of racism throughout the world, *post abolition*, should make us chary of explaining slavery in its terms. Yet slavery was abolished, the most powerful world leaders, for the first time in recorded history, deliberately set out to get both the slave trade and slavery suppressed. It became politically and socially viable for them to pursue such a policy. Slavery began to appear as archaic and its personal brutalities and restrictions were anathematized. Slavery became the antithesis of modernity. It cannot be an accident that the leadership of the anti-slavery agitation on a world-wide scale was conducted by the most industrialized nation in the world, namely Great Britain. However, that is another and a longer story. The point that I wish to emphasize is that a study of slavery, disengaged from the general history of the exploitation of labour, has inherent dangers, leading to a false emphasis and to a too simplified causation. It is even more confusing to see slavery entirely in terms of racism.

1969

10

*Plantation Power**

Now that the 1960s have closed, it is fitting to salute Eugene Genovese and the salutary, disturbing, critical effect that he must have on the writing of American history – performing, indeed, for his own country the service which Christopher Hill and Eric Hobsbawm did for Britain in the fifties. The rise of very sophisticated, scholarly and sensitive Marxist history has been a feature of the cultural life of both countries, making the historians of an older generation look curiously dusty and old-fashioned and bringing the English-speaking historians much closer to those of France and Italy. Not that I can accept in totality the analysis of Genovese any more than I can that of Hill and Hobsbawm: often there is a twist and slither in their arguments in order to achieve the hoped-for consistency with doctrine. But of that, later. Let us stress their virtues.

They are the heirs, the inheritors, of a vital change which began to take place in historical study at the turn of this century. For most of the nineteenth century, historians were concerned either with annals or with biographies. They wrote multi-volume histories of countries, reigns, wars or people. They told stories splendidly, dramatically, and they pointed morals and taught lessons so that all who read them might be made wiser. History, narrative history, was, they thought, a high calling, none perhaps higher. About 1900, however, there was a shift. The development of what one

* *The World the Slaveholders Made*, Eugene D. Genovese (London, 1970). *Slavery in the New World: A Reader in Comparative History*, ed. Laura Foner and Eugene D. Genovese (New York, 1970).

might call 'concept' history: the most obvious and best known example of this being Turner and his concept of the moving frontier as a factor in American history. The historian's new aim was to discern the dynamic processes controlling social change. The proliferation of specialized fields of historical study, the growth of learned journals, the rapid expansion of graduate schools of history (again in some ways Turner was a pioneer) soon made 'concept' history the dominant scholastic form of historical study. True, the old style annals and the old style biographies went on, but with less and less impact on the intellectual life of history and historians, particularly in the universities. The excitement lay in economic history, in the history of ideas, in the application of new ideas in anthropology and sociology to historical situations. Obviously this was an ideal seedbed for Marxist historians.

Naturally, in this new analytical game, both slavery and the Civil War acted like powerful magnets, drawing shoals of historians into their orbits. The cautious pursued eruditions piling up the ammunition for the conceptualists. And new concepts flew thick and fast. Slavery was an archaic, unprofitable method of economic organization; slavery was patriarchal and less hideous than rampant capitalism; slavery bred a special mentality in the slaves which reduced social tension; slavery was a red herring disguising the real motive, of the North. For fifty years or more some of the best historical minds in America have been concerned with what is, after all, its greatest social and historical problem.

True, these historians have been a minority. Often those most widely read by the public and most earnestly listened to by the Establishment have done their best to ignore slavery and write off the Civil War as an 'unnecessary conflict'. For, as conservative historians know, analysis tends to lead, not to national self-approval and euphoric self-confidence, but to criticism and doubt. Since the radical element in American life strengthened in the later fifties and throughout the sixties, so too has the quality of work on slavery strengthened. If anyone doubts this, then he should buy

Slavery in the New World, edited by Laura Foner and Eugene D. Genovese, which brings together a collection of brilliant papers in the comparative study of slavery in the New World. The new masters are all there, Stanley M. Elkins, David Brion Davis, Winthrop D. Jordan, Elsa V. Goveia, H. Orlando Patterson and M. I. Finley: only the Grand Master, C. Vann Woodward, is absent. The challenger for his title – Genovese – is naturally well represented: I find his, Winthrop Jordan's, and M. I. Finley's contributions the most suggestive in a book which is alive with intelligence and perception. Indeed, here is another admirable illustration of what I have said before – the writing of history in America is, at last, acquiring that sophistication and analytical insight which has been the hallmark of the best European scholarship for fifty years.

The burden of the book, its lesson, is that slavery cannot be studied as a separate institution, divorced from time and place. Slavery, like poverty, changes with changing society. Poverty in Pennsylvania cannot be the same as poverty in Peshawar. And poverty in Pennsylvania in 1930 was not the same as poverty in Pennsylvania in 1690. Trite. Maybe, but like many other simple approaches to historical problems, it becomes complex and revealing when applied, and the results are compared. If one studies slavery in Cuba before and after the development of the great sugar plantations, the difference is almost as startling as the difference between domestic industry and the factory. Again, such comparisons, as Genovese rightly points out, make one very wary of accepting some forms of slavery as mild and benevolent, others as harsh and exploitive. In a fascinating and perceptive essay Winthrop D. Jordan shows how in Jamaica, where blacks were worked more vigorously than almost anywhere else, at an almost death-haunting pace, the mulatto had far greater chance of freedom and social opportunities than in the somewhat milder slavery of the Southern States, where race and slavery were more closely related.

These comparative studies lead, as Genovese and Foner meant they should, to a realization that slavery can only be

116

understood in relation to the class structure of the societies that practise it. And that class structure, of course, will be intimately related to the economic activity upon which the society is engaged. This is the theme of Genovese's new book, *The World the Slaveholders Made*. Here he attempts to explain why slavery differed so markedly in the New World, and compares not only the ruthless and intense system in Jamaica with the milder forms in Martinique and Guadaloupe, but also the variations within Brazil and elsewhere. He makes short shrift of the old argument that Catholicism, because it encouraged the baptism of slaves and so elevated them to the rank of Christian, gave the blacks a passport to common humanity and, therefore, an easier social situation than they enjoyed in Protestant slave societies.

After all, few Catholic clergy in Brazil pressed for abolition. C. R. Boxer has produced in his recent book, *The Portuguese Seaborne Empire*,* plenty of evidence of harsh treatment, reluctance to permit baptism, and as rabid a racism in parts of the Portuguese empire as would have delighted the most fervent Southerner.

Again, as Genovese shows, the Puritans were themselves no more averse to slavery when it suited their economic needs than their Southern cousins. Slavery did not root itself throughout New England (it did in patches) simply because economic necessity did not require it. The commodities in which New England traded did not demand a huge labour force in their production; tobacco, sugar, cotton did. Short of people, the South had to acquire a working population, and that could only be done forcibly. It is Genovese's view that slavery will be the more economically exploitive the closer the economy is to the world markets, and this is the reason for the most fundamental differences in various forms of slavery.

At this point it is important to remember that all slave societies of the New World were colonies, attached closely not only to the economies of their mother countries, but also to their social and constitutional structures. Absolutist,

* London, 1969.

paternalist mother governments will create absolutist and paternalist colonies. Bourgeois capitalist societies, such as Britain or the Netherlands, will produce colonies in which high production and high profit will override all other considerations. Hence the difference between the Jamaican slave code and the Colbertian Code Noire of the French West Indies: one the result of bourgeois, the other of absolutist government. Again this reconciles the conflicting views of Freyre and Boxer with regard to Brazilian slavery: Freyre was mainly using evidence derived from domestic slavery, which naturally reflected the patriarchal, absolutist social pattern of Portugal. Boxer, however, derives his evidence from the profit-conscious sugar plantations that, in some ways, were exceptional in Brazilian society as a whole.

Genovese argues his thesis with a subtlety and breadth of scholarship that we have now come to expect in his work. He dismisses mechanical Marxism, and his own dialectical skill possesses the flourish and deadly intent of an expert duellist. And how well he writes – no deadly jargon, no laboured pages. So easily is one persuaded by so much of Genovese's argument that it is difficult to stop oneself from swallowing it whole.

The trouble lies, of course, in what Genovese himself recognizes as his major conundrum. The society which gave birth to Jamaican slavery was also the one which fathered the Old South – namely seventeenth-century Britain, which Genovese, following dutifully in the footsteps of English Marxists, regards as a strongly bourgeois society dominated by the economy of the market place. This explains Jamaican slavery, but does create a difficulty for the Old South, which Genovese regards as a patriarchal slave society, perhaps indeed the most highly developed patriarchal slave society the modern world has known. After all, elsewhere in the New World it was seigneurial societies – Spain, France, above all Portugal – which spawned paternalistic slave systems. So how come this startling exception? Genovese's handling of his conundrum is very neat.

Paternalism, he argues, is inherent in all slave–master relationships, and the special historic situations in the Old South, particularly the system of large plantations, turned a potentiality into a reality. Hence Genovese can fit all that he believes about the Old South into his general theory of slave systems. Naturally the argument is more complex than is possible to sketch here. But this bridge safely crossed, Genovese is then able to discuss the highly developed slave society of the Old South, its philosophy and its prophet, George Fitzhugh, in order to underline once more his view that its quality of life, its ideals and aspirations, as well as its social structure, differed radically from the North.

To understand the Old South is also to appreciate it. There were human values in slavery as well as inhuman ones – a theme which Genovese has consistently developed. Not, of course, that he condones slavery. Nor, and this should be made clear, does he think, as many of his critics mistakenly believe, that the slave society is a feudal society or even a variant of it. The Old South was a slave society, no more, no less, with its own developed pattern of class relationships and with its own *persona*: distinct from the capitalist worlds of both New and Old England whose evils the slaveholders saw with clarity and which they regarded as far more monstrous than the benign if disciplined servitude they practised. And no one else put his point of view with the urgency and conviction of Fitzhugh.

Nearly a half of *The World the Slaveholders Made* is devoted to George Fitzhugh. Fortunately Fitzhugh's blistering attack on capitalism, *Cannibals All: Or, Slaves Without Masters*, is available. And all should read it, giving particular attention to C. Vann Woodward's excellent introduction.* Of course, Fitzhugh seized on a central contradiction. How could abolitionists prate about liberty and human dignity when the conditions of their factory system were more horrible than plantation slavery? Fitzhugh quoted largely from the revelations of the parliamentary inquiries into factory conditions in England, with their appalling evidence of the exploitation

* Harvard, 1960.

119

of women, children, and men in terrible conditions for excessive hours at very low wages. Against these horrors, he opposed the picture of patriarchal plantations – stern masters certainly, discipline certainly, but there was always food, always a roof, even in old age. Slave workers could not, like factory workers, be turned out to starve in bad times, or left to die in destitution in old age. Both societies, the North and the South, were slave societies, but the South at least retained moral responsibility for its slaves.

Indeed Fitzhugh maintained that all societies, whether free or not, would be slave societies, for the nature of man demanded it. 'Some were born with saddles on their backs, and others booted and spurred to ride them.' All talk of progress, of betterment, was illusion. There would always be masters and men, and the master–slave relation was one of the best, far superior to a free labour market.

Genovese rightly sees that Fitzhugh was making a serious case. Exploitive industrial capitalism could be vile, some plantation slavery by comparison was almost benign. However, I believe that Genovese puts too high a value on Fitzhugh and does not allow enough both for the contradictions in Fitzhugh's own thinking, often more apparent in private than in public, and for Fitzhugh's desire to shock.

The World the Slaveholders Made enriches our understanding of the slave system of the New World; it sparkles with originality and it is a most important contribution to the swelling historiography of slavery. But there are weaknesses. The major one for me is the rigidity with which Genovese distinguishes between seigneurial society, or patriarchal society, and the competitive, bourgeois, market-dominated societies – principally New and Old England and the Netherlands. Moreover, Genovese has relied too heavily on Christopher Hill and Maurice Dobb for his analysis of English society. England did not secure a full bourgeois revolution in the seventeenth century. Patriarchalism remained a powerful feature in English social attitudes; aristocracy recovered much of the ground which it had lost before 1640 after the Restoration in 1660. A profound respect for rank, hierarchy and status infused the very marrow of seventeenth-century England, as indeed one may see from the original constitution of South Carolina devised by no less a 'bourgeois' apologist than John Locke. True, some feudal trappings had been abolished, and a world in which the bourgeois could develop and expand had come into being, but the structure, worm-eaten though it might be, was still monarchical, aristocratic and patriarchal; and in some ways the divisions between the social structures of New England and the Old South only reflect in a more extreme way the divisions which existed in the mother country itself.*

The same sort of insistence on the two opposed societies – patriarchal and bourgeois – also inhibits Genovese's appreciation of the exceptionally strong patriarchal streak in early industrial capitalism. Indeed, words that he applies to the best resident planters, the care for the housing, food, health, and old age of the slaves, could be written with equal justice about Wedgwood and his workers or Jedediah Strutt and his. I do not know enough about early industrial capitalism in New England but, I suspect, one could find easily enough similar examples of benevolent patriarchalism. And it does make one wonder if Genovese has not somewhat overdone the differences between North and South and whether they had not more in common than he allows. Others have pointed out that many Southerners had feelings of guilt about slavery, indeed even some planters, and that Fitzhugh himself could write in praise of Northern industry and hope for a closer relationship between it and the South. I find it difficult to accept Fitzhugh as presented by Genovese.

Fitzhugh's claims are, I think, somewhat inflated although his importance needs to be stressed. In the end what worries me most is the distinction between patriarchal and bourgeois societies that is made too hard and fast for my liking. As in England during the seventeenth century, so in America

* A fact which Fitzhugh seized upon. He realized that these two aspects, symbolized by Filmer and Locke, existed together very uneasily in seventeenth-century English society. After all, he resuscitated Filmer to refute Locke.

during the nineteenth, they were inextricably mingled. However, if the lines of Genovese's argument are drawn more vehemently than, perhaps, the evidence allows, they surely are drawn in the right places. Our understanding of the slaveholders' world has been greatly enhanced by Genovese's work, and he has established himself without question as one of the leading historians of the South. In Genovese, America has a Marxist historian in every way as gifted and as subtle as Hill, Hobsbawm or Soboul, and at times just as opaque.

1970

Part Two

IN THE LIGHT OF HISTORY

I

Secular Heretics

In late February 1967 a stark naked man stood near the sanctuary of the Glide Memorial Church in San Francisco; about him men and women, waving incense, chanted to the throb of the Congo drums; topless belly dancers wove in and out; psychedelic colours flashed across the church; and time and time again the sad, humanity-haunted face of Christ was projected above the crowd. Adolescents caressed and loved by the altar or withdrew to another room provided with a plastic bed. And so it went on until the early hours of the morning when the church elders 'lost their cool' and called it a day.

In Cologne about 1325 the Brethren of the Free Spirit met in their luxurious secret chapel: there a live Christ celebrated mass, a naked preacher exhorted the Brethren to return to primeval innocence, to strip, to love: for those who had become one with God there could be no sin, no church, no property. Love and the ecstatic experience was all. The church of the pope and the kingdoms of princes were evil. Take from them all that was needed, cheat them, lie to them, for innocence and love were beyond crime as well as beyond sin. The celebrants responded to the preacher and loved hard, there and then. What better place than a church for copulation that was beyond sin?

In Hampshire in 1649 William Franklin and his soul-mate and bed-companion Mary Gadbury found God within themselves, gave up work, lived in voluntary poverty, rejected sin and encouraged their little flock of Ranters to revel in obscenity, promiscuity and drink. They were not alone, little bands of these religious hippies buzzed like wasps' nests throughout Cromwell's England. They were stifled, not by the savage laws of the Commonwealth, but by their first cousins, the Quakers, whose early philosophy was hip with a difference. The first Quakers sometimes walked naked through the villages of Leicestershire: both to show disapproval of the accepted world of materialism and darkness and to proclaim their salvation and their purity as Children of Light. They too rejected the religious establishment as well as the differences of social status; wearing their hats in church to demonstrate one and calling all men 'thou' to prove the other. And they would not pay tithes. They went to gaol. Nor would they take oaths, or fight, so off to gaol they went again. And although they eschewed physical love outside marriage, the love of all men and women, whatever suffering it might bring, lay at the heart of their creed.

Much of the content of hippie philosophy has a long history in such religious heresies: even to drugs, for Ranters and Free Brethren and Spiritual Libertines used alcohol in excess to provide ecstasy: and as for promiscuity clothed in an aura of religiosity, this almost stretches back to Adam himself. The hippies, ignorant of history, are but a part of a chain stretching back into the Middle Ages and beyond. Why do these philosophies, heresies, call them what you will, recur so frequently in Western society? And is the present-day hippie world illumined by the light of the past?

The hippies are secular heretics, for they reject the moral principles of society, claiming to return to a purer, less hypocritical morality. What is common to this new secular heresy and religious heresies of the past, to which it possesses so many resemblances, is that it has occurred in a very affluent society. The Brethren of the Free Spirit, who were so similar to the hippies, flourished in the prosperous towns of Flanders and the Rhine where society and the Church had grown materialistic, given to wanton luxury and guilt-free extravagance. Also, as now, it was a time of war and of social dislocation. And the same conditions prevailed in England in the days of the Ranters and early Quakers. The philosophy of the market place had spread like bindweed over ancient morality and stifled it: political and social anarchy, with turbulence and riot, combined with seemingly meaningless civil war, gave a loathsome luminosity to the material world in the eyes of the Ranters and Quakers. Better get right out of it, and dwell with Brethren, led by the inner light.

Such antipathy to the material world and to the world of government, order, discipline and force goes, however, deeper than heresy. It is a constant theme in most religions except the Chinese. Sometimes the Church has contained it and been revivified by it. Think of St Francis, the son of a prosperous merchant, who divested himself of all material things and treated all that lived – birds and beasts and insects – as aspects of God. He pursued poverty like a lover and preferred the broken, the tormented, the simple and the foolish. A hippie-saint if ever there was one. He and his brethren battened on the conscience of the material world that they despised – taking the food, the alms, the shelter as the hippies did in Haight-Ashbury. Indeed some founders of religion seem uncomfortably close to the hippies. Beyond St Francis looms a larger, more formidable figure, who amidst the vast riches and stupendous power of the Roman Empire had no use for it, nor for riches, nor for strife, nor for hypocrisy, who preferred a prostitute to a prude. In the West, religion that is intense, personal and deeply felt has always been at odds with the world it has to live with.

Yet no matter how closely one presses the resemblance of this new secular heresy, with its total rejection of the principles and morality of the middle-class establishment, to the religious heresies and movements of the past, or indeed sees it as a part of the cycle of rejection of materialism which has been a constant factor in Western life and thought, there remain very important differences. The hippie world is compounded not only of social heresy but of acid. Here surely is the break with the past.

Drugs date back, at least, to the neolithic revolution, when men first discovered wine and beer: both were given sacred and ritualistic functions, which they have maintained.

This is true of all communities, primitive and advanced, communist or capitalist. Almost the whole of humanity has been sodden, at some time or another, with alcohol. And its use is deeply embedded in social rituals. Billions of gallons of wine, spirits and beer are needed to sustain the social conventions of group activity. Minor drugs and narcotics, after much initial opposition, also secured social acceptance, and became a part of the social ritual. After all, James I of England hated tobacco as much as Harry Anslinger hates hemp, and coffee houses were thought by Charles II to be dens of decadence and political treachery; but the public craving would not be denied.

Artists, particularly from the nineteenth century onwards, sought powerful hallucinations through drugs. Opium, laudanum, ether and hashish were plentiful in bohemian and artistic circles in nineteenth-century Europe, a process which reached its zenith in Rimbaud, who deliberately attempted a '*dérèglement de tous les sens*' and wrote psychedelically of the colours of vowels. But this experimentation was a means to art, an attempt to heighten consciousness for art's sake – not a way of life.

In the hippies, therefore, two historical strands have intertwined in an odd way – social heresy and the artist's quest for heightened perception through drugs. The need for the latter is, of course, due to the absence of God. Ecstasy and elation could be achieved by the mystical heretic through ritual, fasting, contemplation or flagellation, so long as they were intensified by a sense of God within and without. For the hippie, God is scarcely existent, replaced by a vague sense of the oneness of humanity which is quite insufficient to create the heightened consciousness needed for hallucinations or ecstatic experience.

The hippies' ancestry, however, is European rather than American, which, perhaps, is one of the reasons why their impact has been so shocking. During the nineteenth century the American artist occasionally toyed with decadence or drugs but, like Poe, he was an oddity. There were no Coleridges, no Baudelaires, no Rimbauds, no Verlaines, no

Wildes, not even a Byron or a Shelley. The American bohemians were a tiny sect and their free-love utopias were small, isolated and without dramatic social impact. In America the need to fly from materialism, from the grossness of a conscious world, was assuaged by the West, either actively or imaginatively. Nature, wild and untamed, was there in abundance to soothe a Thoreau or to ease a Parkman. Nothing was easier in nineteenth-century America than to contract out of urban, commercial civilization. Now it is impossible, as it has been in Europe for many centuries. Not because there are not enough ponds for putative Thoreaus, or Oregon trails for embryonic Parkmans, but because the myth has grown feebler: myths can only be sustained and given meaning by the needs of society. This aspect of American life – half dream, half reality – has lost its social dynamic. Pioneer America is meaningless, not only to hippies, but to the nation at large. It has been commercialized to package tours down the Grand Canyon or up the Santa Fé trail. Escape is easier within oneself. Indeed, there is nowhere else to go.

Furthermore, America is beginning to be afflicted with those ills which beset Italian and Flemish towns of the late Middle Ages – a contraction of opportunity for their middle class or their artisan young. Medieval heretics were often drawn, as were the earlier Quakers, from the class of skilled artisans in times of depression and economic contraction, or in periods of rapid social and technological change which proved inimical to their crafts. The hippies are largely the waste products of extensive university education systems; the drop-outs who are creatively or intellectually unsuited to the intense competitive system of Horatio Alger America. The acceptance of failure and withdrawal from society are deeply satisfying solutions to stress, anxiety and strain – especially if there is the ultimate safety net of middle-class parents. Religious heresy was rare amongst the abject poor. They preferred saints and miracles, and hippies are not common in the black ghettos of America.

And therein lies a danger, for although individuals and

groups can opt out of the political and moral structures of society, the majority of the nation cannot. And opting out changes nothing but the individual. No religious heresy of total or partial withdrawal from society has changed a nation for better or worse. Advancement in social and political justice can only come through political action, revolution or civil war, as indeed the history of America demonstrates. If the hippies develop a philosophy of active civil disobedience the picture may change. If they do not there will be enormous *political* danger in the growth of hippiedom. The aesthetes and decadents, as well as many sensitive liberals, withdrew likewise from active politics in Germany in the twenties and early thirties. Politics for them were corrupt, violent and dishonest, and withdrawal seemed to possess a higher morality, to be a more sensitive reaction. A withdrawal of a large segment of the younger generation of the middle class from participation in politics may easily lead, as it did in Germany, to a situation ripe for totalitarian politics. One of the most disquieting aspects of the hippie world is the cultivation of the Indian and the withdrawal from the Negro and his problems which create the central crisis of American politics. Lucy may be in the Sky with Diamonds but it is the Negro in the ghetto who matters.

But will this secular heresy grow? After all, medieval heresies rarely lasted. They were quickly destroyed if not obliterated. They were sporadic fires which only ravaged briefly the healthy body of the Church. And even the Ranters were quietly absorbed by the Quakers who disciplined themselves to live alongside if not within the society they despised. (Will this happen with the hippie rural communities which are growing such splendid vegetables?) Other less ecstatic and more socially orientated heresies such as occurred at the Reformation, however, established themselves successfully. Printing in the fifteenth century broke down the localization of medieval heresy: social dislocation and economic change in the sixteenth century gave new heresies opportunities for growth and victory denied to heresy in the Middle Ages.

Indeed, the potential for the growth of heresy is in direct proportion to the means of communication that are available. At the present time secular heresy has an even greater communications system at its command than that enjoyed by Luther and his allies. Hippies are news, to be exploited by every means of modern communication – press, radio, television and film. Hence their message and their way of life spreads like a virus, leaping from state to state, from country to country, from continent to continent in the briefest possible time. And they provide by their dress, their buttons, their posters, paint and pot quick bucks for the commercially adroit. The consumer society they hate manures and fertilizes their growth. And like the great religious heresies of the Reformation which succeeded in establishing themselves as orthodoxies, this new secular heresy has begun to spread internationally in a way the beats never did: nor for that matter the London teddy-boys or the mods and rockers. Groups of hippies have emerged in London, in Cambridge, in Oxford, even in the provincial towns of England. Leicester has its flower people and its park has witnessed its first love-in. The Provos in Holland will soon be riding their white bicycles with tulips in their hair and bells on their handlebars. Already there are feeble attempts, and they will grow stronger, to give these seemingly spontaneous growths international organization and common propaganda.

For any religious or secular heresy to succeed requires a social context that will nurture and strengthen it. In return it must meet the aspirations and create the opportunities not merely for a handful of folk but for considerable and diverse sections of a community. This was true for Christianity, for Lutheranism, for Calvinism, for the Quakers, Unitarians, Mormons, Methodists and the rest, all of which began as heresies. It is as true of intellectual heresy as of religious. Is there a resonance between the hippies and new situations in our society which may echo louder and more clearly in the near future? Maybe. Youth has achieved a freedom and an affluence that in previous societies was limited to the aristocracy and to very small sections of the rich middle class. What was once the privilege of a narrow segment of society has acquired a mass basis. Throughout history youth, especially its élite in intelligence and creativity, has rarely been drawn to the adult world, but it was forced to accept it and to obey it. The weight of society was too great, the structure of family life too firm, the acceptance of the Christian morality of the Churches too widespread for more than rebellion and rejection on the part of gifted individuals clustered in small groups. Most children and adolescents accepted, worked, obeyed and joined the adults. Those days may be over.

The opportunity for youth to rebel successfully is made easier because society itself is no longer sure either of its institutions or its morality. After all both were derived from a basically agrarian and craft-based society. The unitary family proved a remarkably viable basic unit in pre-industrial society and so did the extended family in the Orient. In the early stages of industrialization the family proved adequate though far weaker; but it may be doubted if it will survive into a world moulded by technology and science. Certainly its sanctions are crumbling at every level. Few fathers today possess a tenth of the authority of their grandfathers, either over workers or children, and the father is the core of the family as we know it. One has only to contrast Jewish and Negro family life to see the truth of this statement. To the sensitive young the social structure of the adult world must seem hypocritical and luminous with decay, as ripe for revolution as the Tsardom of Nicholas II. And I suspect that attitude is acquiring the force of truth in Moscow as well as New York. Because social institutions have lasted ten thousand years, it does not mean that they are eternal: ten thousand years is a very brief span in the history of mankind.

The family, as an institution, may have reached a danger point; just as the aristocracy did in 1789 or the Roman Catholic Church at the time of the Reformation. The situation, oddly enough, is not dissimilar. Institutions that are unsure of themselves, given to practices that are at odds with their avowed ideals, often crumble before a sharp radical attack, so long as this has a wide base, and this is the current situation between youth and its social targets in the adult world – marriage, monogamy, family life. It may not be too far-fetched to conceive of the Western world being caught up in a new type of social upheaval: a social revolutionary young attacking the institutions not of political life but of adult living. Possible, but, I think, unlikely. For the hippies do not possess the most important weapon in all revolutionary movements – a coherent ideology that interlocks belief and action, that combines philosophy with the strategy and tactics of action. If one looks back at the successful historical movements or the triumphing political and social revolutions of the past, they have always possessed, as well as deep emotional drives, a strong intellectual content. An active ideology – coherent, rational within its own principles – marks Calvinism as well as Communism, the Quakers as well as the Jacobins. But the hippie world is a flight from the intellect and all that the intellect implies. It does not wish to dominate reality but to flee from it: to mock the adult world, not capture and change it. It possesses attitudes but not an ideology.

The hippie movement remains adolescent – confused, emotional, idealistic, protest rather than propaganda, an experience but not an ideology. And its social criticism remains merely a personal expression, not a dynamic of political action. In this it relates most closely to those ecstatic heresies of the Middle Ages that were also savagely anti-clerical, that dwelt with bitterness on the riches, the greed, the corruption of the clergy, and the simplicity and poverty of Christ: the contrast between the ideal and the reality. In this, the hippies' criticism, by implication and by action, of the straight world – its self-indulgence, its hypocrisy, its materialism – may lie their greatest contribution to society. The alarming gulf between avowed intention and action, as in Vietnam, is leading to moral bankruptcy. The American Dream, like America's Manifest Destiny, is dissolving, giving way to a future not of hope but of night-mare.

If the hippies force us to look at ourselves morally and spiritually naked, then well and good – but they may provoke a blinder and less sensitive reaction. They are playing as dangerously with social passions as any heretic played with religious passions in the Middle Ages. And remember how society turned on *them*, how its inquisitors tortured them, burnt them, extirpated their women and children, rooted them out, purged society of its danger. America, faced by insoluble problems, made frantic by riot and by the prospect of moral defeat, may vent its spleen and crush all liberal attitudes, using as one of its excuses the social noncon-formity of the hippies. Heresies without ideology or the discipline necessary for political action have usually ended in disaster.

The hippies are a part of a social and historical process, and many strands are united in their beliefs and actions; but so far in man's long history no movement that has ignored power has ever succeeded, and all groups who have made a cult of social anarchy have either been defeated or destroyed. In the absence of a political creed and of a programme the hippies must be regarded as a symptom, not a social force – they are a living phantom bred by the decadent hypocrisy of so much of America's social and political morality.

1968

2

Were They Right?

There they were on a Sunday morning in the 1890s, pedalling with determination across the windswept George Washington bridge, wheeling right along the New Jersey Palisades until they found a quiet stretch of river, then they stripped off their serviceable knickerbockers and blouses, and bathed, glowing with high-minded morality, quite naked. Refreshed, they sat down to a healthy picnic of wholemeal bread, raw carrot, fruit and nuts. They sang a few glees, danced 'Gathering Peascods' or 'Jack's Maggot', mounted their bicycles and, full of virtue, pedalled back to New York. Men might scoff and women might scorn, but they were the *avant garde*, the pioneers of a better life, the leaders of the new way, the social reformers who, by the shining example of their lives, would help to dispel the moral squalor, the filth, the commercialization, the savagery and sadism of their day.

Across the Atlantic, similar knots of men and women were hiking across the Chilterns or pedalling along the dusty roads of the Kentish downs, or up in the North, clambering about the Pennines or the Yorkshire wolds. The men wore sensible clothing – tweed plus-fours, open-necked shirts, a straw boater. Some of the women might be hatless, all, except the youngest, were shapeless, as they disapproved of girdles, corsets, bustles and the like. They were clothes reformers, pacifists, vegetarians, nudists; they made pots, carved wood, weaved on handlooms, forged iron, printed by hand, played recorders, folk danced, cultivated gypsies and explored Celtic mythology, supported civil liberties, voted socialist, opposed child labour, advocated birth control, abhorred churches, yet attended séances. They were free with children, gentle to animals, hated fox hunters, loathed fur and despised, indeed hated, feathered headdresses; in fact they organized a protest movement to stop the use of birds' feathers in clothing. Wood fires, cold baths, wide-open bedroom windows, Japanese prints, Gothic furniture and Morris chintz adorned their homes. On their bookshelves could be found Thoreau, Ruskin, Whitman, Morris, W. H. Hudson, Shaw, Wells and the Webbs. The more adventurous had taken up camping, canoeing and mountaineering in order to get close to Nature which for most of them had replaced the anthropomorphic God. They were the faddists.

Of course, they were not uniform. Some ate meat, some even eschewed eggs and milk as a violation of natural diet, many would not under any circumstances eat cooked food or drink anything but water. Some refused to marry, others did: some went nude and others would not. Some women arrived at a bizarre sack-like garment. Most of the women were feminists and their men supported them. Most of the men were pacifists and socialists and their women supported them. They all belonged to innumerable societies for social protest or amelioration.

Intelligentsia, bohemians, faddists or cranks, call them what you will, they are the spiritual grandparents of our children; the first to drop out of their society and attempt to make their own. They were numerous enough to catch the public eye, to be pilloried by *Punch* and *Le Canard Enchaîné*, but far too small to sway public opinion or become a social problem. At most, like the suffragettes, they were an irritant. They could be and were ignored, dismissed as fools, cranks and self-important prigs. The men of authority assumed that they were wrong-headed, at best eccentric, at worst anarchistic, but always a ripe target for reactionary abuse. And yet, were they wrong? Perhaps they were right? Has the world of authority been so free from madness, so full of sound sense and thoughtfulness for mankind? Ninety million men and women killed in war this century. Stalin and Hitler. Were they sane?

Wherever one looks in late Victorian or Edwardian England, and the same is true of America, one finds small bands of dedicated men and women, usually of middle-class origins, but sometimes joined by bank clerks, insurance agents and skilled artisans, who had come together to reform the life that they detested. A typical society was the Fellowship of the New Life, founded by Thomas Davidson in the 1880s, which believed passionately in fraternity, open air, sensible clothing, folk pastimes, freedom of thought and intense suspicion of commercial and industrial society, which they believed destroyed life's harmonies, devastated the countryside and polluted food, all for the sake of profit and grab. It was in this Fellowship that Havelock Ellis, who outdated Kinsey by two generations in his approach to sex, met Edward Carpenter, who preached the virtues, naturalness and inevitability of homosexual love before and after Oscar Wilde was clapped into gaol. This same Fellowship spawned the tough-minded Fabians whose incisive criticism of society created the intellectual bone structure of the English socialist movement.

These men and women reacted violently *against* their society, giving their enthusiasm to myriad causes that their own world thought screwball – vegetarianism, nudism, opposition to blood sports, freedom for homosexuals, equality for women, abolition of censorship, nature cures, etc., etc., etc. John Galsworthy belonged to the stuffier middle class by origin, but his sensitivity, his intelligence, his deep sense of moral obligation drove him into bohemia – towards the world of the Fabians, the Webbs, the Guild Socialists and the Art and Craft movement that derived from William Morris. The causes which he supported from time to time give a fascinating insight into the huge constellation of faddist and do-good societies of our great-grandparents, ranging as they do from politics to the protection of birds. They were: abolition of the censorship of plays, sweated industries, minimum wages, labour unrest, labour exchanges, women's suffrage, ponies in mines, divorce law reform, prison reform, aeroplanes in war, docking of horses' tails, for love of beasts, slaughterhouse reform, plumage bill, caging of wild birds, worn-out horse traffic, performing animals, vivisection of dogs, dental experiment on dogs, pigeon shooting, slum clearance, zoos, Cecil houses, children on the stage, the three years average income tax.

Much that Galsworthy and his allies fought for has been won. Cats are no longer skinned alive in the streets of London and New York for fun. Children cannot be beaten insensible by their fathers with impunity. There are no earth closets left in London, not even in the slums, which indeed themselves are rapidly disappearing. Women no longer wear aviaries in their hats: birds and beasts are protected. Wives are no longer slaves. Sex is no longer a shameful word: nudism unbearably comic. All of these things are *their* victories, the result of their bravery in withstanding social ostracism, harassment by police, sometimes, as with Carpenter or Ellis, prosecution. Social disapproval did not deter them. They were right, overwhelmingly right, sometimes for the wrong reasons, sometimes for right: but their suspicion of science, of the more artificial aspects of modern living, of exploitation of women, children and animals was utterly sound and, as we know to our cost, many of their battles are far from over.

But our modern protest groups rarely realize that they are the heirs of a long tradition, just as most of the late Victorians and Edwardians were ignorant of those who had protested long before them. Concern about the treatment of children began in the eighteenth century, societies to protect animals from human cruelty were established in America and in England by 1840. Food reformers were active before 1850, especially in America where Sylvester Graham preached the virtues of wholemeal flour in the 1830s and crusaded against the eating of meat. Freedom for women was several generations old by the time the suffragettes demanded the vote. Amelia Bloomer was crusading for clothing reform in America by the middle of the century. And the back to nature cult had its apostles even before Thoreau and Ruskin.

Were They Right?

But the voices had been lonely: rarely were they institutionalized in clubs, societies and fellowships. By the 1880s the faddists had become a social if not a political force. Since then their reputations have fluctuated, but increasingly as we discern the violence that we have done to our environment, the pollution in which we have drenched ourselves, and the crippling effect society has had on our emotional lives, we realize that these men and women were not cranks, not faddists, not screwballs, but that they were right.

1969

3

The Woman's Burden

Sir Robert Walpole, England's prime minister, who stayed in office for longer than any prime minister has done since, lived in very great splendour. His bills for food and wine were quite prodigious – in 1733 his household consumed well over one thousand bottles of white Lisbon wine, merely one brand amongst the score that stocked his cellar. As with wine, so with food; every week oysters came in by the barrel load; about once a month chocolate was purchased 100 lb. at a time, along with a load of mixed nuts. And there lay the rub, for Walpole's kitchen had to set about making the chocolate bars that Walpole loved. Indeed, back at Houghton Hall, his vast house in Norfolk, his mother always, and sometimes his wife, with an army of servants, was busy preparing, preserving, boxing food that they then dispatched by ship, by coach, by wagon to London.

As with Walpole, so with the rest of the nobility; so too the merchants, lawyers, doctors, tradesmen, their kitchens were active all the year round to a degree which would daunt and depress even the most dedicated housewife today. Wives and daughters made everything, the processes were slow, the labour, even with the help of servants, back-breaking. Beer, cordials, lemonade, herbal and medicinal drinks, fruit wines, all had to be made; everything preservable, from pigs to mushrooms, had to be preserved; fruits were jammed and crystallized. No mixers, no shredders, no liquidizers; patiently and endlessly the women worked, over wood, coal and charcoal fires – in Leicestershire they were reduced to dried dung for fuel.

Nor was it merely food they had to prepare; as a boy Walpole's shirts, nightgowns and cravats were made at home or by a gentlewoman who lived ten miles away and was noted for her splendid needlework. And, of course, his sisters' petticoats and dresses were, like everyone else's, made by themselves or by their mother. The same with household linen; one bought it by the yard and made sheets, pillow cases, bed hangings and the rest. There were worse drudgeries. The streets of London as well as the roads of the countryside were, in foul weather, a loathsome mess of mud, water and dung, and houses could only be kept clean by getting down on the knees and scrubbing. So periodically Mrs Samuel Pepys and her maid rose at 2 a.m. and set about first the laundry and then, with the copper's fill of hot water, about the house. They finished late in the day.

We can scarcely begin to imagine the toil that went into even a modest household of the eighteenth and nineteenth centuries. Water had to be fetched from wells, candles constantly trimmed, lamps filled, earth closets and close stools emptied; fires in every room meant toiling up and down stairs with loads of wood and coal. Nor were servants plentiful. Pepys, and men in his class for long after his death, had to manage with one serving girl, perhaps no more than fifteen or sixteen years old. Except in the highest ranks of the aristocracy the women worked, perhaps slaved would be a better word, in their houses. This, as much as childbirth, led to the subjection of women.

True, childbirth could be a burden. There are plenty of examples of middle-class women in eighteenth- and nineteenth-century Europe having up to twenty children during their bearing lives. And it is even more appalling to think of these constant pregnancies combined with the toil of a household. Naturally, with their lives so wretchedly encumbered, they had little or no time to cultivate their minds. Even in the eighteenth century an upper-class female could rarely spell correctly, and their education, other than the acquirement of social graces, was sadly neglected. Of course there were a few exceptions, a few enlightened fathers, a few very gifted women, such as Mrs Elstob who, even in the seventeenth century, was one of the founders of Anglo-Saxon studies. But mostly they were as securely locked in the prison of their households as any convict in gaol and, like them, condemned to a daily treadmill of toil. And therefore they were regarded by most men as inferior in intellect, a weaker vessel that had to be both disciplined and protected. Of course, this life had its compensations, the love of children and dominance over them, the authority, rigorously maintained, over the occasional drudge of a servant. Human beings fortunately can derive consolation from almost any condition and, at least, the fundamental biological necessities of women were fulfilled – nest-building, children, a husband, the provision of food and clothing.

But for many it was a wretched fate, made more wretched because their marriages were so closely bound up with the transmission of property that they were arranged in accordance with social and economic considerations; they were rarely made for love. And naturally some women sought escape. Occasionally by sheer business acumen a few succeeded in trade, frequently obtaining release from drudgery by the death of husband or father. There were excellent female purveyors of silver long before Hester Bateman – Mary Makemead, and before her, Eliza Godfrey. And naturally there was always a sprinkling of women amongst the trades which battened on fashion. Probably it was always easier for a craftsman's or shopkeeper's wife to struggle free and participate in the more active business world of men. The same is true, of course, of innkeepers' wives. But it must be stressed that these were few; just as it was a minority of country girls or servant girls who fled to freedom through prostitution.

Naturally, although exploited by males, married and unmarried, the prostitute was constantly denounced. Morality pictured her driven through certain disease to early death – a fate not far different from many devout and chaste wives. Probably there were thousands of whores who had a far more enjoyable life than they would ever have known had they stuck to the harsh morality preached to them from the pulpit. The subjection of women – enslavement is not too harsh a word – is also reflected in the codes of law as well as of social custom throughout all pre-industrial societies. In many, adultery – because it threatened property relations, the status of males and the labour of the household – was regarded as a capital crime for women. In ancient Assyria they were stoned to death: in Victorian England they lost everything that they possessed. Their husbands had the right to fling them on the streets without a penny – and did. As with any form of slavery, tyranny was capricious. Some husbands could be indifferent, some could be compassionate, but as always in slavery, the terror of tyranny was always there; husbands could be, and were, tyrants.

This was but a hundred years ago: although women still cry for liberation, and links of their old shackles still hobble their lives, yet the freedom, the opportunities, the range of experience open to women borders, for the perceptive historian, on the incredible. This change is one of the most profound, the most remarkable, of modern times. And like their previous subjection, which was a commonplace of oriental despotism as well as of Christian Europe, this change too is universal, a feature of Kosygin's Russia, Mao's China as well as Nixon's America. Even in the Latin countries, or in Japan, where subjection has lingered longer than elsewhere, the fetters are being struck off. Even Italian women may now get a divorce.

Such liberation as women have so far enjoyed has usually been explained by three major factors – the growth of contraception, the spread of education and the dedicated fighting spirit of women themselves; especially those magnificent suffragettes, who chained themselves to railings, threw themselves under horses' hooves at the Derby, or starved themselves to the point of death in prison. These heroic women certainly helped their cause, but only because the tide had already set towards their goals. Increasingly men, for reasons which they did not understand, could no longer maintain those emotional and intellectual attitudes which condemned women as an inferior, if enchanting, race; and quite incapable of coping with the world outside the home or the bed. Such a view, as the Victorian world vanished amidst the glitter of the Edwardians, became increasingly archaic. And certainly education of women had helped. Those Victorian women, so rugged if so deliberately feminine, who had become doctors and lawyers, and even engineers, had demonstrated that they could excel in so many careers that were thought to be particularly reserved for males. Their missionary spirit in founding their own academies – Ratcliffe and Smith in New England, Girton and Newnham in Britain – had, like the suffragettes themselves, shown to a half incredulous world that the talents of women had been almost inconceivably undervalued. And both the suffragettes and the female academics produced excellent propagandists who hammered at the conceits and illusions of a male-dominated world.

Nor would it be possible to deny the immense value of the third strand – the spread in the knowledge and use of contraceptives, helped as they were by exceptional technical improvement from the exploitation of rubber in the nineteenth century to the pill in the twentieth. No woman, a prey to constant pregnancies, can lead a full life outside the home. Planned pregnancies obviously make a career far, far more feasible. Yet one should not place too great an emphasis on the liberation provided by birth control. Birth control has been widely practised in pre-industrial societies; primitive methods – *coitus interruptus*, herbal abortients, acid douches, lengthy periods of lactation combined with ferocious taboos on intercourse, even the exposure of babies – have all been practised with some success from Tahiti to seventeenth-century New England. What happened with birth control in the late nineteenth century was that it became technically, thanks to the industrial revolution, very much more efficient and, because of the growing need for women in industry, it spread to the lower middle and working classes. Certainly it eased the problems of women but it was, as with education or the suffragette movement, but an aspect of a far deeper revolution at work in human society.

The Woman's Burden

What is hard for people to grasp is the fact that the technological and scientific revolution in which mankind has been involved with ever-increasing momentum this last century has profoundly affected every social and personal relationship, no matter how seemingly private. Politics, organized religion, children, the family, the arts and music, the use of leisure – nothing has been left untouched by it. And, furthermore, it is a process whose end is nowhere in sight. Scientifically based industry has brought affluence and freedom – even in the end to the poor and the disadvantaged.

This affluence, and the personal freedom it creates, springs from two sources – the rise in the value of labour and the growth of that much maligned consumer society. Go to West Africa and you will still see women pounding for hour after hour the cassava roots from which their flour is made. Go to the most wretched ghetto in urban America or to the desolate villages of the Appalachians and there will be canned goods of every description, wrapped and sliced bread, packaged meats, vegetables from the four quarters of America, and even in the most broken homes there will be iceboxes, vacuum cleaners, electricity, water, heat. Move from the ghettos to suburbs of modest affluence and the ease of household management becomes even more marked – washing machines, dish washers, electrical gadgets for quick food preparation, so efficient and so quick that even the most dedicated, the most traditionally orientated housewife cannot use up much of her time on household management. Furthermore, it is all so easily learnt, so that a man, pursuing his career, can perform many of the household jobs as easily as a woman. A hundred years ago, women had to learn scores of traditional ways of managing their household, from diagnosing and treating children's diseases to drying fruit. Their apprenticeship was long and arduous and as soon as they had young daughters they, too, became teachers. Now domestic management is taught in schools, cooking can be learnt by anyone who can read.

The industrial revolution has steadily provided women of

all classes with more leisure in the home. This has given opportunities for the working-class woman to get into the factories and give that economic buoyancy to the blue-collar family which is such a marked aspect of advanced industrial societies. For the middle-class woman, however, the new freedom has created almost more problems than it has solved. With commercial, technical and professional activities still male dominated, with their lives still cluttered by the vestiges of household duties and motherly cares, and still, alas, the victims of social ideologies that regard women as essentially decorative or domestic, many middle-class women are faced with the boredom of ever-increasing leisure – hence the increase in alcoholism, adultery, to say nothing of bridge, tennis and the arts. Indeed one might argue that women are now the victims of liberation. They have been freed from the age-old tasks, from their vital and never-ending toil within the basic social unit – the family – yet they have been given little in exchange. Society pretends that the basic role is still there, even though it is obvious that it is vanishing fast. The freedom of women from their burdens derives more from electricity, more from the supermarket, than from the suffragettes or the pill. But, sadly, attention to their fundamental plight – the erosion of their social role without satisfactory replacement by another – is distracted by the ravings of female radicals who seem more bent on destroying the concept of femininity than on creating a more satisfactory life for their sisters. Sex is easy enough these days to get and enjoy, a deeply satisfying social role is far more difficult to achieve. And woman's historic role – hearth and home – is, like so many social institutions, eroding fast.

1970

4

The Dying Family

I was rather astonished when a minibus drove up to my house and out poured ten children. They had with them two parents, but not one child had them both in common as mother and father, and two of them belonged to neither parent, but to a former husband of the wife who had died. Both parents, well into middle age, had just embarked, one on his fourth, the other on her third marriage. The children, who came in all sizes, and ranged from blonde nordic to jet-haired Greek, bounced around the garden, young and old as happy as any children that I have seen. To them, as Californians, their situation was not particularly odd; most of their friends had multiple parents. Indeed to them perhaps the odd family was the one which Western culture has held up as a model for two thousand years or more – the life-long union of man and wife. But it took me a very long time to believe that they could be either happy or adjusted. And yet, were they a sign of the future, a way the world was going?

Unlike anthropologists or sociologists, historians have not studied family life very closely. Until recently we knew very little of the age at which people married in Western Europe in the centuries earlier than the nineteenth or how many children they had, or what the rates of illegitimacy might be or whether, newly wed, they lived with their parents or set up a house of their own. Few of these questions can be answered with exactitude even now, but we can make better guesses. We know even less, however, of the detailed sexual practices that marriage covered: indeed this is a subject to which historians are only just turning their attention. But we do know much more of the function of family life – its social role – particularly if we turn from the centuries to the millennia and pay attention to the broad similarities rather than the fascinating differences between one region and another: and, if we do, we realize that the family has changed far more profoundly than even the bus load of Californians might lead us to expect.

Basically the family has fulfilled three social functions – to provide a basic labour force, to transmit property and to educate and train children not only into an accepted social pattern, but also in the work skills upon which their future subsistence would depend. Until very recent times, the vast majority of children never went to any school: their school was the family, where they learned to dig and sow and reap and herd their animals, or they learned their father's craft of smith or carpenter or potter. The unitary family was particularly good at coping with the small peasant holdings which covered most of the world's fertile regions from China to Peru. In the primitive peasant world a child of four or five could begin to earn its keep in the fields, as they still can in India and Africa: and whether Moslem, Hindu, Inca or Christian, one wife at a time was all that the bulk of the world's population could support, even though their religion permitted them more. Indeed, it was the primitive nature of peasant economy which gave the family, as we know it, its wide diffusion and its remarkable continuity.

Whether or not it existed before the neolithic revolution we shall never know, but certainly it must have gained in strength as families became rooted to the soil. Many very primitive people who live in a pre-agrarian society of hunting and food-gathering often tend to have a looser structure of marriage and the women a far greater freedom of choice and easier divorce, as with the Esquimaux, than is permitted in peasant societies. There can be little doubt that the neolithic revolution created new opportunities for the family as we know it, partly because this revolution created new property relations. More importantly it created great masses of property, beyond anything earlier societies had known. True, there were a few hunting peoples, such as the Kwakiutl Indians, who had considerable possessions – complex lodges, great pieces of copper and piles of fibre blankets, which periodically they destroyed in great battles of raging pride – but the property, personal or communal, of most primitive hunting people is usually trivial.

After the revolution in agriculture, property and its transmission lay at the very heart of social relations and possessed an actuality which we find hard to grasp. Although we are much richer, possessions are more anonymous, often little more than marks in a ledger, and what we own constantly changes. Whereas for the majority of mankind over this last seven thousand years property has been deeply personal and familial: a plot of land, if not absolute ownership over it, then valuable rights in it; sometimes a house, even though it be a hovel by our standards; perhaps no more than the tools and materials of a craft, yet these possessions were the route both to survival and to betterment. Hence they were endowed with manna, bound up with the deepest roots of personality. In all societies the question of property became embedded in every aspect of family life, particularly marriage and the succession and rights of children. Because of property's vital importance, subservience of women and children to the will of the father, limited only by social custom, became the pattern of most great peasant societies. Marriage was sanctified not only by the rites of religion, but by the transmission of property. Few societies could tolerate freedom of choice in marriage – too much vital to the success or failure of a family depended on it: an ugly girl with five cows was a far fairer prospect than a pretty girl with one. And because of the sexual drives of frail human nature, the customs of marriage and of family relationships needed to be rigorously enforced. Tradition sanctified them; religion blessed them. Some societies reversed the sexually restrictive nature of permanent marriage and permitted additional wives, but such permission was meaningless to the mass of the peasantry who fought a desperate battle to support a single family. And, as we shall see, the patterns of family life were always looser for the rich and the favoured.

But a family was always more than property expressed clearly and visibly in real goods; it was for thousands of years both a school and a tribunal, the basic unit of social organization whose function in modern society has been very largely taken over by the state. In most peasant societies, life is regulated by the village community, by the patriarchs of the village, and the only officer of the central government these villagers see with any regularity is the tax-gatherer; but in societies that have grown more complex, and this is particularly true of the West during the last four hundred years, life has become regulated by the nation state or by the growth in power and importance of more generalized local communities – the town or county.

This has naturally weakened the authority of heads of families, a fact that can be symbolically illustrated by change in social custom. No child in Western Europe would sit unbidden in the presence of its parents until the eighteenth century: if it did it could be sure of rebuke and punishment. No head of a household would have thought twice about beating a recalcitrant young servant or apprentice before the end of the nineteenth century. For a younger brother to marry without the consent of his eldest brother would have been regarded as a social enormity; and sisters were disposable property. All of this power has vanished. Indeed the family ties of all of us have been so loosened that we find it hard to grasp the intensity of family relationships or their complexity, they have disintegrated so rapidly this last hundred years. Now nearly every child in the Western world, male or female, is educated outside the family from five years of age. The skills they learn are rarely, if ever, transmitted by parents: and what is more they learn about the nature of their own world, its social structure and its relationships in time outside the family. For millennia the family was the great transmitter and formulator of social custom; but it now only retains a shadow of this function, usually for very young children only.

The Dying Family

Although the economic and educational functions of the family have declined, most of us feel that it provides the most satisfactory emotional basis for human beings; that a secure family life breeds stability, a capacity not only for happiness, but also to adjust to society's demands. This, too, may be based on misjudgement, for family life in the past was not remarkable for its happiness. We get few glimpses into the private lives of men and women long dead, but when we do we often find strain, frustration, petty tyranny. For so many human beings family life was a prison from which they could not escape. And although it might create deep satisfactions here and there, the majority of the rich and affluent classes of the last four hundred years in Western Europe created for themselves a double standard, particularly as far as sex was concerned. In a few cities such as Calvin's Geneva, the purity of family life might be maintained, but the aristocracies of France, Italy and Britain tolerated, without undue concern, adultery, homosexuality and that sexual freedom which, for better or worse, we consider the hallmark of modern life. Indeed the family as the basic social group began firstly to fail, except in its property relations, amongst the aristocracy.

But what we think of as a social crisis of this generation — the rapid growth of divorce, the emancipation of women and adolescents, the sexual and educational revolutions, even the revolution in eating which is undermining the family as the basis of nourishment, for over a hundred years ago the majority of Europeans never ate in public in their lives – all of these things, which are steadily making the family weaker and weaker, are the inexorable result of the changes in society itself. The family as a unit of social organization was remarkably appropriate for a less complex world of agriculture and craftsmanship, a world which stretches back some seven thousand years, but ever since industry and highly urbanized societies began to take its place, the social functions of the family have steadily weakened – and this is a process that is unlikely to be halted. And there is no historical reason to believe that human beings could be less or more happy, less or more stable. Like any other human institution the family has always been moulded by the changing needs of society, sometimes slowly, sometimes fast. And that bus load of children does no more than symbolize the failure, not of marriage, but of the role of the old-fashioned family unit in a modern, urbanized, scientific and affluent society.

1970

5

Children, the Victims of Time

Within the circle of the family the affections which bind parents and children seem so natural that one assumes that these relationships are a part of our humanity. Certainly some aspects are. Mothers protect, look after and feed children. One can see *that* biological urge at work whenever one glances at animals or even birds. But once one moves away from this deep biological urge, then one moves into a world of change, of varying social attitudes of remarkable diversity. And certainly our own attitude to children is not only widely different from our fathers' and grandfathers', but immensely so once we push back into the early nineteenth century and beyond. The world which we think proper to children – fairy stories, games, toys, special books for learning – even the very idea of childhood, is a European invention of the last four hundred years. The very words which we use for young males – boy, *garçon, knabe* – were until the seventeenth century used indiscriminately to mean a male in a dependent position and could refer to men of thirty, forty or fifty: indeed there was no special word used to denominate a young male between the age of seven and sixteen. Even the word 'child' expressed *kinship* rather than an age state.

About the ancient world's attitude to children we know next to nothing. Certainly we are somewhat better informed about training and education of youth in Greece, and especially in Sparta. In classical China the situation is similar: deep reverence for parents, particularly the father, was insisted on, but we know very little of what was thought of childhood as a state. The common pattern amongst most primitive people, and there are discernible relics of this situation in most advanced societies, about children is this: they are regarded as infants until seven years of age; little differentiation is made between the sexes, often, indeed, they are dressed alike; then at seven infancy goes, and the boys begin to follow men's activities – herding cattle, hunting for food, working on the farm or at their father's craft. Usually they are not men in two important aspects, the making of love and the making of war. The entry into full manhood is usually marked by a specific ritual, sometimes simple, sometimes elaborate, almost always painful – Spartan boys were viciously flogged, Arab boys were circumcized without anaesthetic, so were aborigine Australians. Nuer boys had their foreheads incised to the bone.

Usually the boys undergoing this operation were regarded as being of the same tribal age. They remained 'class' mates for the rest of their lives, although their actual ages might vary by as much as four or five years: most of them, however, would be unaware of their own precise age – indeed this is true of the majority of men and women of medieval Europe. In some cases their ages would be associated with a village event, sometimes fairly decisively, but often in the vaguest way: a child of 'about seven' could be anything from five to nine. Precision of age is a remarkably modern phenomenon. Most societies until modern times grouped the young in blocks – infants, non-initiate boys or girls, and the like – in which calendar age was irrelevant.

Again, it is very rare to find children depicted as children before the beginnings of the modern world at the time of the Renaissance. Usually in Chinese paintings, as in medieval manuscripts, they are shown as small adults, wearing the same clothes, often, too, having the expression of men and women. The Greeks did not pay any attention to childhood as a special state and there are no statues of children: the *kouroi* are young men, representing youth at its triumphal entry into manhood. It is true that in the late Roman empire there is the hint of a change. There are a few remarkable heads of young boys, ten or twelve years of age, very lifelike and obviously individual portraits, most of which seem to come from funerary monuments. They display a quite remarkable sense of age, of the young and growing child, which was not to be found again in Western art until Renaissance times. And there was Cupid, who fluttered in and out of frescoes, who as Eros was sculpted time and time again in the Hellenistic period. He is the ancestor of the naked *putti* that flit through the pictures of so many European artists from the fifteenth to the nineteenth centuries, mischievous, impudent and sentimental. Eros however was not a child but a stylized symbol. Similarly towards the close of the Middle Ages, angels appear in illustrated manuscripts, singing, playing musical instruments, and they are quite obviously neither infants nor adults, but children. Yet they, too, like the infant Jesus or Cupid, fulfil a special function: and they do not lead to the portrayal of actual children, who are still depicted as if they were small-scale adults – one has only to look at the church monuments of Elizabethan England to see how distant the concept was of childhood as a separate state. There, lined up behind father, will be three or four little men, all dressed like himself in the formal clothes of the age, and behind his wife will kneel a group of little girls wearing the habits of women. Only infants will be dressed differently. They will be shown either tightly bound in their swaddling clothes, or dressed in the long-skirted robe worn by girls and boys alike until they were about seven.

Fortunately enough records survive for us to be able to state with confidence that pictorial representation is but a reflection of a social attitude. And we can trace the slow evolution of our modern concepts of childhood over the last four hundred years. The journey, though slow, was immense – the development of a separate world of childhood. This seems so natural to us that it is difficult to conceive any other state of affairs.

First we must remember that infants died more often than they lived. 'All mine die,' said Montaigne casually, as a gardener might speak of his cabbages. And until they had reached the end of infancy, between five and seven, they scarcely counted. Indeed a character in Molière, when talking of children, said, 'I don't count the little one.' Men and women of the sixteenth and seventeenth centuries would not have regarded the exposure of children by the Spartans, Romans and Chinese as callous, as we do. Indeed, it is likely that the poor of Renaissance Europe treated unwanted infants with a similar brutality. Life was too harsh to bother overmuch about an infant who probably would not survive anyway. At that time the attitude was much nearer to an animal's – immense concern whilst the infant lived to feed it and protect it, indifference once dead, and death was expected.

A new sensitivity towards infant mortality can be discerned towards the end of the sixteenth century, when dead children are represented on their parents' tombs. The fact that they were dead, not living, children is made grimly clear. They either have skulls in their hands, or kneel upon one, or have one hanging above their heads, and even tiny infants, still in their swaddling clothes, which indicates that they were probably younger than two years of age, occur. Children, even babies, were ceasing to be anonymous, yet if this is the beginning, the dawn of a new attitude to childhood, its fulfilment was still far in the future.

Certainly there was no separate world of childhood. They shared the same games with adults, the same toys, the same fairy stories. They lived their lives together, never apart. The coarse village festivals depicted by Breughel, showing men and women besotted with drink, groping for each other with unbridled lust, have children eating and drinking with them. Again, in the soberer pictures of wedding feasts and dances, the children are enjoying themselves alongside their elders, doing indeed the same things. Nor need we rely on paintings, for we have a wonderfully detailed record of the childhood of Louis XIII. His physician kept a diary, every day, of what the young Dauphin did. From this we can perceive how his father, Henri IV, and the Court treated him. It gives one an insight into aristocratic attitudes towards childhood,

and indeed into middle-class attitudes, for we have other
corroborative sources, though none so rich, from the period
just before some of the most momentous changes were to
take place in adults' attitude to children.

The young prince was involved, like the peasant children
of Breughel, in adult life to an outstanding degree. At four
Louis was taking part in adult ballets, once stark naked as
Cupid, at five he enjoyed hugely a farce about adultery, at
seven he began to go to the theatre often. He started gambling at the same age, indeed he was playing crambo at three.
He frequently went off with the King to watch wrestling,
tilting at the ring and the like, and by seven he was learning
to ride and shoot and hunt. He relished blue stories as well as
fairy stories. He enjoyed both, with a group of courtiers of
all ages; fairy stories did not belong to children, and courtiers,
particularly the ladies, loved them. Similarly the games he
played – hide and seek, fiddle-de-dee, blind man's buff –
were all played with adults and adolescents as well as with
his child companions.

Although the adult and childhood worlds intermixed very
intimately, there were some differences, particularly before
the age of seven. The Dauphin when very young played with
dolls, rode the hobby-horse and rushed about the palace
with his toy windmill; and these were very specifically the
activities of infants. Also before he was breeched he was often
dressed up as a girl, and of course wore always the robe of an
infant. More surprising, however, was the amount of open
sexuality permitted before he reached seven. The Dauphin
and his sister were stripped and placed naked in the King's
bed and when the children played sexually with each other
Henri IV and the Court were hugely amused. The Queen, a
pious and rather austere woman, thought nothing of seizing
hold of his genitals in the presence of the Court. The
Dauphin often displayed himself, to the amusement of his
very staid, middle-aged governess. He acquired the facts of
life as soon as he could talk. At seven, however, all changed.
He was severely reprimanded for playing sexually with a girl
of his own age, and the need for modesty was constantly

impressed upon him. The importance of this very detailed evidence from the Dauphin's doctor, who saw nothing odd in it, stresses that the world of children and the world of adults were deeply involved – children, even infants, were not thought of as requiring a special environment, special entertainments, special clothes, or as needing to be kept apart from the sophistications and ribaldries of adult life. There were, however, some distinctions: actions that could be permitted, indeed joked about, in very young children had to stop as soon as they left infancy and became young adults at seven.

In some ways the court was old-fashioned and by 1600 there was growing up a new conception of childhood. This had been developed by the schoolmen of the fifteenth century, and adopted and adapted by the educationalists of the Renaissance, especially Erasmus, Vives and Mosellanus. It became the stock in trade of the Jesuits, who were to dominate the education of the aristocracy and the richer middle class of seventeenth-century Europe. This new attitude was based on the concept that childhood was innocent and that it was the duty of adults to preserve it. The child, surely, was a prey to passion and to irrationality, but just as innocence could be preserved, so passions could be repressed. The protected child could be guided by remorse-less effort into the world of rational behaviour, innocence could be transmogrified into adult morality. So even whilst the Dauphin was playing with his naked sister to the ribald amusement of the Court, the Jesuits were purging school-books of indecencies, the religious at Port-Royal were editing Terence so that he might be read at school. In many educational establishments discipline was becoming extremely stringent and the dangers of childish sexuality legislated against – boys were no longer put two or three to a bed, there was a steady separation both of the sexes and of age groups.

Parallel with this developed the cult of the Infant Jesus, which symbolized childish innocence. Increased attention was given in religious literature and education to the holy childhood of Jesus and one of the most common devotional prints of seventeenth-century Europe was a Christ summoning the little children to His knee. Increasingly the child became an object of respect, a special creature with a different nature and needs, which required separation and protection from the adult world. By 1700 for a child of middle-class family to be outwardly licentious would have been deeply shocking, to be allowed to gamble for money at six would have appeared outrageous: by then too, the child possessed his own literature, books carefully pruned of adult sophistication or broad humour, but also especially written for the young mind. The age between seven and adolescence was rapidly becoming a world of its own.

In the eighteenth century this new vision of childhood became the accepted social attitude of the affluent classes. Amongst the poor, the old attitudes lingered on – poverty bred proximity and so forced adults and children to share the same world and naturally the adult world dominated, with its coarseness, its ribaldries, its simple humour: in villages and in slums, children and adults still played games together, listened to the same stories, lived lives much more closely bound together. Their lives could not be separated.

Nor was it only in manners and morals that changes took place in the lives of children between 1600 and 1800. This period also witnessed a revolution in the attitude towards the education of children – and many of the assumptions that we regard almost as belonging to human nature itself were adopted during that time. For example, everyone assumes that the processes of a literate education should develop with the developing child – that reading should begin about four or five, writing follows and then gradually more sophisticated subjects should be added and become more complex as the child grows. Education, indeed, is tied almost inflexibly to the calendar age of children. In the modern world, at least of Europe and America, a class of children at a school will all be very nearly the same age – a few months, may be, either side of the average, but only rarely as much as a year.

As with manners and morals, there were for a very long

time two worlds of education: one that belonged essentially to the Middle Ages which persisted amongst backward people for a very long time; and the other which is basically our own, which took centuries to achieve its final organization and definition. The medieval child learnt his letters with the local priest or monk from a nearby monastery, more rarely in the singing schools attached to cathedrals, but the age at which he started his primary education would be due to his own personal circumstances. Often, and this was true right up to the late seventeenth century and in backward areas even much later than that, a boy would not start to learn the rudiments of Latin, without which all but the most basic learning was impossible, until he was in his teens, sometimes even twenty or older, simply because his economic circumstances prevented it. In the seventeenth century Giradon, the French sculptor, worked at home until he was sixteen; when, prosperous at last, his father sent him off to begin his studies.

Still not unusual in Giradon's day, it had been customary in the fifteenth century, when old men, young men, adolescents and children could all be found sitting in the same class, learning the same lessons. No one thought this in any way odd. They turned up for classes but no one cared about the rest of their lives. Students young and old lived together under their own rules, with their own tribal customs, as best they might. Sometimes, as we learn from Thomas Platter, who wrote the story of his schooldays in the early sixteenth century, groups of students ranging in age from the early twenties to a mere ten would wander in search of learning from France to Germany and back again: the young boys would be bound to an older boy, beg for him, be beaten by him, and might occasionally be taught by him, but always fed and protected. Occasional jobs would enable them to attend classes and lectures: but usually they begged and education proceeded by fits and starts. They lived like hippies and wandered like gypsies, begging, stealing, fighting, yet always hungry for books, for that learning that would open the doors of professions. Platter was nineteen before he could read fluently, yet within two years his hunger for learning led him to master Latin, Greek and Hebrew. And in the end he became Rector of Basel's most famous school.

Even in Platter's day, however, things were changing. The late Middle Ages, particularly the mid-fifteenth century, witnessed the proliferation of colleges, particularly at Oxford and Cambridge and the university of Paris. Students entered the university at a very early age, usually at fifteen, sometimes as young as twelve, and, of course, there was no bar to the very mature. But residence in colleges fixed them in one place and parents could be certain that their sons would be subject to discipline and sent regularly to lectures and classes and that they would be protected from the excesses of drink, the temptation of fornication and the dangers of gambling. College rules became very strict, obedience insisted on, and whipping frequent for delinquency: inexorably a world of learning, quite separate from the adult world, was created, indeed one carefully protected from it.

As time passed so further regulation, further systematic organization followed, for example the division of pupils into classes with work especially assigned to that class for one year. And this gradually, but only gradually, had an effect on the physical organization of the school. In the sixteenth and seventeenth centuries all Etonians were taught in one large room. The boys were divided up into groups in accordance with the progress of their studies and the usher and master would go from group to group. At this time few grammar schools or *lycées* had more than one master and one usher. Both taught at all levels. Hence teaching hours were long, for otherwise it was difficult to supervise the habits and activities of the schoolboys.

This system began to change towards the end of the eighteenth century and by 1820 or 1830 a new system had been established. Schoolrooms were divided up or added, boys of the same age were moved steadily from class to class, and as the numbers swelled, fees grew and so did the number of masters employed. Yet much of the adult world lingered on, even in the boarding schools which became increasingly popular in England. We know that at Eton, Harrow, Rugby and elsewhere there was drinking, smoking, fighting with local boys, a great deal of gambling and a considerable amount of surreptitious wenching. But reform went relentlessly on to create a separate world of childhood and early youth. Even the leisure and amusements of schoolboys were differentiated – organized team games replaced casual, individual sporting activity; innocence was insisted on and incessantly preached about, sex before entry into the adult world came to be regarded as a social crime, literature was even more carefully censored – the headmaster of Harrow in the mid century would not allow the reading of any novel in case it corrupted the reader; naturally gambling was forbidden, alcohol banned; even food became different, far plainer than adult food and dominated by milk and suet puddings that you may still hear an old-fashioned Englishman dismiss as nursery food.

School clothes became different too. In the seventeenth century two ribbons at the shoulder marked a child's dress, otherwise it was the same as an adult's. In the eighteenth century children were frequently clothed in semi-fancy dress – sailor's costume, the kilt and bonnet of the Scottish highlander, Vandyke dress for special occasions – rather as if society were searching for difference. Also greater freedom was permitted to the child and children were allowed trousers long before adults would wear them. But gradually two basically separate forms of costume for children and adults evolved. By the early twentieth century, boys between infancy and puberty wore short trousers, and their clothes were always far more drab than adults', confined to greys and blues and blacks. At school, whether a day school or a boarding school, they were put into uniform and the same was true of girls. Children were, indeed, clamped into uniform, as socially distinct as a soldier's or policeman's, or prisoner's.

In the European upper classes the children were, in the nineteenth century, even excluded from adult society *in the home*. The children were forbidden most of the house and lived in day and night nurseries with nurses, governesses or tutors, visiting the rest of the house and their parents only for very short periods. Indeed the difference between the life of a sixteenth- and late nineteenth-century child is so vast as to be almost incomprehensible. Four centuries had created a private world for children.

Although this new attitude to children developed in the middle classes, it seeped down into society as time passed. The pictures of working-class children of Victorian London or Paris show them still dressed as adults, usually in their parents' worn-out and cut-down clothes, and we now know that they drank, gambled and rioted sexually and in fact participated in every form of adult life – indeed they physically had no escape from it. But as affluence spread the working class too was caught up in mass education and their children began to have a separate world forced upon them. Social legislation, too, took a hand. In the nineteenth and twentieth century children were excluded from public houses, forbidden to gamble or buy tobacco, and their sexual lives were regulated by the concept of the 'age of consent': for it was assumed that they would be innocent and prefer innocence unless a corrupt society forced sex upon them. So by the First World War, speaking broadly, there were three ages: infancy, which had been shortened to four or five years; childhood, which ran from infancy to late puberty for the lower classes and to early manhood for the rest, and adult life. And no child anywhere in the Western world was expected to share the tastes, the appetites, the social life of an adult.

And then the change came. The change from medieval to modern had taken four centuries. The revolution in attitude which frightens modern society is scarcely a decade old. To understand it, one must learn why children had gradually been separated from the adult world, and their lives and education carefully regulated. The short answer was social need: from 1500 onwards the Western world grew ever more complex, demanding more skilled and trained men for commerce and the professions. And for these activities boys rather than girls were needed and that is why attitudes to the young male changed most of all. Also the great empires –

the French, the British, the Spanish and the Dutch – required men with the habit of authority. The proconsuls of empire had to be stamped with the image of a gentleman, aware of obligations as well as privileges. Discipline, conformity, best enforced by a regular schooling, proved the most efficacious mould for the colonial bureaucrat.

But society is never still and even as the new attitudes to childhood grew fully fledged, there were counter movements in social structure that were to make even profounder changes. Science and technology invaded more and more of economic and social life. From 1880 onwards the speed increased until they dominated the activities of Western society. Their growth demanded a longer and longer education. Before the First World War sixteen or seventeen was a not unusual age for a middle-class boy to leave school either in America or Europe. After the Second World War huge segments of the population, female as well as male, remained in the educational system to twenty-one and beyond, and the number doubles and trebles every few years. Such a vast social change must necessarily have affected attitudes to childhood and youth; but there were other complex social forces at work as well. The great European powers lost their empires. Their need for conformity to an accepted middle-class pattern weakened. And America filled up, became urban, and its accepted social images of youth became blurred and confused at the same time. The whole purpose of education, other than the learning of crafts and skills, became entangled in debate. Add to this the psychoanalytical attacks on the Victorian concept of childish innocence, and the social confusion about how to treat childhood is easy to comprehend.

There were other muddying factors: the middle classes grew very much richer and the pressure on their children towards economic and social goals eased too. They were pressurized neither to be Christian gentlemen nor Horatio Algers. And yet in spite of myriad warning signs that attitudes to children needed to be changed, those belonging to an earlier and simpler world were still enforced. Children were not allowed to drink, parents and educators insisted on old patterns of overt deference and unquestioning obedience. Behaviour, clothes and hair styles had to conform to archaic standards, juvenile reading was still censored; sex was regarded as belonging to the adult world and certainly not to be practised by those being educated. Repression, conformity, discipline and exclusion were until the last few years the historically bred attitudes of most educationists and parents. Kept out of the adult world, the adolescents naturally created a world of their own – their own music, their own morals, their own clothes, their own literature. And they, of course, began naturally to capture the minds and imagination of the children who, younger in age, nevertheless lived with them in the same basic educational territory. In consequence, in the last few years the period between infancy and adolescence has been sharply reduced, and probably will be reduced even further.

Social movements and tensions in the adult world can be, and often are, adjusted by politics, but adolescents and children have no such mechanism for their conflicts with the exclusive world of adults. And so the result has been and must be rebellion. That rebellion, however, is not due to mistakes or difficulties of these last few years. Rarely do we look far enough into the past for the roots of our present problems. This revolution of youth has been building up for decades, because we forced the growing child into a repressive and artificial world, a prison, indeed, that was the end product of four centuries of Western history, of that gradual exclusion of the maturing child from the world of adults. We can now look back with longing to the late medieval world when, crude and simple as it was, men, women and children lived their lives together, shared the same morals as well as the same games, the same excesses as well as the same austerities. There is something to be said for the view that childhood is like a physical blemish, best ignored whenever possible. In essentials youth today is rebelling against four centuries of repression and exploitation.

1970

6

De Mortuis

The British have hilarious fun at the quaint funerary habits of the Americans. The death of Hubert Eaton, the world's greatest entrepreneur of death, and the recent discovery of a funerary home for pets by a wandering British journalist, released another gale of satirical laughter in the English press. The mockery was hearty but sustained, yet was it deserved? Well certainly much of Forest Lawn is hard to take: the wet, nursery language for the hard facts of dying – 'the loved one' for the corpse, 'leave taking' for burying and 'slumber' for death; the cosmetic treatment – the contortions of death waxed away, replaced by rouge and mascara and fashionably set hair; all of this is good for a gruesome joke. The place names of the Lawn are appalling – Lullabyland, Babyland. The piped guff, the music that flows like oil and the coy fig-leaved art give one goose-flesh. It is hard to repress a sense of nausea, and one turns, almost with relief, to a harsh fifteenth-century representation of the Dance of Death – livid corpses, jangling bones and skulls that haunt. How wholesome, after Hubert Eaton, seem the savage depictions of Bonfigli of the ravages of plague: or even the nightmares of death painted by Hieronymus Bosch. And how salutary in our own age to turn from Forest Lawn to the screaming, dissolving bodies of Francis Bacon, for surely this is how life ends for most of us, in pain, in agony.

And if Forest Lawn nauseates, what of the Pets Parlour? – 'Blackie' combed and brushed, stretched out on the hearth rug before a log fire, waits for his sorrowing owners. The budgerigar is naturally wired to its perch. The Ming Room houses the Siamese cats and if you want to do your pussy proud, you can spend three hundred dollars or so on a stately laying out, a goodly coffin (if you're worried about its fun in the after life, you can put an outsize rubber mouse in with it) and naturally a special plot in 'Bide-A-Wee', the memorial park for pets. Certainly it takes some taking, although it seems President Nixon took it, for his dog, Checkers, had the treatment: he lies amongst the immortals in Bide-A-Wee, like Hubert in Forest Lawn.

However, this will become all very cheap, a mere second-class death, if deep freezing really catches on, as it shows every sign of doing. The Life Extension Society is spreading, and the entrepreneurs have smelt the profit in immortality. As soon as the breath goes, get yourself encapsulated in liquid nitrogen and stored in one of the specially constructed freezers that are springing up all over America from Phoenix to New York. And so wait for the day when they can cure what you died of, or replace what gave way – the heart, the brain, the liver or the guts – or simply rejuvenate your cells. Naturally it is not cheap: the capsule costs $4,000 and then there are the freezing costs and who knows what they may be in fifty years, so it would be imprudent not to make ample provision. And then, of course, I cannot imagine the revitalizing process will not dig a big hole into quite a considerable personal fortune. Forest Lawn may be death for the rich; this is death for the richer, death for the Big Time. And in America there are a lot of very rich, so maybe soon now, outside all the big cities, there will be frigidaires, as huge as pyramids, full of the frozen dead. This surely must be a growth industry. Perhaps, by the year 2000, Hubert Eaton will seem but a modest pioneer of the death industry, for who does not crave to escape oblivion? All rich people have tried to domesticate death, to make death seem like life. The American way of death is not novel, nor, *pace* Hubert Eaton, is it nauseatingly comic: seen in proper historical perspective it reaches back not only down the centuries but down the millennia, for it is a response to a deep human need.

Some of the earliest graves of men, dating from palaeolithic times, contained corpses not only decked out with bits of personal finery but also sprinkled with red ochre, perhaps the symbol of blood and life, maybe in the hope of a future resurrection. After the neolithic revolution, which created much greater resources and very considerable surplus wealth, men went in for death in a very big way. Doubtless the poor were thrown away, burnt or exposed or pushed into obscurity, back to the anonymous mud from which they came.

The rich and the powerful, high priests and kings, could not die, they merely passed from one life to another, and the life hereafter was but a mirror image of life on earth, so they took with them everything they needed – jewels, furniture, food and, of course, servants. In the royal graves at Ur, some of the earliest and most sumptuous of tombs ever found, a row of handmaidens had been slaughtered at the burial – death's necessities were life's. No one, of course, took this elaboration of funerary activity further than the Egyptians. And the tombs of pharaohs and the high officials of the Egyptian kingdom make Forest Lawn seem like a cheap cemetery for the nation's down and outs. After all, one must use one's imagination. What should we think of vast stone mausoleums outside Washington, stuffed with personal jewellery from Winston's, furniture from Sloanes, tableware by Steuben, food from Bloomingdale, etc., etc., and in the midst of it all the embalmed corpse of a Coolidge or a Dulles? We should roar with laughter. We should regard it as vulgar, ridiculous, absurd.

Pushed back three millennia, such habits acquire not only decorum, but also majesty, grandeur, awe. The Egyptians were as portentous in death as in life, and their grave goods only occasionally give off the breath of life, unlike the Etruscans who domesticated death more completely, more joyously than any other society. A rich caste of princes built tombs of singular magnificence, filling them with amphorae, jewels and silver. And they adorned their walls with all the gaiety that they had enjoyed alive. There was nothing solemn about their attitude to death. In their tombs they hunted, played games, performed acrobatics, danced, feasted; their amorous dalliance was both wanton and guiltless. Deliberately they banished death with the recollected gusto of life. No society has brought such eroticism, such open and natural behaviour to the charnel house. But in the annals of death, Etruscans are rare birds.

How different the grandiose tombs of medieval barons, with their splendid alabaster or marble effigies. There they lie, larger than life, grave, portentous, frozen in death, a wife, sometimes two, rigidly posed beside them, and beneath, sorrowing children, kneeling in filial piety, the whole structure made more pompous with heraldic quarterings. These are yet another attempt to cheat death, to keep alive in stone what was decaying and crumbling below. And even here a breath of life sometimes creeps in. The Earl and Countess of Arundel lie side by side, dogs beneath the feet, pillows under the head; he in armour, she in her long woollen gown, but, movingly enough, they are holding hands. The sons of Lord Teynham cannot be parted, even in death, with their hawk and hound. Nor were these tombs so cold, so marmoreal, when they were first built to keep the memory of the dead alive. They were painted, the faces as alive with colour as corpses in the parlours of Forest Lawn.

Seen in the context of history, Forest Lawn is neither very vulgar nor very remarkable: and the frigidaires at Phoenix are no more surprising than a pyramid in Palenque or Cairo. If life has been good we, like the rich Etruscans, want it to go on and on and on, or at the least to be remembered. Only a few civilizations have evaded expensive funerary habits for their illustrious rich, and these usually poverty-stricken ones. Even the Hindus, burning bodies and throwing the ashes into the Ganges, austere as they are, have maintained distinction in their pyres. Not only were widows coaxed or thrown on to the flames, but rare and perfumed woods were burnt to sweeten the spirit of the rich Brahman as it escaped from its corrupt carapace. Cremation à la Chanel!

What is tasteless and vulgar in one age becomes tender and

moving in another. What should we say if we decorated our tombs with scenes from baseball, cocktail bars and the circus, or boasted on the side of our coffins of our amatory prowess, as erect and as unashamed in death as in life. And yet when the Etruscans do just these things, we are moved to a sense of delight that the force of life could be so strong that men and women revelled in it in their graves.

So the next time that you stroll through Forest Lawn, mildly nauseated by its silly sentimentality, think of those Etruscans; you will understand far more easily why seven thousand marriages a year take place in this Californian graveyard. After all, like those Arundels, Eros and Death have gone hand in hand down the ages. The urge to obliterate death is the urge to extend life: and what more natural than that the rich should expect renewal. How right, how proper, that Checkers should be waiting in Slumberland.

1967

7

Games with a Serious Purpose

The British pioneered the view that games formed character. They even came to believe that Waterloo was won on the playing fields of Eton. The Poet Laureate, Henry Newbolt, wrote a moving poem on the heroic nature of a school cricket match. 'To play the game' was a sign of candour, of upright moral character, of emotional integrity. The school fields bred *esprit de corps*, a sense of selflessness and dedication. The rough and tumble of football, the strenuous rowing battles, the vigorous athletics, the long, long hours on the cricket pitch purged the body and cleansed the mind. *Mens sana in corpore sano* became the most fashionable of tags; games were essential to healthy boyhood and naturally enough they became a way of life. What few, if any, schoolmasters in English and American boarding schools realized was that the games which they played were the feeble shadows of ancient rites. Games when they first began in the dawn of history had not been an embodiment of bodily joy, but a celebration of death.

Travellers to Mexico, when they visit the ruins of the Mayas and Aztecs, learn with astonishment that both these civilizations played complicated ball games in stadiums specially erected for the purpose, with tier upon tier of seats for the spectators. Indeed these courts are both intimate and surprisingly modern. But the flash of recognition, the half expressed delight to observe so close, so comforting, a common association quickly turns to horror as the guide goes on to explain that the captain of the losing team was ritually slaughtered by the waiting priests – a fate known and expected by player and spectator when the macabre play began. When Russia struggled against America and blacks pitted themselves against whites in the new splendid arena at Mexico City, with its powerful Aztec overtones, how few realized that the angel of death rather than the dove of peace was the symbol of gamesmanship.

It is true that when the Olympic Games emerged into the light of history, they had largely sublimated the old fertility cults, with their emphasis on human sacrifice, from which they sprang. The boxing and wrestling, the duel fought with swords that ended in death, all the earliest of the games are linked to the sacrifice to the dark gods, to celebrate the birth and death of Pelops or to make the sacred marriage of Demeter. The footrace, from which all modern sprint races derive, originated in the race between Demeter's suitors. Her priestess, the only woman allowed in the Olympic stadium, sat on a throne at the finishing line: winner take all. The discus and javelin throwing, the archery and chariot races, all have profound links with the ancient fertility religion and it was not until the innovation of the contests for boys in 632 BC that the Olympic Games broke out of their structure of religious ritual in which blood sacrifice and death were symbolically if not actually involved.

Elsewhere the relationship with death was not so easily sublimated, nor did games players evade the penalty of defeat. Outside Greece, the story of games is bloodier, more closely related to the death of men and of animals which, poor wretches, were early used as substitutes for human slaughter. The Etruscans were fascinated by the story of Patroclus. Time and time again they painted on the walls of their tombs the ritual that celebrated his death, including the slaughter for his funeral pyre of twelve noble Trojan youths by Achilles. And what regaled them in death, they enjoyed in life. They loved butchery. Three hundred and seven Roman prisoners of war, Michael Grant reminds us in his splendid book on *The Gladiators* (London, 1967), were slaughtered on one day as a sacrifice in the forum of the Tarquinii. However, the straightforward sacrifice became transmogrified. Either it proved too boring or too wasteful: better make the prisoners fight for it, kill off the defeated, and use the victors to fight another day. Hence began the gladiatorial games which the Romans adopted from the Etruscans. The Etruscans were a merry people as far as death was concerned and they never jibbed at blood and carnage, and as a refinement in their sports they introduced wild animals, and pitched them against sometimes armed, and sometimes unarmed, men. And so the gladiatorial games were born, occasionally mingled with the age-old chariot races that harked back to Troy and beyond.

But death still kept its vigil both in the stadium and in the rationale for the games. Games celebrated death. When Achilles mourned Patroclus, he not only slaughtered cattle and horses and noble Trojan youths and flung them on the pyre to keep company with Patroclus to Hades, but also celebrated the burning with the traditional games. What greater honour could Romans do themselves than follow the noble example of Achilles? So men vaunted their lives in lavish funerary games in which gladiators killed each other in their honour. And naturally, men being what they are, they grew as whimsical about their games as their tomb-stones. One insisted, as a light relief, on a duel between women; another on a contest between his boy-lovers. The macabre-minded Emperor Commodus collected all the dwarfs and cripples that he could find and made a holocaust of them. Most, however, vaunted their power by getting as many gladiators and animals in the ring as possible.

The taste for slaughter spread and gladiatorial shows became as regular as football matches in the Roman empire – every petty little provincial town had its stadium, a tiny replica of the Colosseum where the orgies of blood were on a stupendous scale. Naturally emperors needed to be imperial. Augustus set the pace, but his successors out-distanced him. Trajan in AD 107 brought ten thousand animals and ten thousand gladiators into the amphitheatre: that year blood flowed like a river and the Roman people lapped it up. Huge crowds attended these fiestas of ritual murder, for the

Colosseum could hold fifty thousand spectators: even Pompeii's stadium had room for twenty thousand. The gladiatorial games became an object of attack by the Christians, but they were not ended until early in the fifth century AD, whilst the practice of pitting criminals against wild animals lingered on for another hundred years.

A monstrous public entertainment had grown out of the dark primitive rituals of death and such blood-baths as the Romans enjoyed have never again stained human history; and yet sadism, brutality and even death itself have remained intimately linked with sport, indeed with organized games. I do not mean merely symbolically, although the symbolism is often clear enough. One has only to listen to the braying of a football crowd to sense the horrific atmosphere of a Roman stadium. The association has remained closer. Spain and those countries within the penumbra of Spanish culture still celebrate death in the afternoon – the stylized drama between men and bulls. And the bull fight is as much ritual as game, perhaps more so. The tension lies not only in the balletic skills of the matador, nor in the ritual slaughter of horses and bulls, but in the shadow of death that hangs over the performers themselves.

Nor need the rest of Europe feel smugly superior to the Spaniards; the risk of death in games still titillates Western man. The immense popularity of motor-car racing, which draws its tens upon tens of thousands of spectators, is based as much upon the scent of death as of skill. Most of the crowds can see little or nothing – the flash of a car perhaps once in a quarter of an hour – but death is always waiting and claims victim after victim. The life of a *grand prix* motor driver compares in uncertainty with that of a first-class gladiator. Nor has the ritual slaughter of animals ceased since it was stopped in the Roman amphitheatres. The *battues* of European monarchs in the seventeenth and eighteenth centuries, in which stags and birds were driven before the seated slaughterers, were little different from the sport enjoyed by Nero or Trajan. It was blood and death that counted.

Games with a Serious Purpose

Our ancestors were far more addicted to blood sports than we are. They relished the sight of blacksmiths fighting with bare fists for hour after hour until one was battered into bloody insensibility. They revelled in a main of cocks in which maybe fifty or sixty birds were done to death. They rode for hours to be in at the death of a stag or fox, torn to pieces by their dogs, and ritually they daubed their sons' and daughters' faces with the hot blood. They were not averse in their more bucolic moments to watching rustics playfully trying to pull off the greased head of a goose whilst riding at full tilt. Such pleasures, true, might be remote from the Roman orgies, but death was their purpose.

If many of these so-called sports still linger, they are contracting, and no longer unchallenged. Foxhounds now can scarcely meet in the English shires without being subject to a campus-like protest. Even the 'manly' sport of boxing (gladiatorial shows were manly too) has its dedicated critics. And even if the ravening wolf that lurks in most of us is occasionally stirred by the violence of games or the ritual sadism of sport, he is no longer given a free run. And better an animal than a man, though best of all, neither.

Nevertheless, even in the most ritualized and sublimated of games, athletic contests, there is still not only the historic link with the death of gods and the funeral of heroes, but the faint, faint shadow of death itself. We expect our athletes to drive themselves to the very limit of human endurance and we are never surprised to see them writhe in agony as they collapse at the tape. Just as the companions of Patroclus challenged death and celebrated life in their races before the walls of Troy, so do we. Apart from the blood sports, mankind can look back with some pride on its attitude to games: in the vast majority there has been a growth of compassion and of civility. Much that fascinated our ancestors is unthinkable. No society would tolerate the spectacle of ritual human slaughter for fun. A positive and real gain. If only a like civility, a like humanity, a like compassion could infuse the other competitive and murderous instincts of man. Is there not more than a hint of hypocrisy in being revolted by murder in the arena, yet indifferent to slaughter in the concentration camp or mangling of the innocent by bombs?

1969

8

Riot

The Senate House in flames; mobs roaring and rioting in the Forum, full of hate, hungry for blood; off they went looting and pillaging; confronted by rival gangs they fought and killed even in the Via Sacra itself, not once, but year after year as the Roman republic crumbled. And the empire of Augustus only brought an uneasy peace: social welfare, free food and free fun, kept the excesses down, but it required little – rumour, bribes, stirring oratory – to bring the mob back into the streets. Demagogues played on their fears and exploited their savagery for their own ends. When the capital of empire moved to the East, the mob was not lost. At Byzantium they rioted with equal panache, played on by oligarchs and factions in politics and religion; for centuries the mob rose and destroyed, tearing buildings down, pillaging, burning, looting and howling as they went.

In June 1780 London erupted: by the 7th it was a sea of flames; the prisons were broken open, the breweries looted and the gutters flowed with beer; Roman Catholic chapels and households were first desecrated, then wrecked and finally burned. In all 285 rioters were shot dead, 173 wounded, 450 taken prisoner. But these, the famous Gordon Riots, were unusual only in their extent. There had been wild rioting, burning and looting in the 1760s and 1770s; in 1753, 1736, 1733 London had been at the mercy of its mob, as it had been time and time again during the previous century. Nor was the situation in London unknown either to the rest of Britain or to Europe. Again it was summertime – the last week in July 1766 – when the rioting started in Devonshire. It spread like a prairie fire and for the rest of the summer the mobs flared up into violence throughout the kingdom: every market town of consequence had shops broken open, looted and burnt. The government shot down the rioters, hanged a selection of those they caught and transported the rest to the colonies. To little effect, because periodically for the next eighty years mobs swept the towns and countryside, howling destruction, threatening and offering violence and, above all, looting. Generations of Englishmen in those centuries had to learn to live with the riot as they lived with disease or death. It became a part of the nature of society.

Nor was rioting an Englishman's vice; across the Channel they were just as violent. In the 1620s, 1630s and 1640s France erupted in bloody riots that turned into a peasants' war in Normandy; for the rest of the century scarcely a year passed without the mob coming out in the streets of some provincial town, or in Paris itself. It wreaked its vengeance on those it hated, on those whom it thought responsible for its misery and its deprivation. Each wave of violence sank back into the sea of misery only to gain fresh force and momentum; inevitably the wave reared up again, crashing itself against the walls of society, bringing death, destruction and hate.

The French revolution changed the European riot quite fundamentally. The mob acquired more than a directing intelligence (it had rarely been without *that*): it now fell under the leadership of political strategists bent on using it for long-term ideological ends. Gradually the dispossessed and the frustrated acquired a deeper, a more ruthless sense of identity which accepted violence, tragedy, pain, even death for the sake of the future, the unborn generations. And so riot became an instrument of revolution. The European towns and countryside became more violent, not less, in the nineteenth century and that was true, too, of England, at least until 1850. Every capital city experienced street warfare, the barricades up, shooting, burning and destruction. The lesser towns fared little better than the great cities; and the villages and market towns often experienced the worst savageries. The delightful green shutters that one sees on houses great and small in France, in Germany and in Italy, the stout iron bars set in the stone of the windows, the huge oak doors almost too heavy to move, were not placed there for decoration, but protection. Europe had to live with the riot for decade after decade, generation after generation.

Things got better towards the end of the nineteenth century. Baron Haussmann drove his great boulevards through the riotous heart of Paris, providing excellent vistas for the rifle and later the machine gun and the tank: the weapons at the command of authority out-distanced the capacity of the mob to retaliate once the issue was joined. Of course there were still opportunities, for even the most brutal tyrannies hesitate to use the full weight of their firepower against their own people. Nevertheless, mobs tended to decline into demonstrations of protest with a fringe of sporadic violence. It required the para-military formation of the Fascists, Nazis and the Action Française on the one hand and the Communist party on the other to resuscitate the riot in the 1920s and 1930s. The military fanatics having been crushed in Europe, the riot has declined once again into demonstration and protest that teeters along the borders of provocation and violence.

In 1968 Europe burst again into flames from Colchester to Cracow with student riots. Although these were provoked by academic situations, they were exploited by acute political leaders. The students became a type of false proletariat (a California professor wrote 'a student is a nigger') and they were exploited as such and attempts were made, in France in early summer with success, to harness their idealism to the political programmes of the working class. These riots in Europe belonged to the classical tradition of both radical socialism and anarchism, but they were different in dimension to American student riots.

The near-riot, the student-mob, which Europe has recently experienced, however, is quite different from the riots of its historic past. Student violence is organized for purely political ends, and lacks the mass basis of class or the spur of social and economic deprivation, and is therefore totally different in kind to the rioting which America is experiencing. The American ghetto riot is, as it were, the grandchild of the classical riot which was bigger, more incoherent, more desperate, a deeper convulsion in the very bowels of society than the recent disturbances in Europe. The present American experience is more akin to the riots of pre-revolutionary Europe, before the mobs became infiltrated with political agents and exploiters who turned the riot to social revolutionary ends. This second stage may be beginning, however, in America and could develop with great rapidity.

The riot, urban or rural, with which Europe had to live over so many centuries was rarely an act of despair by starving peasants or slum dwellers. The old view of the traditional historians was that riots and mobs were sudden hysterical outbursts of anguish and despair. Certainly poverty played its role: high prices, scarcity of corn, brought out the rioters. But usually they had leaders – journeymen, artisans, skilled craftsmen, modest yeomen farmers – and often such people made up the hard core of riot and led it to its targets. Their aim was usually direct: to break open the granaries, to lower prices by threats of destruction or to improve wages or even secure work, for workers rioted as often as peasants. But the root causes of most riots were economic and specific. They were never aimed to overturn the structure of eighteenth-century society, any more than most rioting Negroes in Watts or Newark wished to overturn American capitalism and its social structure. The rioters were out to secure immediate benefits; economic, social and *local*, not revolution.

In England in the seventeenth century rioters tore down the hedges by which landowners had enclosed the peasants' common fields, or in the eighteenth century they ripped up turnpike toll-gates that taxed the movement of their goods. By threatening in 1696 to burn down Sir John Brownlowe's new house about his head they secured free beer and emptied a granary of corn. By starting to dismantle a textile mill at Stroud, the workers got a penny rise in wages. Riot worked more often than not. True, some rioters were always caught, some hanged, some transported, some imprisoned, but the rioting mass escaped scot free, often with loot, and many times they were successful in winning their immediate, short-term aims.

The American urban riot is working, as yet, in the same way as its historic counterparts. 'A little early Easter shopping,' said a Negress, going off with a coat in the Washington looting that followed the murder of Martin Luther King. The urban riot is for the rioters like a mildly hazardous game of bingo with plenty of prizes. And apart from immediate gains there are two others, one psychological, the other practical. The practical one is quite simple. Large losses of physical property scare owners into action. An urgent sense that something positive and quick must be done for the Negro in regard to integration and civil rights immediately follows riot. It is a sobering fact that, as in the past so in the present, riots rarely fail and the rioters always win; not a long-term victory, of course not, but in the short term.

The other gain is the release of social emotion. Before the nineteenth century, the lower classes, that is small craftsmen as well as labourers, had little social hope. Societies, as far as they could see, never changed. There had been and always would be rich and poor. Those who laboured all the years of their lives to eat sometimes well, sometimes badly were as eternal as nature. It was a changeless world and riot, therefore, brought revenge as well as a windfall. They beat with fury at their fate and burned their hatred across the countryside and into the cities in an orgiastic release of frustration. For the overwhelming majority of Americans, black or white, rich or poor, a fundamental change in social structure is just as unthinkable as it was to eighteenth-century Englishmen. Few Americans can accept the fact that the land of opportunity may have closed its doors: that a black pool of poverty will stretch like slime across the cities, spreading and growing so long as the economic and social structure remains unchanged. And as long as these conditions prevail, the riot with its emotional release and its material windfalls and illusory social gains will go on and on, hot summer after hot summer, as it did for centuries in Europe.

But in Europe riot turned in the end, in most countries, to revolution; in England, and England alone, it faded into insignificance in the nineteenth century. France in 1789 led the way; it proved through the Terror that social change and political power could be achieved through riot and mobs harnessed to a political ideology of social hope – a lesson which neither the French nor the countries to which they exported their ideas forgot. England nearly followed suit – right up to 1850 revolution was possible. Then Britain was saved, on the one hand by the enormous affluence of its industrial revolution in full spate, supported by a dependent and exploited empire, and on the other by creating a pattern of social hope for all classes through universal elementary education and full political participation. There were other and more complex factors at work but these were the primary causes.

America is, in a sense, entering a political phase curiously akin to Europe in the nineteenth century, a world of savage social conflict and possible revolutionary turmoil. Which way will riot develop; will it be moulded by revolutionary leaders into a revolutionary movement, dedicated to social change and if need be civil war? Or will the riots fade away, as in Britain, by the creation of true, not false, social hope and by full, not spurious, political participation? I am not suggesting that the British governing classes made that social hope easily realizable, nor that full political participation quickly prised their hands from the wheels of government. Of course not. But classes, like men, leap at a glimmer of real hope. But it must be real and true. If time and time again hope proves illusory, a false and deliberate mirage, then the looting will stop, the rioters will become disciplined, ferocious, dedicated, willing to die in their tens of thousands so that they can kindle an unquestionable spark of hope in the hearts of their own people. They will start fighting not for the present but the future.

1968

9

Their Excellencies

Mobs of blood-hungry students surge through embassy gardens, tear down flags, break windows, push into the embassy itself and insult the ambassador and his staff with impunity. Consular officers are daubed with glue and feathers: others spat on and reviled. The Chinese may have set new standards for contempt of ambassadors, but Western diplomats do little better throughout the Middle East and Africa and indignities also occur in Moscow, Paris and London. Indeed the ambassador has become a target for abuse. Not long ago nations would have gone to war for such affronts offered to their sovereign representatives. The ambassador's person was as sacred as the emperor or potentate whom he represented. But imprecations, mud and physical violence are but the outward symbols of a cataclysmic fall in the ambassador's status. Hot lines proliferate – Moscow–Washington, Washington–London, Paris–Moscow – so that the button-pressing men can talk instantly as they teeter on the brink. Any negotiation of importance sends foreign secretaries or special emissaries scurrying about the globe. Khrushchev or Kosygin rush to the United Nations; Johnson jets over the Pacific to meet Ky. Foreign Secretaries meet in clusters in Kuwait or Geneva or Lagos.

The power of diplomats has, of course, been fading for decades. The growth of modern communications, first the steamship, railway and telegraph and recently jets, telephones and radio, have deeply undermined their purpose and usefulness. Yet it was the thirties with its steady diplomatic retreat before the bullying threats of Hitler and

Mussolini that brought diplomacy into total disrepute. Ambassadors are the shadow of what they were and embassies now are little more than centres for propaganda and intelligence. One of the ironies of history is the steady growth of diplomatic personnel and of maintenance costs at a time when diplomacy has almost vanished from an ambassador's work. The immunity which protected an ambassador and his servants because he was the personal representative of his sovereign now masquerades and protects the activities of spies, formerly regarded as the most disreputable part of his duties. To some it might seem that the world would be healthier if ambassadors and their immunities were abolished. How the mighty have fallen.

Just about two hundred years ago, when ambassadors were at the height of their powers, they met in solemn conclave to settle the problems of Europe once and for all. As their coaches rattled down the long roads to Cambrai, dashing horsemen in brilliant liveries led their cavalcades; fanfares of trumpets greeted their entrance to towns; mayors and aldermen turned up to meet them and waited humbly in the drenching rain, expecting nothing but a lofty greeting and a word of praise for the munificent hospitality that they dispensed. It was as if the kings and emperors themselves were passing by.

At Cambrai two years were spent in the examination and acceptance of credentials. Most of this time was taken up with the infinitely thorny question as to whether the Holy Roman Emperor could possibly, through his ambassador, address the King of Sardinia as 'Good Brother'. Problems equally grave beset them on all sides: could the Papal representative be a member of the Congress or act merely as an observer? Which ambassador had precedence, England's, France's, Spain's? Their excellencies whiled away the weeks and months with gigantic banquets whose magnificence became a matter of national honour. The English ambassador's health broke down under the strain and he was forced to request a separate table at his rivals' dinners so that he could keep to his diet. Even when precedence was settled, business moved at a snail's pace – trivialities such as the ownership of two decrepit palaces in Rome kept them busy as one winter followed another. Only modern disarmament conferences are in this grand old tradition of diplomatic activity. But there was this difference, that, slow though it might be, the Conference of Cambrai did settle some issues and settle them permanently. Even so the mechanics of the Congress were worthy of the satire of a Swift – who could doff hats, who could sit on a stool, whose consul should go first. National pride, it might seem, was carried to the point of lunacy.

One might, indeed, be tempted to regard ambassadors as a gigantic and expensive fraud: men who achieved nothing, who neither stopped war nor made peace, men whose whole manner of living and acting was but an extravagant symbol of national pride taken to grotesque lengths. And can these monstrous men of straw, decked in the garish national regalia, be said to have ever achieved anything? In this century their record is appalling. The British Ambassador in Berlin became a tool of Hitler; his policy of appeasement led to Munich. Throughout their attempt to secure peace with Hitler, Europe's diplomats staggered from one disaster to another. The persistent attempts to secure a *détente* before the First World War had scarcely any better results.

Is not the history of diplomacy, therefore, a history of disaster and failure? Surely war settles issues. It stopped Louis XIV, Napoleon and Hitler. Where would diplomacy have left Israel? A sharp blow in Sinai is, surely, worth years of talk. Diplomacy is dead, even if it was ever alive. Blunt statements across the hot lines call statesmen's bluff and rearrange the chequer board. Neither peace nor wars are matters any longer for ambassadors. Nowadays an attitude of conflict is regarded as far more realistic than a willingness to take part in a dialogue for peace. Even the very mention of a dialogue for peace leads to a cry of the old shibboleth 'appeasement'. Suggest diplomatic discussion with Ho Chi Minh and 'Munich' will be thrown in your teeth. Nowadays diplomacy is the double-talk of the weak. Action alone speaks strength. And yet in the light of the past how erroneous all this is!

There is a great necessity to think clearly and historically about the diplomatic history even of the last fifty years; to separate out real problems from the Nazi method of dealing with them – the question, for example, of Sudeten Germans was not a matter merely of propaganda or even agitation. They existed, and their plight required discussion. Or take even the Nazi Anschluss with Austria. There was, and is, an obvious economic and cultural case for Austro-German unity. The problem lay not so much in what was discussed, nor even in the diplomatic discussions themselves, but with whom they were made. Why diplomatic action became appeasement was because of Hitler's ideology: his appalling racial theory, his irrationality, his aggressive nationalism and his utter refusal to accept the results of any diplomatic decision. But it is absurd because of Hitler to dismiss all negotiations, all diplomatic bargaining as a meaningless exercise that can only weaken one side and strengthen the other. Instead of diplomacy's failures, let us consider some of its greater successes.

Europe has experienced aggression and war far more than any other continent. It has been torn by ideological strife to a degree unknown elsewhere in the world. And it was these conditions – war, aggression, ideological conflict – which gave rise to the ambassador and all his works. And these men, the diplomats, helped to settle some of the gravest problems which have ever beset mankind. To realize the horror, the passion, the blind hatred and fury that Catholic felt for Protestant and Protestant for Catholic in the six-teenth and seventeenth centuries one needs to use a most active imagination. To get one's religion wrong did not mean merely sudden death but eternal death; so heresy needed to be burnt out. In Spain, Protestants and Jews were terrifying heretics, fit only for the flames which consumed them. In France Protestants were exiled, killed, bullied. In Elizabethan England Catholics were traitors, neither more nor less, and the fate of traitors awaited their priests. Their bowels were torn out and burnt before their eyes. Religion indeed heightened to a fever the conflicts between nations and the divisions within them to a degree which makes quarrels between capitalist and communist look like the petty squabbles of children. During these centuries war, civil and international, raged, not for four or five years, but for decades, and the problems that war strengthened or created seemed incapable of solution. Armageddon had to be lived with.

In this maelstrom ambassadors and diplomacy raised their status and began to create linkages, maybe as fine as gossamer and as easily ruptured, between the conflicting ideologies. These men were not saints. Philip II's ambassador in England was deeply involved in the plots to murder Elizabeth I. The Tudor poet, Sir Thomas Wyatt, whilst on an embassy to Spain agreed to secure the death of England's leading expatriate Catholic, Reginald Pole. For such crimes they were neither arrested nor tried, but sent back to their own countries. All viewed their activities realistically – of course they would work for their masters, and work, in a world of violence, meant violence. Yet for whatever iniquity they might commit, Grotius, the great international lawyer, thought they should go scot free because their utility as a class was more important even than the danger that stemmed from them. And again that active imagination must be used. The Dutch sent Calvinists to Paris and Venice: James I's Court accepted Catholics from both France and Spain. And these ambassadors flaunted their religion, insisted on having their chaplains and chapels within their embassies: rather as if the Devil himself were permitted to open a small shop for the purchase of souls, or a Red Chinese embassy gave open lectures to schoolchildren on the thought of Mao Tse-tung in Washington every Sunday afternoon. But the ambassadors were patient, professional, and by their profession committed to seeking for peace.

Diplomacy had a wealth of failures, but some outstanding successes. The Calvinist Dutch who had wrested seven provinces from the Spanish Netherlands – rebels, therefore, as well as heretics – finally secured recognition of their independence after generations of both hot and cold war in the great diplomatic settlement which goes by the name of the Treaties of Westphalia and Münster, signed in 1648. This was the result of patient, hard-headed, determined bargaining by ambassadors who were loyal Spaniards and loyal Dutch, aided and abetted by their equally hard-headed allies. Of course, the Dutch Stadtholder could never have met the King of Spain and settled this issue. They were the inviolate symbols of ideological principles that could not be compromised, as Mao Tse-tung, Mr Kosygin and the President of the United States are today. And there is all the difference in the world between a leader, a figurehead of a nation, and a negotiator. Symbols could, or should not be, wheelers and dealers. And if diplomacy helped to solve problems in a war-torn and hostile Europe, far more hostile and war-torn than the present world, why should it not today?

First we must get rid of the insane notion that all nego-tiation is a preliminary to appeasement. Secondly, we must learn again that bargains have to be two-sided, that con-cessions need to be mutual and fairly balanced. Bled to death and exhausted, the Protestant and Catholic powers gradually learned this simple lesson in the first half of the seventeenth century. And they learned more than this. They discovered that the self-interest of a nation is not always identical with its ideological aspirations. France realized that alliance with Protestant powers was a necessity for its own survival, even more daringly that an under-standing with Moslem Turkey added strategic strength to her position. Amongst modern statesmen only General de Gaulle had a similar sense of the virtues and possibilities of classical diplomacy. Independent, rigidly concerned with French power, deeply conservative, disdainful of cries of Munich or appeasement, he was willing to bargain with Ben Barka, Nasser or Ho Chi Minh.

The world is a sorry place, less so than seventeenth-century Europe, but bad enough. Korea, Vietnam, Israel – which spell out bloodshed, violence, destitution and misery for millions of ordinary men and women who only want to eat and love and breed and die. And these are the conflagrations only; dangerous flashpoints elsewhere crackle and splutter every month or so. Is it too much for humanity to ask that men should attempt not to win, but to bargain, and to keep the bargains made? After all, when Catholics and Protestants learned to live in suspicious friendship, is it too much to ask that communists and capitalists might do so too? If the world survives, perhaps, the hostility between capitalist and communist – both mere routes to industrialized society – will seem as foolish as the old religious hatreds. To achieve that desirable result will require years of patient negotiation; let us therefore revive the negotiators, give them back their status. To tar and feather an ambassador or his staff should seem, even to a Red Guard, like an affront to humanity and its aspirations.

1968

10

Clothes

Clothes, like so many aspects of life, have suffered an almost complete revolution. Now they indicate primarily age and group, and to a lesser extent wealth. In the Far East and in the less Westernized parts of Africa, clothes still play a different social role, conferring status and grandeur as, indeed, they used to in the West. Now, this is not true, not even for the greatest in the land. President Nixon dresses like tens of thousands of other prosperous, well-groomed, middle-aged Americans: sombre suits, somewhat gayer leisure clothes. The Queen of England does not wear, except on very special occasions, anything different from any other middle-aged woman of her country – style, colour, cut, differ in no way.

What a marked contrast this makes with the ancient great. The emperor of the Romans wore nothing but purple – purple toga, purple underwear. He sat on a purple throne, surrounded by purple curtains, and indeed stood to receive on a purple marble circle. Purple was imperial and preserved for the emperor and his family. Similarly the Chinese emperors, the Sons of Heaven, wore yellow, the symbol of the earth, the centre of the universe, embroidered with a special five-clawed dragon, reserved for them alone. Even Elizabeth I, perhaps especially Elizabeth I, would have been amazed, probably outraged, by the inconspicuous modesty of her namesake. For clothes used to set apart men and women, enhance their glory, touch them with a divinity to which the men who toiled and worked, or bought and sold could never hope to aspire. True, at no time did aristocrats

and courtiers deck themselves in their hierocratic finery
every day, but even when dressed up for work in the Council Chamber they always managed a discreet and costly
ostentation. William Cecil, Elizabeth I's devoted secretary
of state, dressed in gowns of sombre hue, but they were
edged with beaver, the most costly of furs – a quiet symbol
of his magnificence in strong contrast to the unquiet symbol
of his vast Renaissance palace at Theobalds.

There is no doubt that the sixteenth century saw a changed
attitude to dress. There had been extravagant fashions
before – long pointed toes to shoes that curled backwards
almost to the knee, strange and complex wimples for women
that hid even a wisp of hair. Colours had varied from dark
brown to staggeringly psychedelic effects of yellow and
green, doublets indeed that would have made Harlequin
envious. The rich, the well born, members of courts had,
even in the darkest ages, marked themselves off from the
mass of the population. So, too, had professions: monks had
their habits, soldiers their armour, whether the monks and
soldiers were European or Japanese. Doctors, sages, lawyers,
professors all had their distinctive quirks of dress, slowly,
very slowly, changing with the generations.

Even today a few vestiges remain. Black barristers in
Ghana still sport the vestigial grey-white legal wig: the
sixteenth-century professor's gown comes out of its mothballs
for encaenia in Enid, Oklahoma: the dons of Oxford and
Cambridge even sport them to eat their dinners. But in
everyday life who can now tell a general from a banker, a
surgeon from a scholar? The disappearance of clothes that
establish the profession of the wearer is, however, far less
dramatic than the collapse of the use of clothes to indicate
power and dominion. This rose to quite extraordinary
heights between 1500 and 1600 and unless one grasps the
almost religious significance, the fantastic aura which clothes
acquired in that era, one will be baffled to understand much
of its art, even some of Rembrandt's greatest pictures.

One of the reasons for the excessive preoccupation of
monarchs and aristocrats in the sixteenth century with

clothing may be due to the establishment of printing and engraving. This opened up not only the opportunity for creating awe and adulation but also for satire and ridicule on a scale which was unthinkable in all previous ages. Before printing, only coins could circulate the god-like image of kings to the multitude, but printing, and particularly the development of the art of engraving, as the popularity of Dürer's *Erasmus* had shown, opened up vast new possibilities. It is not surprising, therefore, that Elizabeth I's Privy Council forbade printers to publish any likeness of the Queen until they had agreed on an authorized portrait. Although there were scores of pictures of the Queen painted during her long reign, they were all derived from six official portraits. In these she never aged; she was as young, as fresh, as virginal, as god-like in 1590 as in 1560, especially god-like. The verses painted on most of them are equally adulatory and always refer to her as a goddess – a Cynthia, a Diana, a Gloria, or even a Pandora.

Her clothes, of course, marked her divinity. She wore ruffs and lace of almost inconceivable complexity; her hair elaborately adorned with pearls and jewels, her vast and ornate dresses alive with rubies, sapphires and diamonds. And nor were these clothes kept for portraits only: so bedecked, she was carried in a litter through London and through the countryside on her famous progresses, like some monstrous painted but living idol. Naturally this divine monarch was surrounded by her high priests and priestesses, whose clothing, too, marked them off from the common herd: aristocrats with velvet breeches studded with elaborate emblems in gold thread, sporting codpieces that proclaimed their more than mortal manliness, and ladies-in-waiting whose beflowered skirts and intricate ruffs were the result of years of patient embroidery that no mere mortal could afford. The cost was prodigious, for gods and goddesses must never appear old-fashioned and their clothes always had to be radiant and new. Viscount Montague spent £1,500 on two dresses for his daughters. Sir Edmund Bacon wore 138 gold buttons on one suit which was no sooner worn than discarded. As one puritanically inclined member of the House of Commons burst out, women 'carry manors and thousands of oak trees about their necks'.

Of course, ordinary mortals were forbidden such clothing by law, or even to ape such rich and fabulous fashions. Like the imperial purple or the Son of Heaven's yellow, this clothing was the external visible sign of the divinity of kings and queens. Such divinity was given a nasty shock in England by the execution of Charles I, but elsewhere it lingered on and Louis XIV, the 'Sun King', not only wore extravagant and costly clothing, but each day was ritually dressed by his highest nobility, and to hand the King his shirt was bliss and fame and jealously guarded.

As in life, so in death. Aristocratic funerals, in which horses and hearse, corpse and coffin were as fabulously dressed as the mourning crowd, reached a cost and an elaboration that surpassed all other ages – cortèges, preceded by heralds and gentlemen-at-arms, were at times over two miles long, and it cost about £60,000 to bury Elizabeth's Leicester in 1588. This was the last age of human gods, marked out by wanton exhibitionism, in Western Europe. And so one should not dismiss the rich furs, the costly velvets, the golden, gleaming silks of Rembrandt's pictures as mere visual delight on Rembrandt's part. They proclaimed grandeur, nobility, *virtù*.

Slowly, slowly, aristocratic ostentation was eroded by middle-class values. In the eighteenth century aristocrats sported their orders and decorations; their silks, satins and velvets which they wore for court occasions and for balls still marked them off from the common herd, but their styles were steadily approximating more and more to the affluent middle class. In the country and in the morning in town there was little to distinguish the courtier from the well-to-do citizen. And Beau Brummell, rapidly followed by the French revolution, gave the *coup de grâce*: Beau Brummell, the arbiter of fashion in late Georgian England, believed in buff and blue and austerely cut lines – elegance not ostentation proclaimed the gentleman – and so the Prince Regent, whose imagination, as we see in his Brighton Pavilion, ran to fantasy, dressed plainly, letting himself riot only in his frilled shirts and cravats or the occasional fancy dress of Scottish costume. Naturally the citizens of France were even more austere and although Napoleon made his Court somewhat grander, the days of aristocratic excess were quite over. Only feeble, decadent relics linger on, such as the black tail coat and white tie, which were *de rigueur* for Victorian middle-class dinner parties, but which was itself court dress transformed and rendered funereal for the multitude. Now it is primarily the dress of waiters.

Clothing indeed has come full circle: it is cheap clothing that is ostentatious, wild, extravagant, aristocratic in its diversity, and instead of marking out the socially secure, the grandees of authority, it is the badge and symbol of revolt. The Queen of England might pass almost unnoticed in Bond Street, but who could miss Jerry Rubin on Fifth Avenue?

1970

I I

Angst

Anxiety, anxiety, anxiety, the endless round of unease, the hesitation, the fear, the unquiet age that has never known security, decade flowing into decade, generation into generation: the bomb over one, death over the other, no ease between. So it would seem. So, indeed, are we told, over and over again. Of course, there was a golden time not so very long ago. It used to be the spacious days of those four-square Victorians whose morality and sense of purpose were as solid as their bankbooks. Then faith was secure; status certain; morality rigid but acceptable; peace abounded. But the Victorians are faltering, Bosch-like horrors are beginning to peep from behind the aspidistra: their secret lives are too disturbing. Sex combined with hard cash on the one hand and hypocrisy and impotence on the other is not much to the taste of the present generation.

We are far happier with the permissive Edwardians. The glitter of their decades now beckons the anxious present. Sexually loose, may be, but how skilfully they blended marriage and dalliance. How much better a marriage that bent rather than broke: the home, the child, secure. And the world, how good it was, how plush, so dollar-sprung and cosy. War, then, was still distant; true the atom was split, but the scientists assured the world that it could only be of theoretical interest. Social change might threaten but the cloud, if black, was tiny and easily dispersed. The Emperor was in China, the Tsar in St Petersburg, the Kaiser in Berlin: and no one fretted overmuch if they, or even Mr Rockefeller, shot their workers down. And the odd pogrom

in an unpronounceable Polish town was just in the course
of nature. It could hardly worry the Rothschilds with
Edward VII in Baden-Baden. And as for the starving
peasantry in India and Africa, their outrageous naked bodies
were not advertised in the Sunday newspapers, but decently
forgotten, the conscience eased with a dollar |for famine
relief or missionary enterprise. Was not the fertility of death
Nature's answer to their thoughtless concupiscence? Over the
not so distant past there was a sheen, a golden haze, a sense
of relaxed and untroubled life, when authority and wealth
bred a serene stability. At least for those who knew no history.

For some intellectuals, aware of Bloody Sunday, of the
revolutionary seethings amongst the workers and the clash
of battle armour amongst the great powers, these times
seemed less glamorous, more foreboding, licked with the
orange flames of Armageddon. Like the wistful New England intellectuals of the late nineteenth century, their
golden age, their age of equipoise and tranquillity, was discovered in the Middle Ages – when common men were close
to nature; when all was folded in an harmonious ritual of
the changing seasons; when men and women lived out their
lives within a spiritual framework of a Christian community,
catholic and universal. But some could not deny the hunger,
the pestilence, the dark superstitions of the medieval mind.
Others searched further still but in the present not the past,
particularly the agnostics, who discovered a more sophisticated refuge. They turned to the savages. Their primitive
cultures emerge as exquisitely sophisticated. Have they not
reached the perfect ecological balance with their environment, tamed time, subjugated the past and obliterated the
future? How could this be bettered? If life was short, it was
serene, untroubled by change.

Over the last hundred years a social nostalgia for the
past has become almost obsessive. Does it spring from a
growing sense of anxiety, of unease, of dislocation? Is it true
that the world man has created for himself can only be lived
in at immense emotional cost to himself? Has it grown so
complex that the mind and the passions shrink in terror and

tremble not only at the future but at the present? Is the most complex society in the history of mankind also the most neurotic?

The arguments for the affirmative, of course, are very powerful. Man is being urbanized at an incredible rate: in Asia, India, Java, Mexico, Brazil, wherever one turns, streams of humanity are pouring into the cities. Packed as dense as a shoal of whitebait, they are harried by noise, choked with filth and cramped by a city's routine. Nothing, it would seem, could be more alien for an animal of savannah and forest, mountain and sea shore, whose complex and delicate senses are tuned to explore the natural world. What use his miraculous vision in the smog of Los Angeles? Surely anxiety and neurosis must result. And the signs of it seem obvious enough: the growing addiction to drugs of every variety – oceans of alcohol, mountains of nicotine, millions of pills, down they go, drug after drug – mental breakdown spreading, suicide rising. An incapacity to control change or stabilize society drives more and more, particularly the young, into a febrile search for identity and release. Hence the sexual promiscuity, hence the sexual experimentation, hence the rejection of inherited social and personal standards. As the Moloch of industrial society goes marching on, the individual becomes weaker, bewildered, lost: a screaming ball of *Angst* in an urban prison whose lights wink at him like a crazed and uncontrollable computer. Poor man.

But has he ever found peace here and now? From those far-off days in the savannah when the great cats pounced and tore him apart, anxiety as sharp as toothache has dogged his life. Can we even begin to realize the anxiety of an agrarian society which lived on the margin of existence, dependent entirely upon the whims of weather? One year may be abundance, a glut of food, for all; and the next maybe with crops shrivelled or blackened on the stalk; starvation certain for all and death for the old, the weak and the young. And yet this is how our ancestors lived in Western Europe and Africa. The vast majority never knew security in their basic needs. The average span of life in

Elizabethan England was twenty-six, less than the hungriest and most famine-ridden Indian peasant of today. The pot bellies and protruding eyes of starving children were more a part of the Elizabethan scene than madrigals.

Such fears about the harvest bred anxiety, heightened fear and made the peasant hysterical, hag-ridden with fearsome spectres. The terrors of hell, of Armageddon, of sorcery, of witchcraft, of devilment everywhere abounded. That the world might suddenly end is not a new anxiety created by the bomb, merely an old anxiety renewed. As the year AD 1000 approached, men and women and children quaked with fear, certain that the Day of Doom was at hand, that God was coming to judge them all. And that meant, as Pope Gregory had told them long ago, that the majority would boil in God's wrath for eternity. The day passed, but not the anxiety. A sudden sense that the world's end was near could grip the mind of the medieval peasant and craftsman with the power of hysterical obsession and lead him to actions as extravagant as any the world has seen – nudity, mass flagellation, communal love, pogroms. Often they behaved like wild animals caught in a savannah fire. They fled and killed.

The wrath of the Lamb did not only blow up in spasmodic social whirlwinds, though they were as constant and as terrifying as gales at Cape Horn. The anger of God, as well as the horror of the Beast, was a daily, an hourly presence, for the Devil and his temptations, together with his horde of demons, monsters and goblins, lurked everywhere – in the milk churn, in the wind, above all in the minds of men, women and children. Ritual, holy relics, priests, bell, book and candle might keep the terrors at bay, but they rarely defeated them. Suspicion and fear hung about medieval lives like fog from a swamp, making our own anxiety-ridden lives seem serene and sunny by contrast. After all hippies may annoy, and homosexuals give one goose-flesh, but they can hardly be regarded as witches and wizards, responsible for all our ills and ripe for brutal extermination at the stake.

Angst

Nor did the world become much more comfortable as peasant society gave way to commerce and industry. Plague stalked the cities year in and year out as famine had stalked the land. And the puritan ethic was scarcely insouciant. The Devil still roared at large although his utterances seemed to be more personal, more concerned to capture the individual soul than bring on Armageddon. But one can begin to imagine the anxieties of adolescence when every lustful thought was charged with sin, when the Devil itched in one's fingertips. From day to day one's immortal soul was in jeopardy; the tortures of hell were no fantasy, but real, gloatingly dwelt on by preacher after preacher. Can worry about being called up, or bewilderment about one's identity, match terrors such as these?

Within this last century enormous burdens of anxiety have been lifted off the shoulders of men and women, particularly in the highly industrialized West, to a degree that they can scarcely appreciate. How rarely now do parents fear the sudden illness of children – the quick hand of Death through diphtheria, poliomyelitis, meningitis, scarlet fever and the rest which were commonplace but a generation or two ago. Deadly disease is no longer a lodger in the home but a remote contingency. And better still, the spiritual fears have vanished. No devils, no witches, nothing but a necessary wantonness in those fingertips.

Of course we are still far from sweetness and light, remote from a stable, rational and loving world. Anxiety can still lead to pig-headed and cruel policies, particularly anxiety about loss of prestige or loss of wealth. At times the fear of social change or of cracks in the political structure blinds the hearts and minds of men as completely as the fear of the Day of Doom did men and women in the Middle Ages. And, although the Devil has been abolished from the nursery, is not social shame almost as effective in creating worry about sexual habits we deplore? Nor are the old taboos broken: the sense of a future alien to our habits still disturbs the depths of our natures. We find lives lived along lines totally different from our own curiously menacing. Allen Ginsberg, naked, fakir-like, high on pot, has the same effect on the conventionally minded as a medieval heretic on a college of cardinals – and for similar reasons. He threatens the structure of respectable ritual. Hence the violent need to get the kids off Sunset Strip. Unconventional behaviour that preaches a golden age, a millennium, a paradisical way of life menaces the frail structure of society, makes breaches in it through which anxiety can sluice: so anxiety transmutes into action, which means as ever war, violence, brutality, repression. Kill what you fear, that was the lore of the savannah and forest, a lesson that man learned when he first stood upright: a lesson, it seems, that he can neither forget nor exorcise.

Anxiety, like sex or hunger, is probably a part of the structure of our instincts; one can only wish that it received the same recognition. Certainly it has infused all societies through the ages of man and usually led to cruelty, stupidity and repression. If only there was more fear of fear: more anxiety about anxiety. What is wanted is more preoccupation with it and less expression of it. What should disturb us about Ginsberg or the children on the Strip is the disturbance in ourselves. And we should feel cooler, more at ease, if we compared these outbursts to the millenary rantings of the Christian past, when hordes of hysterical believers worshipping their saints stripped, flogged and copulated in an orgy of religious ecstasy. The motives were much the same: driven frenzied by the anxieties of their age, they wanted paradise here and now. How quiet, how serene seems a 'be-in' compared with that.

1967

1 2

The Stars in their Day

Are you Taurus or Gemini, Pisces or Capricorn? Does your eye furtively glance at the column headed 'The Stars and You' and are you relieved when you read that you could have a 'speculative benefit' or worried when you see 'changeability in relationships may pose problems'? Or does a slightly sheepish, shame-faced smile flutter across your face as you turn hurriedly to another page in your newspaper?

I suspect it strikes few readers that the silly astrological columns are the sad end of an extraordinary human enterprise stretching back to the very dawn of history. The persistence of the belief that the movements of the stars are related to man's destiny goes back to the very earliest days of the neolithic revolution, if not beyond. And the fact that popular, non-élite newspapers in America, England, France, Germany, Italy, India, indeed in all non-communist countries, find it worth while to publish astrological columns day in day out, indicates the persistence of that belief. And as well as popular astrologers, high priests of the cult still exist, dedicated astrologers, masters of intricate calculations, who cast horoscopes and predict the fate of individuals with the conviction of a scientist, men and women who believe as intensely in the stars as the magicians of ancient China.

True, over the last three centuries the belief in the stars has steadily weakened and the market for horoscopes dwindled. With the coming of industrial society and the scientific revolution which has given us an accurate knowledge of the stars, astrology has become the plaything of the credulous and the ill-educated. But two hundred years ago its power in the West was still strong: both Cagliostro and Casanova cast horoscopes and interpreted the stars in order to bamboozle aristocrats, merchants and attractive women. A further hundred years back, however, the stars were still playing a vital part in human affairs, although historians rarely pay any attention to this aspect of seventeenth-century belief.

The Earl of Shaftesbury, the violent Whig who nearly toppled Charles II from his throne by exploiting the hysteria of the Popish Plot in 1678-9, believed absolutely in astrology. John Locke, the rationalist philosopher, lived in his household, but made no impression it would seem on this aspect of Shaftesbury's beliefs. A Dutch doctor who dabbled in the occult had cast his horoscope and so, Shaftesbury thought, foretold all that would happen to him. Nor was Shaftesbury an isolated crank. The great German general, Wallenstein, who dominated the Thirty Years War, took no action, military or political, without consulting the stars, and no one thought him either eccentric or pagan.

Astrology in these centuries lived quite comfortably with Christianity. Many kings kept astrologers at Court and consulted them regularly. Dr John Dee, the great Elizabethan magician, who consulted the spirits in a polished obsidian mirror which he had somehow or other acquired from Aztec Mexico via Spain, also used the stars to predict the future. He created a sense of fear, but the great Elizabethans consulted him and he died comfortably enough in his bed and not at the stake. Magic he might practise, but even in that age, terrified as it was by the fear of witchcraft, he survived. The stars were beyond the Devil and his works. They belonged to the mechanism of the universe, a piece of God's handiwork: therefore good and open to interpretation. And, in this respect, Catholic and Protestant did not differ, and a belief in astrology covered all creeds and heresies: Protestant, Catholic, Jew and Moslem did not differ in this particular. And in this respect, at least, they were at one with the Hindus and Chinese, and with the remoter civiliza-

tions of the Middle East. The stars dominated the lives of
Sumerians, Akkadians, Babylonians and Egyptians.

The greatest historian of classical China, Ssŭ-ma Chi'en,
gloried in the title of the Grand Astrologer, possibly because
the earliest archives to be kept systematically were those
which dealt with astrological matters. Indeed the Chinese
not only consulted the stars but devised the most elaborate
instruments to determine their precise conjunction at a
precise moment of time. One of the most elaborate and
complex astronomic clocks of antiquity was built by the
Chinese so that the position of the stars, even if the heavens
were cloudy, would be known, should the empress conceive
when the emperor paid a visit to her bed, for Heaven would
naturally be disclosing its hand at such an auspicious
moment, either to foretell happiness or doom.

Long before the Chinese had developed their elaborate
system of star-gazing, the Assyrians and Egyptians had been
studying the heavens just as intensely. Of all civilizations,
perhaps, the Assyrian was the most addicted to astrology and
no king of Babylon would act in minor, let alone major,
matters without consulting them. A great reference library
was built up in their palaces, so that prediction and result
could be studied and referred to. By the time Babylon fell the
Assyrian astrologers and divinators had reference material
which dated back nearly a thousand years. The ancient
Egyptians too studied the stars and believed in their benign
or malevolent influence. Nor was belief in astrology derived
from a single centre for, without any contact with Europe,
the Mayas in the Yucatán and Guatemala built huge
observatories and watched the stars. From China to Peru
throughout many millennia, men's lives were star-haunted
and the heavens wrote in cryptic symbols the fate of nations
and the destiny of men.

So those foolish columns in the newspapers have a long,
long history; a history heaving with portent. The stars have
terrified men, made them jubilant, provided dreams of
ecstasy and fear and, above all, strengthened a sense of un-
alterable fate, not only in the heart of the peasant and

craftsman, but also in emperors and kings, priests and soldiers. It is easy, of course, to see how relevant initially the position of the stars was to all communities which depended on the soil, for changes in the constellations indicated the coming of spring or winter or foretold that rains would come in Yucatán or the Nile flood in Egypt, events which, if delayed or inadequate, could mean famine. To the peasant the sky and the seasons were in mysterious harmony, yet capable of discord. The constellations might appear and yet the rains, in spite of sacrifice and religious observance, stay away; and then for years the juxtaposition could be close. The will of the gods and the stars were interconnected but not obvious: they needed to be studied with intense and minute care, and only then could they be used safely for prediction.

But humanity's need for the stars goes deeper than the need to discern the changing seasons or the coming of rain and water, deeper than the need to foretell the fate of kings, or the hopes and fears of men. There is a need in man to know and to rationalize his universe through magic and through very precise and detailed knowledge. He derives a sense of security from knowledge, whether it be the very precise and detailed knowledge of territory, of its trees and flowers and animals, such as the most primitive tribes of men acquire, or from the complexities of the modern science of physics or biology. His aim has always been both to control his environment and to banish anxiety. Man has always been, as it were, scientifically orientated even if his earlier and more primitive sciences did not work very well. Only gradually did he learn the precise way to investigate and control (perhaps one should rather say exploit) his environment, but he put the same intellectual effort, the same passion to observe and to accumulate knowledge into his earlier attempts.

Magicians, astrologers, were but mankind's first scientists. They were men of great intelligence and keen observation, no different in quality from Newton or Rutherford and, essentially, dedicated to the same task. Many of their facts were right and beautifully observed; their pursuits led them to invent instruments of great ingenuity. What was wrong were their premises. And in the vapourings of a Katrina one sees the pathetic end of a once majestic and comprehensive study of destiny: a science which for thousands of years interpreted men's hopes and fears and which seemed to give them a chance of evading disaster and controlling their fate.

1968

13

Genealogy

In the early summer discreet advertisements appear in *The Times* offering the services of a specialist in genealogical research. They are but the tip of the iceberg. Most genealogists never bother to advertise; their books are full of work for years ahead. About the same time, the secretariats of the Scottish clans are organizing jamborees of McNabs, Frasers, MacDonalds, so that Australians, Canadians, Americans and even Eurasians of that name can swarm together in the highlands of Scotland and feel at one with their mythical past. A family tree is a precious link, providing roots for millions of the rootless. Nicely emblazoned, it can decorate the study wall and provide an opening gambit in conversation in Sioux Falls, Montego Bay, Buenos Aires, Manitoba, Auckland, Alice Springs or Allahabad. Wherever the Scots or Irish go, their clans go too: but all men and women of European origin cling to their ancestors as frantically as any mandarin of ancient China or scion of the House of Jesse.

At first sight, it seems easily explainable. During the great migrations of the nineteenth century hundreds of thousands of Europeans tore themselves from their homes, villages and farms to root themselves in the far ends of the earth; the Welsh tending their sheep on the desolate slopes of Tierra del Fuego or the Polish miners burrowing into the rich lodes of Pennsylvania naturally clung to the memories of the past. Their money made, they wanted longer, more visible antecedents, with preferably a noble lurking in the higher branches of the family tree. Genealogists rarely failed to provide them with what they wanted. When William Morris, afterwards Viscount Nuffield, England's great motor manufacturer, endowed the multi-volume history of the English peerage, its professional scholars had no difficulty in providing him with an ancestry that reached back into the fifteenth century, making him nearly, if not quite, a Plantagenet. Yet we should not mock. Year in, year out, strangers from overseas drive to the villages of Europe, stroll about the churchyard, glance at the cottages and manor house and feel momentarily a nostalgic link with the great web of life that reaches back beyond the memory of man.

And if one turns from the present to the past, the same relish for ancestors seems to reach back to the earliest records of man. But we should be quite wrong if we thought that the Egyptians', the Greeks', the Chinese or even the Elizabethans' interest in genealogy was the same as our own – merely a mixture of snobbery and human longing. Like all continuing social activities, genealogy, the need for ancestral tables, has served many social purposes, and at times acquired a power, an authority which we find difficult to imagine.

The king lists of the pharaohs, inscribed on the Palermo Stone, look dreary enough. Yet they are magical with power, designed to perpetuate the endless continuity of kingship, right back to the gods themselves. Similarly the famous genealogy of the Memphite priests, that so impressed Herodotus, which lists sixty generations from c. 750 BC back to c. 2100, descending in an unbroken succession of fathers and sons, fulfils the same purpose. It uses the overwhelming authority of the past to enhance the status of those who possess the genealogy. Such an ancestry implied not only the blessing of the gods, but the right to power, the right to rule and to subject others. A claim to ancestors was always exclusive: after all, the Chinese mandarins did not allow peasants to participate in the rites of ancestor worship. Workers and ancestors do not mix: they never have.

All aristocracies have, very sensibly, made a cult of genealogy in order to underpin their special status. And it is interesting, if not surprising, that outbreaks of genealogical fervour occur most frequently when new classes are emerging into status, a new faction pushing its way into the ancient aristocracy, or when the established ruling classes feel threatened by the *nouveaux riches*. When, as happened in England between 1550 and 1650, all of these three factors were present at the same time, the effect on the cult of genealogy was dramatic. '. . . As early as 1577 Walter, Earl of Essex was boasting of his fifty-five quarterings, so England was clearly already well set on the road to the heraldic fantasy world whose finest hour came at the end of the eighteenth century with the 719 quarterings of the Grenvilles depicted on the ceiling of their gothic library at Stowe,' writes Lawrence Stone of the Elizabethan aristocracy.

Where the service of the past has been urgently needed, truth has ever been at a discount. As most of the Elizabethan aristocracy's true genealogies tended to disappear after a generation or so, either into oblivion or, even worse, into a yeoman's family, they forged medieval charters, cut ancient seals and invented ancestors with panache. Lord Burghley, the scion of a modest Welsh family, got himself back to Edward the Confessor's day; others were less modest and claimed Charlemagne, Roman consuls and even Trojans. Not to be outdone, the Pophams indiscreetly placed an ark in their family tree. Normans, Saxons, Romans or Trojans were as essential to the Elizabethans as Priam, Hector or Achilles to the Greeks; just as Gaul and Charlemagne were to the aristocracy at the court of Louis XIV.

But this was no joke, no game, no fantasy; both arms and pedigrees were of vital use. The great painted genealogies had a purpose every whit as definitive as the great stele of Sethy I at Abydos, where he is depicted venerating the names of his seventy-six predecessors. So has the power descended, so is power confirmed. As it was for Sethy I, so it had to be for the first Lord Burghley, and so it was to be, but in how diminished a sense, for many New Englanders caught up in the genealogical craze which swept America in the 1880s and 1890s.

Genealogy

The newly arrived Americans, daunted by the Winthrops, the Cabots and lesser families who could trace their pedigrees to the Pilgrim Fathers and beyond, required a personal share of the past to bolster their new-found social status and authority. Alas, there was no American College of Arms to provide their wants, no Garter King of Arms to bribe, no Bluemantle to suborn; but the New York Public Library did its best, and acquired the largest of all genealogical departments; so-called genealogists worked, with about the same sense of historical accuracy as their Tudor predecessors, in the major record offices of Europe. Ancestor worship in America, if pale by Chinese standards, acquired a certain respectability. But, like so many uses of the past that reach back to the dawn of time, the force of genealogy withered, and what was once an essential need for social and political authority became the plaything of snobbery or of mere nationalist obsessions.

Nearly, but not quite, for history delights in irony: there remains one great body of men and women for whom genealogy is more than snobbery, more than intellectual curiosity, more even than a technique for investigating the past. For the Mormons it is a vital activity, and one full of the deepest religious significance. The genealogical past used to sanctify the present; now the living Mormons sanctify the dead. Their ancestors, once truly and accurately traced, name by name, can be retrospectively baptized and given their passport from limbo to heaven. And so in Utah are monuments that the pharaohs might have envied, huge caverns quarried out of the granite, proof against bombs nuclear or bombs biological, in which the keys to Mormon ancestry are preserved for all time.

How much simpler but how much less human would it be retrospectively to baptize everyone, for one does not have to go back very far to be everyone's cousin. After the lapse of a mere twenty generations, everyone has 1,048,576 direct ancestors – great, great, great, etc., grandparents. Apart from a few immigrant groups, every Englishman of English grandparents may claim to be descended from everyone who was alive in England at the Norman Conquest – so much for Norman descent. Everyone's genealogical table, even Queen Elizabeth II's, is a deception. Only by clinging resolutely to one branch, and occasionally swinging to another, can a family tree be made to look like one: otherwise it vanishes quickly in a complex spider's web. All men are brothers – genetically, ancestrally: descended from all who were alive two or three millennia ago. It is hard to grasp: most of us would rather not do so. We cling to false distinction and like any Tudor gentleman hanker after a Trojan, a Norman baron, a Roman senator to link us with borrowed distinction to the living past.

1970

14

The Anarchy of Art

Wandering through the galleries of London, New York or Paris is a bewildering experience for a liberal-minded man of fifty. After all, in our youth we had our moments of excitement and protest. We were seized by bitter fury against the Establishment when the police suppressed D. H. Lawrence's etiolated nudes. And how we laughed at the glossy horrors of Munnings – those beautiful scrubbed gypsies, the scented winds blowing through their tresses and the horses – oh, the horses! So worthy of a royal behind. And what derision we felt for the heavy momentous portraits of tycoons that littered the boardrooms of London and New York. And we thronged to the surrealists – disturbed, perhaps, by those weird landscapes of Tanguy, seemingly full of coloured, floating contraceptives, worried somewhat by Dali's soft watches, by Ernst's terrifying forests and by Magritte's meticulously painted shocks. But we had read our Freud and we knew the language of dreams, so we could participate in the pictures without great difficulty. Nor did Picasso's distorted females nor the abstractions of Nicholson trouble us overmuch, any more than the new sculpture of Brancusi, Archipenko or Moore. Again, we were in touch, less perhaps with pure abstraction than the rest but, even here, the persuasive effects of scientific ideas made it seem relevant: that pure form and pure mathematics might have a resonance seemed possible to the untutored humanist. And the traditional art that we knew had always possessed both geometric and algebraic qualities. And so one could reach through to Jackson Pollock – painting without language, but decorative, memorable, at times haunting. But with Pollock I was getting near the boundaries of contact, feeling not only a lack of intuition but also a deadness of response, as if chords were being hammered on a dumb piano.

But now, how does one find one's way through the present anarchy of art that ranges so wildly from the meticulous studies of Wyeth, to the hollow forms of Moore, to the near abstractions of Sutherland, to the screaming, bleeding faces of Francis Bacon, to the cartoon horrors of Pop, to Bridget Riley's literally painful Op, or to the junk and graffiti schools, or to the dry-edge types or to these anti-art artists who just paint shapeless boards one colour and leave them lying on the floor or propped up against a wall? And, of course, this is far, far from exhaustive: there are the mobiles of Calder, the squashed motor engines of César, the plaster casts of living people; bits and pieces of flotsam and jetsam stuck in boxes; waxworks; the shop window dressers with a difference like Claes Oldenburg; and so on and so on. Above and beyond it all sits, enigmatic as ever, that supreme doodler of genius, Picasso. Must one turn one's back on most of this, denounce it as infantile, regressive, anarchic or mad: neither decorative nor meaningful? Has art after living within one broad context for centuries, shattered into fragments? Is there anywhere to go?

Of course, there has always been a mad fringe to art, an exhibitionistic desire to shock, to blitz the viewer out of his compliant acceptance of the reality that he sees. After all, Bosch did not paint to soothe, but to terrify, to hammer home the evil in men's nature and its terrible consequence: no different perhaps from Francis Bacon, no matter how far apart in technique or subject. And, after all, Arcimboldi must have given his viewers a bit of a turn to see the human face composed of fruit or vegetables. This was not at all the iconography to which they were used. And the boldly erotic in art was not discovered in the twentieth century – Fuseli's ferocious, devil-haunted lesbians still, even in this age, can make us feel very uncomfortable, much more so than the scribbled graffiti of a Bruce Whiteley that might have been taken straight from the scribblings of a fourteen-year-old boy on a lavatory wall. And Pop art has a long history behind it, back really through Daumier, Doré and Hogarth and beyond. There is, oddly enough, a curious Pop quality in those strange women of Lorck, painted in Germany back in the sixteenth century. Few abstract impressionists have been as good as Turner, even though he called his compositions steam and sky.

Some artists have always wanted to give us new eyes, to make us learn a new language of the heart; others, and these usually have been the major artists, have accepted the artistic conventions of their day, bent and exploited them to the limits of their ingenuity and need, but kept always just within the context of the language of art of their time: Leonardo, Michelangelo, Velasquez, Rembrandt, Chardin, Goya are firmly embedded in the artistic tradition of their age, no matter how adventurous they might be in technique or subject matter.

Indeed about most great ages of art there is a harmony between painting, sculpture, music, architecture and the decorative arts that is unmistakable and clear. That the music of Handel should be heard in the Assembly Rooms at Bath adorned by the pictures of Gainsborough and embellished with the furniture of Chippendale, seems as natural as the powdered hair, the satin clothes, the enamelled snuffboxes and the tea-cups of Chelsea china. They are as harmonious as notes in music, as harmonious as the golden stone of the city that blends with the Cotswold hills. That we ourselves endow such a scene with some measure of unity and harmony, I do not doubt, but try as one might it is impossible to unite the elegance of the Seagram Building with the painted bedsteads of Rauschenberg or the cacophonic horrors of *musique concrète*.

In the eighteenth century this overriding unity of taste was established and maintained by a small *côterie* of well-informed connoisseurs who could insist on their standards because they were the sole patrons. And even if this made for some conservatism against which a Mozart might chafe to our loss, yet it did provide a welcome balance against ignorance, vulgarity and a heedless search for novelty. There can be no doubt that the growth of the middle class and its wide-reaching affluence led to diversity and insecurity in artistic taste and production. Already fissures were appearing in the eighteenth century and divisions multiplied in the nineteenth. Bougereau on the one hand and Manet on the other are indicative of the onset of schizophrenia, and worse still, of the onset of intense commercialization of art, much more competitive than any previous century had known. Dealers multiplied, the one-man show started towards the end of the century. The search for artists with a difference was on and the *avant garde* proved as exploitable as the academicians, and so by our own time were infants, grandmas and chimpanzees. But painting was not alone.

By 1900 a stroll through the suburbs of an English town would have discovered a riot of bastard architecture – mock-Tudor, mock-Gothic, mock-Georgian – to which only the pen of an Osbert Lancaster could do justice. Ignorance combined with money to create a market for any monstrosity which seemed to be in the high tradition, just as in the twentieth century this ignorance has combined with more money to create a market for any monstrosity that seems to violate high tradition: a wondrous circle of irony.

The growth, therefore, of a large market for art helped to break the imposition of taste by the patron connoisseur, but that is only a part of the reason for the present anarchy. Looking back on the Renaissance, it seems a miracle that genius blossomed so freely in Florence, Venice, Rome, Milan, Perugia, Bergamo, Bologna and a score of lesser towns. Where did they come from, these supreme artists – Masaccio, Piero della Francesca, Botticelli, Leonardo, Lippi, Cosimo, Michelangelo, Raphael – and so one might go on and on. But unlike most miracles, it proved repeatable, for the cities of the Netherlands suddenly produced a crop of almost equal magnificence in the seventeenth century – Rubens, Hals, Van Dyck, Rembrandt, Cuyp, Vermeer, and so on and so on – only to be repeated yet again in the middle decades of the nineteenth century in France. And between these great periods painters of astonishing invention and skill littered Europe with their pictures; sufficient to fill the museums, palaces and noble houses of first Europe, then America. Great painters are distinctly more easy to come by than great poets or great musicians, or so it would seem.

Given the basic skills, painting is not a difficult art, and the number of human beings who can reach high technical accomplishment is probably very great. No other explanation can make sense. And of course this is true today: the graffiti scribblers, the junk artists, the abstractionists and the rest have the techniques at their command. They can draw, compose; many have a wonderful sense of colour. Rauschenberg's illustrations of Dante's *Inferno* make that point explicit enough. So the answer does not lie in the suggestion that other ages were more greatly endowed with geniuses than our own. Indeed, the reverse is likely to be true. We probably have far more technically accomplished painters and sculptors than any previous age.

One factor is time: each age makes it more difficult for the next. It was easier to be Aristotle in fourth-century Athens than in twentieth-century New York: easier to be Newton in seventeenth-century Cambridge than twentieth-century Moscow. Creative achievements of the highest order tend to open a wonderful field for secondary talent to exploit and cultivate, but to limit the areas for supreme genius. The Renaissance painters created a magic lantern world of perspective in which the viewer and the artist could participate, but it was a world of myriad possibilities that took over four centuries for artists of the most diverse natures and talents to exploit fully. But by the time of the impressionists its resources had been well-nigh exhausted and pressures on technical ingenuity grew.

And there is a further, more profound, difficulty: skill with the brush or scalpel can be combined with any form of human temperament or physique, with the handsome or the deformed, with the clever or the stupid, with the roistering or the retired, with the erotic or the impotent. Artists can be highly intellectual like Leonardo, passionate like Michelangelo, full of the wisdom of the heart like Rembrandt, hungry for flesh like Rubens or Renoir. But only rarely are there painters who are deeply original both in content *and* technique. Originality is just as rare in painters and sculptors as in engineers or chess players. Yet the development of the last hundred years of art has been to create a cult of the artist as a wayward, misunderstood, yet dedicated genius – the man exiled from society by the originality of his ideas and techniques.

Hence the endless pursuit of novelty in modern art; much of its so-called originality is flat-footed, dull, obvious, jejune. Of course, one can see immediately the point of Claes Oldenburg's sagging ironing boards, of those oversize three-way plugs or those man-size hamburgers. Criticism of our modern, supermarket, consumer society is better done in an essay. It is much more powerfully argued by a Galbraith or a Packard. And so the hamburgers do not shock, they just bore. And the same is true of a great deal of Pop art. Of course one can see the point of a meticulously painted Stars and Stripes in a frame, the trouble is that one can see it in a split second and so the picture is as dead as a dodo before it begins. These varieties of modern art are just as banal, as empty of content as the most tedious forms of salon painting. Many artists once they are driven to be original are lost. They need to work in strong pictorial conventions where technical virtuosity is at a premium, or better still in the wake of a major technical release – such as the exploration of perspective, or landscape, or the nude, or even impressionism or surrealism – where the elements of the language are given. But to expect great painters to be original both in content and technique is rather like asking a novelist or poet to invent a language before he writes in it.

Much modern art is therefore so devoid of meaning as to be boring, or its meanings are so obvious as to be tedious. With such endless variety, however, and with so many people painting or carving, there still remains much to admire. To dismiss it all as worthless is folly. Colour has always possessed beauty for the human eye, and much modern art is wondrous in colour, as decorative as any that the world has given birth to. But decoration is not enough. There is a need to return to the most haunting of all human problems – the human face. This, surely, is the artist's infinity, which neither imagination, technique, passion nor wisdom can ever exhaust. And its rarity is for me one of the more depressing features of modern art.

But where do we middle-aged liberals go, where can we look in order to praise? It is impossible to return to the academics, it seems rather staid to stop dead with Picasso or the surrealists, yet we are too old to put up with being bored to death by the Rauschenbergs, Oldenburgs, Klines and Cohens: too old for childish eroticism or flat-footed social comment. Pop, again, is intellectually too simple, although now and again it produces a picture that pleases not only by its decorative qualities but by its content. Peter Blake's self-portrait is a curiously haunting document. But usually Pop is little better than a good cartoon. So one wanders, as along a sea shore littered with debris: occasionally there are bits and pieces that delight the eye, more rarely a fragment of treasure trove, but the skies are grey, the wind coming in from the sea very cold. There is nowhere to go, and Coney Island is just round the corner.

1967

15

A Walk in Detroit

Late in the fall the sun still blessed Detroit, the blue sky was high, wide and handsome, too inviting to evade in a cab, too warm to be missed by one about to be plunged back into the mists and fogs of London. About 11 a.m. on a Saturday morning I set out from my motel and walked down Woodward Avenue. After five minutes I began to feel uneasy, unsure as to whether I was awake or dreaming. Maybe I had strayed into a film set by Fellini. No human being was to be seen. Cars sped by, buses hummed and coughed, the sun blazed down, but as far as the eye could see the sidewalks were empty. After twenty minutes' walk I saw two white boys waiting for a bus: ten minutes later two black youths slid round a corner and stared at a Cadillac through the windows of a showroom. And I saw no one else, no other living being, not even a cat or a dog, until I reached the art gallery, a walk of some two miles. And what a walk. Cracked and broken sidewalks, with grass and weeds growing through them; desolate parking lots, shabby automobile showrooms; and quite often nothing – just lots. Everywhere dirt, bits of paper, cigarette and chocolate cartons – the excrement of a consumer society thrown out of passing automobiles.

The art gallery, of course, was stupendous: wonderful pictures, splendidly displayed; room after room proclaimed the generosity of Detroit's leading citizens. But the walk from the art gallery to downtown Detroit, another mile maybe, was more searing, if less nightmarish. Broken-down snack bars, stinking of cheap food; grimy shops selling magazines and books; side-streets full of ageing houses, the street corners occupied by a few derelict Negroes. Here and there one or two young black people bustled about, but even they in their pink trousers and lime-green jackets could not stifle the air of decay, of dirt, of hopelessness: a concrete city with a concrete heart that belied the generous warmth of the sun and that pellucid blue of the sky that drew my thoughts to fifteenth-century Florence.

What a contrast! There was a city as vast for its age as Detroit for its; there, too, had been families of fabulous wealth drawn from international trade. These families, the Medici chief amongst them, had set about their city. The *piazza* had been cleared and beautified with staggering works of art that have continued to give joy for hundreds of years and will do so for hundreds more. Church after church, square after square, bridge after bridge, street after street create a world of brick and mortar and stone that delights the eye and lifts the spirit – a city in which anyone, rich or poor, native or foreign, can dwell with pride. Nor is Florence unique; the more anonymous aristocracy of Venice deliberately created the beauty which we see. By deliberate act they cleared and paved the *piazza* and *piazzetta*, built the splendid façades and made the beauty that draws the world to it.

Cities do not grow beautiful by chance. None have. A fact forcibly brought home in *Paris in the Age of Absolutism*,* a brilliant book by a young historian, Orest Ranum. Here we see how Paris grew, not only in people, in commerce, in riches, but also how it became a symbol, an expression of the aspiration of Louis XIV and his minister, Colbert, who wished to emulate Augustan Rome. The beauty of the Louvre, of the Palais Royal, of the surrounding bridges and hotels, springs from their intention of making Paris a city of grandeur as well as of beauty. And what Louis XIV started, Napoleon I and III completed; the splendour of Paris is due to them and their architects. At the same time Paris never lost its human scale. For centuries, and still today, it is a city to be lived in, possessing all the contrasts that are needed –

* London, 1969.

quietude and privacy in the midst of the multitude, sudden vistas, parks, gardens, fountains, places to wander in, places to sit in; above all, places to talk in.

Somehow the great European cities have preserved the quality which created the adjective 'urbane'. True, London is under strain, as streets of Victorian and Georgian houses are ripped out for Manhattan-style office blocks. Although the majority of English towns can still be lived in, patches of Detroit blight are visible in most – the waste areas between the suburbs and the commercial centre, which in American industrial cities has become a chronic disease, an inhuman nightmare land of loneliness and violence. The automobile, the basis of Detroit's fabulous prosperity, started the long death agony of the American city by opening up vast suburbs that gave space, a sense of country, and abolished from sight the poor and the black. The only American metropolises, apart from San Francisco and New York, which still possess something approaching the grace and amenities of European cities all predate industry – New Orleans, Savannah, Charleston, Boston and a few other New England towns.

This tragedy goes far deeper than mere physical appearance. Cities, purposely created, are life-enhancing. If you do not believe me, then study the life of Dr Samuel Johnson or, better still, read Dorothy Marshall's *Dr Johnson's London*.* Turn to the other volumes in Norman Cantor's excellent series, Historical Cities, of which these are a part. Then look at a kindred series put out by the University of Oklahoma Press, *The Centers of Civilization*. And having read, think hard and long about Detroit, Chicago, Pittsburgh, Baltimore and the rest – above all, Detroit.

In Dr Johnson's day London, with its beautiful squares and parks, its amusement gardens and theatres, its taverns, concert halls and academies, produced a brilliant civilization that was thoroughly and totally urban. When tired of London the rich and fashionable went sometimes to the countryside but just as frequently to the beautiful spa cities – Bath, Tunbridge Wells, Brighton, Harrogate and the like –

* London, 1968.

so that they could still enjoy the civilities of urban life. Returning to London, they experienced an invigoration of the spirit, a sharpening of the intellect. As Dr Johnson said, 'Whoever is tired of London is tired of life.'

Of course, it was not all Georgian elegance and refinement. There were slums and there were poor: the sick, the starving, the illiterate and the violent. There were mobs and ghettos, but it was a community, the living centre of culture, the seed-bed of genius, complex and human – never a desert of concrete lots and growing weeds.

As I said earlier, many of the most beautiful of European cities were the creations of a man, a family or a small class of men. Even the staggeringly beautiful city of Bath was due almost entirely to one man, Ralph Allen. Yet scarcely one large American city has captured the imagination, the energy and the dedication of those who have derived their wealth and power from them. Outside Detroit lies one of the greatest industrial complexes the world has ever known. The stupendous generosity of the Fords to the world through their foundation has been commensurate with their mountainous riches. Nor have they entirely forgotten their native city: benefactions to universities, and the art gallery's world-renowned pictures bear witness to their private benefactions. These, however, are but diamonds embedded in cinders scattered across a desert of broken and dirty concrete. If one thinks of what the Medicis and the great Florentine families did for Florence, the plight of Detroit scars one's soul. Surely these great empty wastes could have been planned and modelled to create a city to live in. Yamasaki has shown what could be done with his elegant and entirely human-sized buildings at Wayne State University. If only that university and the art gallery had been surrounded by squares enfolding gardens and fountains as a setting for crescents and terraces of housing to suit the whole range of Detroit's needs! If only the Fords had built a palace in the heart of Detroit and lived in it – if only they would! Then there might be a Florence in Michigan. After all, Florence was and is a great industrial city. The idea is not outrageous.

To cure the ills of American cities, the rich, the middle class and the professional families must live in them again, and attempt to re-create the civilities and urbanities that rightly belong tó great towns. American architects (such geniuses with an office block or public building) must design homes within the city landscape. Perhaps it is too late, the disease too far gone. Perhaps one should destroy these decaying corpses and plan a world that consists of suburbs and centres – industrial, commercial, cultural. Perhaps the city is rapidly becoming merely historic and so has no future: or a future only for the poor. If so, humanity will be the loser, for city life at its best has been one of mankind's greatest achievements.

Part Three

OTHER TIMES, OTHER PLACES

I

The World of Samuel Pepys*

For nearly one hundred years Samuel Pepys's diary, written in seventeenth-century shorthand, lay virtually unknown on the shelves of the library he bequeathed to his old college, Magdalene at Cambridge. At that time his reputation was a modest one: he had been an admirable civil servant, a Fellow of the Royal Society, a benefactor of his college – and that was about all.

The success of John Evelyn's diary in 1818 stimulated interest in the few who knew of the existence of Pepys's journal. A young scholar, John Smith, was put to work, and in three years he made an admirable transcript, which Lord Braybrooke, the editor designate, then slashed to his heart's content with the lofty abandon of nineteenth-century aristocratic scholarship. And so the most famous diary in the English-speaking world was launched. Sir Walter Scott puffed it in the *Quarterly Review*, Francis Jeffrey panned it in the *Edinburgh*, only Thomas Creevey damned it as 'trash'. The public bought it and loved it. Three printings were rapidly consumed, and throughout the century its reputation grew. More of the diary was published in better editions, culminating in Wheatley's edition of 1893–9. By the turn of the century Pepys was a household name, regarded as one of the great writers of English literature, a man who could, without offence, be placed alongside Chaucer, to whom he was frequently compared.

* *The Diary of Samuel Pepys: A New and Complete Transcription*, vols. I–V (1660–64), ed. Robert Latham and William Matthews (London, 1970–71).

Naturally, historians and scholars pillaged the diary to enrich their own books on seventeenth-century England, so that the period came to be seen through the eyes of Pepys; the Restoration, the Plague, the Great Fire were all reflected from his looking-glass. Selections from the diary have been published over and over again, giving delight to millions, but always from the old nineteenth-century edition.

Finally, the long-heralded complete, scholarly edition is with us – five volumes now published, and six to go. This, the editors stress, is the *whole* diary, published for the first time. The additional material is not large – ninety erotic passages, mainly very short, dealing with Pepys's sexual gropings, and accounts of five days that previous editors omitted through carelessness (they add but little). Apart from the erotica, which give a little more insight into the hot and urgent nature of Pepys's sexuality, the most important aspect of this edition is its accuracy. On every page there are a number of small changes, restitutions of Pepys's forthright language and the like, which add immeasurably to its quality. At last we have Pepys's diary as he wrote it. Each year of the diary is given one volume, and the last two will contain an index and a compendium of essays by the leading scholars of the seventeenth century on the major topics that interested Pepys. His pride, never in short supply, would have swelled at the sight of it, and rightly so, for it is admirably done. The pitfalls of too much scholarship have been neatly avoided, yet there is enough to elucidate where elucidation is needed. The editors and particularly Robert Latham, who spent twenty years of his life in the service of Pepys, deserve to be rewarded.

But does Samuel Pepys deserve so splendid a monument or such enduring fame? Or did he just strike a particular chord in the sensibilities of nineteenth- and early twentieth-century Englishmen and Americans, which reverberates less and less in our own times? Is he indeed a great writer, one of those rare human beings who can capture for all time not only our hopes and despairs but also the fleeting moments that make up our daily lives, or is he merely a valuable historical source whose literary importance has been inflated? It is not easy to decide.

Anyone reading Pepys for the first time, and unfamiliar with the London of his day, might easily find him a bore. The early entries in the diary are detailed yet matter-of-fact. They contain next to no self-analysis. There are no descriptions of buildings, nor even descriptions of people – the only physical facts Pepys tells us about Charles II are that he was over six feet tall and walked very fast. Reading the first volume is rather like suddenly awakening in the middle of a man's life, being expected to know everyone he meets and all the places he goes. One must persist for a hundred or so pages; not until then does the miracle work. Like a parasite, one slowly enters Pepys's bloodstream and sees his world with the clarity of his own eyes. This capacity of the diary to absorb the reader totally is extremely important. It heightens the sense of truth, convinces us perhaps too easily of the reality of all that Pepys observes, and so creates dangers for the historian while it makes him irresistible to the general reader. His ability to make the reader a participant in his daily life was certainly responsible for Pepys's success in Victorian England. His preoccupations, so intensely felt, were those of his readers. Pepys's career as recorded in the diary would have gratified Samuel Smiles.

When the Journal opens, on 1 January 1660, Pepys was just beginning to rise in the world. He was twenty-seven. Of modest origins – his father was a London tailor – he was nevertheless curiously well connected, for some of his relatives were minor gentry in Cambridgeshire and Huntingdonshire, and one had married into the great family of Montagu, who became Pepys's patrons. Pepys was well educated, but for a poor, aspiring pseudo-gentleman he made a disastrous start in life. He improvidently married at twenty-two (a phenomenally early age for the 1650s) a penniless girl of fifteen, Elizabeth Saint-Michel, the daughter of a French Huguenot. He remained passionately in love with her until she died in 1669, though he was often maddened by her; quarrels, even blows, litter the diary. Her slightest flirtation provoked Pepys to a paroxysm of jealousy. Before the diary opens, they had separated for several months, only to come together again. Sometimes Pepys took great joy in her; sometimes she seems to have kept him unsatisfied. Maybe, as Professor J. P. Kenyon suggests, she was somewhat frigid, and so drove Pepys to amorous intrigues. Whatever the reason, the relationship is described with such honest realism, with such passion linked to kindness, at times with such worries about her extravagance and sluttishness, at others with such pride in her beauty and finery, that it becomes both absorbing and deeply moving. There is nothing, however, to envy; most men can read Pepys (and this is partly a reason for his popularity) and feel a smug sense of superiority. In spite of Pepys's tantrums and his infidelities, his wife always won. By laying bare all his shortcomings Pepys keeps himself free from pomposity: here is no hypocrisy, only a humanity common to us all.

The fascinating relationship with his wife was, however, merely the spice for the feast Pepys provided to the Victorians. His real grip on their hearts came from his rise from rags to riches. Like all success stories, it was studded with anxieties, with ominous men of power who threatened disaster, with golden-hearted patrons, and cautious and mildly dishonest exploitations of power by Pepys himself.

In 1660 Pepys scarcely possessed a guinea. He held a minor post at the Exchequer and acted as an accountant in the household of Edward Montagu, one of the leading naval officers in the Commonwealth, who, after the death of Oliver Cromwell, began to intrigue for the return of Charles II. And Charles's restoration, brilliantly described in the diary – not in brilliant prose, but with an almost photographic accuracy that creates a far more heightened sense of reality than any fine writing could do – made Pepys's career. When Montagu went over to Holland to fetch Charles, Pepys acted as his secretary. Deeply impressed by his efficiency, Montagu obtained two posts for Pepys: the major one of Clerk of the Acts for the Navy, and a more lucrative one at the Privy Seal. Within a year, Pepys had accumulated over £300. The sweet smell of success rushed to his head. He drank hard, ate wolfishly, and went to the newly re-opened theatre several times a week. But after two years his strong Puritan streak reasserted itself. Pepys forsook plays and wine, and, rising at 4 a.m. with no hangover, found that time for work abounded.

Pepys set himself to learn how to run a navy. He mastered arithmetic, he learned the complex methods of costing timber, hemp and tar. He reorganized his office and its records, and made two powerful allies: the King's brother, James, Duke of York, and Mr Secretary Coventry. At the end of Volume III the road to success was open, and Pepys's love of its trappings was being allowed full indulgence.

Like his private life, Pepys's official career was full of minor peccadilloes. He received large and handsome gifts from merchants with whom he dealt; at times, let's face it, he took bribes. If he placed a man in a job, a return was expected. As with his infidelities, these irregularities filled Pepys with both anxiety and elation. Lacking the awful moral priggery of a John Evelyn, Pepys appears in his journal as intensely human, with a keen appetite for love and success yet so fissured with the common weaknesses that he never loses our sympathy.

I feel, however, that these aspects of Pepys may not capture the imagination of this generation as they did our fathers'. His almost naïve delight in the acquisition of expensive things – clothes, coaches, silver, pictures, books in fine bindings – may nauseate those already glutted with this world's goods. His delight in hierarchy, in being treated with deference and humility, his unbridled joy in seeing 'Esquire' on a letter addressed to him, are unlikely to be shared by those who reject the idea of status. Even so, I think the diary will still be read, for Pepys reveals an era that is as strangely different as he himself is familiar.

Pepys's world lacked the amenities of modern living to an astonishing degree, even though it was a world of constantly widening horizons. Novelties, and there were many in the London of his time, heightened the sense of wonder, of curiosity, that pervaded so much of Pepys's life. Pepys's London possessed no newspapers as we know them, only an official gazette containing a little foreign news, usually stale, so that Pepys had to spend hours every day at the Royal Exchange or in Westminster Hall catching up on events. Rumour was more frequent than truth, and to assess rumour was almost a hopeless task. Coffee houses and taverns were never mere places of refreshment; they were essential sources of news and intellectual entertainment. There Pepys met his sea captains and heard about the far-off lands that Europe was still discovering, in tales where fantasy and fact wildly intermingled. There were few other amusements. After 1660 a few poor theatres came into existence; they revived, year in, year out, English plays of the last fifty or sixty years. The acting was often poor, the scenery primitive, yet Pepys was addicted to this 'most rare' entertainment.

Apart from the theatre, there were nothing but fairs and puppet shows. It was natural, therefore, for men and women to meet and make music, or play games that we now regard as fit only for children, or tell each other stories – mostly fairy tales or wild romances. Gatherings in each other's houses were constant; a day scarcely passed in which people did not visit Pepys's house or he other people's. Indeed, the Londoners of Pepys's day lived more like men and women in a village than in a great city. One is also struck by the poverty. Pepys never had a sirloin of beef in his own house until he was twenty-eight. Luxury goods were rare and expensive, and this is the clue to much of Pepys's delight in finery. Pepys's world, therefore, was both ignorant and poor, yet one in which there was a growing sense of achievement, of advance.

Take books: although printing was two hundred years old by Pepys's day, it was only in his time that a man of modest income might acquire a small library at a reasonable cost. A great diversification in the printing of books had taken place – plays, romances, travellers' tales, maps, and books for self-education began to proliferate. To Pepys and his contemporaries these were marvels to buy, to display proudly in the best bindings, and perhaps to read. And so it was with the new science. It was natural for Pepys to join the Royal

Society. He possessed little scientific knowledge, but he hungered like a provincial for 'the rare and the curious'.

So much of Pepys's delight springs from the limited, primitive age in which he lived, when so much was lacking of what we take for granted. Even at thirty Pepys did not possess a watch. He lived by the church bells of London and an occasional sundial. And so did everyone else; thus very few specific appointments were ever made. Pepys drifted about from public place to public place, from coffee house to tavern, hoping to do business. Often he went to Court to confer with the Lord High Admiral, James, Duke of York, only to find that the Duke had gone hunting. Pepys never displays surprise or resentment. Time had a totally different dimension for him from what it has for us.

Pepys's London was small in another sense. The number of men and women who could afford to dress like gentry was tiny. So, dress gave the entrée – to Parliament, to the Law Courts, and to the royal palaces. Hence Pepys could go and view the Court at play, watch the Queen or the King at supper, and eye Lady Castlemaine, the King's mistress. Never has a court been so accessible as that of Charles in the 1660s. Its gambling, whoring, drinking, and general air of fecklessness and extravagance were common gossip. And this rightly worried Pepys. He had seen Charles I executed. He remembered all too well during the humiliations of Charles II's reign the pride that Englishmen had felt in Oliver Cromwell's success, and fears of a renewed civil war thread the pages of his journal. In this, as in so much else, Pepys conveys the feeling of his age to perfection.

Thus public and private are wonderfully intertwined. In the midst of domestic detail – a lip-smacking appreciation of a dish of udders – Charles II strolls in, as it were, with the other great ones of the time.

And so, if one has patience at the beginning, one can enter through Pepys's diary a world that at first deceives, because Pepys himself, in his interests, his tastes, his personal and social ambitions, seems so like ourselves. The realization quickly comes that he lived in a London far, far removed from the city life that we know. This gives his diary a fascination, a depth of interest, that no other journal of the time possesses. Add to this that Pepys himself was a natural writer of the highest class, and it is easy to understand why his is perhaps the greatest diary of all time. Robert Latham and William Matthews have edited it with the high scholarship it deserves, creating a fit memorial for Samuel Pepys.

1970

2

The Victorians Unbuttoned

The paradox of the Victorian world goes very deep. At first glance it seems both humourless, opaque, rigid and puritanical. Many facets of Victorian society chill the mind: its manic preoccupation with respectability and social convention, its dedication to dogmatic religion and remorseless morality; its ferocious attitude to sin in the young and the weak; its nauseous sentimentality about the innocence of women; its lunatic preoccupation with modesty; its obsessive sabbatarianism; and its rage against drink. Wherever one looks in metropolitan or provincial society, amongst the rich, the prospering or the poor, one finds an agonizing preoccupation with sin, combined with a Jehovah-like inflation of the figure of the father.

Once the historians had got to work on this world of our great-grandparents and ransacked the cupboards and attics for diaries, letters and memoirs, the image of the Victorian world began to change; it developed some of the qualities of a nightmare. Cruel fathers, savage governesses, maniac mothers, abused wives and imprisoned daughters peopled the Victorian scene; fearful repression of sex was followed, as might be expected, by life-destroying neuroses; at the same time the Victorians' moral arrogance, the worship of money, the vulgar and tasteless ostentation became matters for a cynicism worthy of Voltaire. Lytton Strachey did his best in his *Eminent Victorians* and *Queen Victoria*, using whatever gossip suggested or malice supplied to denigrate the stern ideals of the Victorians: General Gordon was discerned to be as addicted to brandy as to the Bible, Florence Nightingale emerges from his book as a tough, interfering busybody, Cardinal Manning as a self-regarding, flamboyant exhibitionist and the Queen herself as absurdly infatuated with her ghillie, John Brown.

Recently an even darker side of Victorian life has appeared in a fantastic pornographic autobiography, *My Secret Life*, which reveals a range and depth of sexuality with which few had credited the Victorian age; a revelation confirmed by the journals of John Addington Symonds, which gave new insight into the extent of practising homosexuality amongst the intellectual élite of Victorian England. Naturally the assumption that the Victorians were hypocrites and that their morality was in itself a perversion has become widespread. And those who rebelled – Thomas Huxley, John Ruskin, Samuel Butler, William Morris, Oscar Wilde – now appear to be the true symbols of their age. The problem, however, is more complex.

Take the most Victorian of all the great figures of that age, William Ewart Gladstone, the prime minister whom the Queen detested. Night after night he would leave 10 Downing Street, stout stick in hand, and walk up to the parading whores in the Haymarket and Regent Street. Once accosted, he would do his best to persuade the prostitute to give up her trade; if there were signs of repentance, he would invite her home for tea with Mrs Gladstone in the hope of persuading her to enter one of the houses for fallen women that he and his wife supported. No ribaldry, no threat of blackmail, no scurrilous rumours about his real purpose could deter him from his work. Odd work for a prime minister! And odder still was his constant attendance at the salon of 'Skittles', the most notorious courtesan of the 1860s, or his very close association with Lily Langtry, the Prince of Wales's mistress. Yet Gladstone was a ferocious Christian, committed to the view that every hour of every day should be in God's service: and the hours he spent with whores were hours spent in service. Nevertheless, what was at work was Gladstone's powerful sexual nature: through these quaint methods of sublimation, in no way hypocritical, he was able to tame his lust and live his life of dedicated respectability. This type of semi-double life, a respectable Dr Jekyll and a sexy Mr Hyde, enabled many a Victorian to cope with his puritanical world.

And there was Lewis Carroll, the Oxford mathematician, who wrote *Alice in Wonderland*. Although this became the great children's book of middle-class England, it is in many ways a nightmare of cruelty and violent sexual symbolism. But it brought Lewis Carroll great fame. His book was considered both pure and delightful, a work fit for the innocents. He was a clergyman and much revered in Oxford and a pillar of its stuffy respectable society. And yet he was constantly falling violently in love with small girls, from seven to eleven, chasing them ardently, and such was his charm, fervour or transparent innocence that he persuaded many a nursemaid to permit him to photograph their little charges stark naked. Piety and photography lived demurely together, and Carroll never strayed beyond the focus of his camera lens.

Again, Alfred, Lord Tennyson, one of the louder voices of the Victorian conscience, who thundered at 'the slope of sensual slime' and hinted so delicately at the adultery of King Arthur's Court in the *Idylls of the King* that most of his readers were oblivious to it, told blue stories in Lincolnshire dialect as soon as the ladies had retired to bed; but, of course, acting the peasant glossed bawdiness: folk tales were respectable for men. Earlier he had written *In Memoriam*, a passionate declaration of love to his dead friend, Arthur Hallam, that some Victorians even found too open and too warm-blooded, used as they were to 'manly' friendships in which they blandly ignored the homosexual undertones. Nevertheless, Tennyson got away with it. But then one of the most popular of all Victorian boys' school stories, *Eric, or Little by Little*, has boys of fourteen kissing each other, weeping in each other's arms and making declarations of eternal love. Nevertheless, hundreds of Victorian fathers gave Dean Farrar's book to their young sons for a birthday present! The friendships described were pure and Christian, therefore the gestures of affection noble. Many Victorians possessed a remarkable capacity for sublimation, an incapacity to see through the sentimental mist to their own unconscious drives. Some, however, came near to recognition; others were forced into it; others broke down under the strain; a few, particularly in the later decades of the century, denounced the whole system of Victorian respectability as cant.

Scholars and scientists were particularly fortunate if they possessed strongly sexual natures. These uneasy spirits could dabble in the new sciences of ethnology and anthropology, or take to bibliography. Cult objects could be collected (indeed phallic cult objects soared in value in Victorian days and became scarce enough to be extensively forged). Lectures were very popular where one could gravely listen to a detailed discussion, naturally with lantern slides, of fertility rites or the sexual habits of primitive peoples. True, some characters, such as Sir Richard Burton, who spoke with such intimate knowledge of female circumcision in Somaliland and the boy prostitutes of Scinde, created a sense of alarm. Yet they bought his translation of the *Arabian Nights*, shocking though it might be, on the grounds of erudition. Along with similar works of curious scholarship, it went into their libraries, but under lock and key. Indeed few ages have collected '*curiosa*' with such fervour. Bibliography, like anthropology, provided a heaven-sent veil for sin. H. S. Ashbee, whose *Notes on Curious and Uncommon Books* is the basis of the bibliography of pornography, left his own collection, the largest ever assembled, to the British Museum. Although the greatest, he was one of many amateur scholars who eased the burden of respectability by a pursuit of dubious scholarship. These, however, were the lucky men.

The burden of respectability, the Himalayan ideals of morality which many Victorians imposed on themselves, proved too much for others. They sinned or became neurotic. Dr Vaughan, the headmaster of Harrow, had been a pupil of Thomas Arnold of Rugby and imbibed his ardent, evangelical Christianity and his desire to convert the brutal schoolboy to a life of Christian dedication and leadership. As soon as he got to Harrow, Vaughan intensified attendance at chapel, increased the time the boys spent in prayer and preached quite terrifying sermons on sin. Alas, the headmaster knew too well what he was preaching about. He taught classics, construed with his pupil by his side on the sofa, but too often his hand strayed to the root of evil; a boy babbled to a friend, whose father sent for Dr Vaughan; the choice, exposure or resignation. Dr Vaughan resigned, preaching without the slightest irony or cynicism his last sermon on the theme 'Yet Once More'. It became a Victorian favourite. Promotion denied him on the threat of exposure, he was exiled to a bleak mining town in Yorkshire; a model, he allowed it to be believed, of Christian self-sacrifice and the abnegation of ambition. A score of Victorians knew the truth, yet the truth remained hidden for three generations; lapses of virtue if they threatened the fabric of society, as a scandal about the most Christian of headmasters would have done, were rushed like skeletons into the cupboard and locked up.

Hypocrisy? No, prudence, for the Victorians saw little virtue in publicizing lapses in virtue; ostracism was their weapon. Sir Charles Dilke and Charles Parnell, the Irish leader, suffered as Vaughan suffered, although their lapses were perhaps less heinous: both politicians and potential statesmen of the highest order had their lives blighted and careers ended because they were co-respondents in divorce cases. Indeed the penalties for transgression of the sexual code were desperately harsh, particularly for women. Lady Ward, married by her parents to a nobleman, found she possessed a strange husband. He ordered her to lie naked on a black sofa in her jewels. Then he sat and stared at her. And that was all of married life she knew. She complained bitterly to her father, who ordered her to obey her husband: after all, it might be odd, but not immoral, to look at your wife, whose duty in life was obedience. In the end the situation became unbearable and, foolishly, Lady Ward took a lover. Discovering her to be pregnant, her husband turned her out of the house in the middle of the night, without any means of support. She turned to her parents, who shut the door in her face. Death was her only escape. No one blamed either her husband or her parents. She had transgressed, they had behaved with propriety.

As soon as George Eliot began to live with Lewis, her brother cut off all communication with her. No one brought a greater sense of duty, of personal and deeply felt morality to the commission of adultery than George Eliot, but few would receive her and her life was made wretched by strain that showed itself in violent headaches, sickness and paralysing neurosis. Again, Dickens had to go to frantic lengths to keep his mistress secret, and his family maintained that secrecy for three generations. The strain of Victorian morality weighed with peculiar heaviness on the sensitive, often driving them into neurosis. John Ruskin, innocent of the nature of female genitalia, was so shocked by marriage that he was driven into life-long impotence and a drooling sentimentality for pre-pubic girls. Indeed, the whole Victorian scene is littered with broken hearts, broken minds, broken lives and broken careers. Men and women were destroyed by a moral code which was either too strict for them to keep, or which, if they did keep it, made them neurotic.

What was this iron respectability that held them in thrall, how was it imposed and why did they feel so strongly its necessity? At the heart of Victorian morality lay the concept that man was accountable for every moment that he spent on earth – this was the reason for the endless and meticulous diary that Gladstone kept, recording every game of backgammon, every sermon read, every rare lapse into masturbation. For over seventy years Gladstone drew up his daily personal account of good and evil. Obviously the day best spent was one spent in the service of God: and the service of God must be the rejection of sin. But sin for Victorians could be very wide. It could mean the playing of cards, the reading of fiction, cooking on the Sabbath, the drinking of alcohol, the smoking of tobacco, the immodest display of an ankle;

not far from sin was indelicacy, the use of any language, gesture, manner that could be so construed, like a young girl walking out alone unchaperoned. Hence the rejection of sin and the practice of respectability were dovetailed neatly together; certainly the former could not exist without the latter. But to achieve both was a constant struggle, a never-ending battle with Satan, who filled the world with temptation. Hence it was exceptionally important to protect the weak and the innocent, namely women and children, the weaker vessels, as the Victorians liked to call them. Children, unless properly educated, might quickly be lost, and women, in their innocence of the world's ways, had to be protected against themselves.

The family, therefore, was the citadel of morality and its defender, whose law must be explicitly obeyed, was the father. If he wished, therefore, the Victorian male could flog his wife, beat his sons and terrify his daughters. He could immure them at home for weeks on end, spend his wife's property, cut his children off without a penny. A few responded to the sadistic opportunities, many created an economic tyranny (one has only to think of Samuel Butler's parents, or Edward Gosse's father, or Mr Barrett of Wimpole Street) in which the so-called best interests of the child excused despotism. The majority of Victorian middle-class parents felt the need to temper affection, for they were conscious of the sinfulness of human nature.

Although no society has prized more highly what it liked to think of as the innocence of children, the Victorian parent and schoolmaster were well aware that the child was always the Devil's target, especially the young male child. In the eighteenth century John Wesley had preached the need to break the child's will, and the Victorian evangelicals set about it with a vengeance. A low diet was thought by many to be essential in restraining the growth of carnal appetites in the young male. Augustine Hare's mother started the discipline young.

I was not six years old before my mother . . . began to follow out a code of penance for me. . . . Hitherto I had never been allowed anything but roast mutton and rice pudding for dinner.

239

Now all was changed. The most delicious puddings were talked of – *dilated* on – until I became, not greedy, but exceedingly curious about them. . . . They were put on the table before me, and then, just as I was going to eat some of them, they were snatched away, and I was told to get up and carry them off to some poor person in the village.

And in case Mrs Hare is thought of as an idiosyncratic sadist, there is ample evidence elsewhere. The boys at Radley College were so hungry that they searched for acorns like squirrels and nibbled at crocus and hyacinth bulbs like mice. One of their greatest delicacies was cowslip roots, for which they scoured the water meadows by the Thames. The food, indeed, provided by Mr Squeers at Dotheboys Hall was no exaggeration.

Even in the richest and most luxurious houses the children were kept to a diet of milk puddings, boiled potatoes, suet and a little meat. Yet their parents' table would be loaded with oysters and lobsters, fish, roasts, game, pastry, cakes, jellies, ices, vegetables and salads of every description. Surely here was hypocrisy of the first order: the guzzling downstairs and the semi-starvation in the nursery and school-room. But, as in so many aspects of Victorian living, there was no hypocrisy. The child had to be protected from temptation, from rioting in his carnal appetites; only after he had learned iron discipline could he remain temperate in the midst of profusion.

Hence the over-ruling need for the headmasters of all public schools to be clergymen, and the greater need for compulsory chapel and constant sermons, prayers and exhortations. Clerical headmasters knew the dangers of youth and its temptations. They insisted on godly habits, godly friendship, a horror of sin, a detestation of drink and infinite circumspection with regard to light literature. The boy had to be converted to the active evangelical principle of a purposeful Christian life; and there was no better moment than puberty. After all the Victorian child had almost certainly been thrashed for touching itself or displaying sexual curiosity in its brothers and sisters; from the

tenderest age the seat of sin had been underlined by punishment, so that when the Victorian boy was suddenly infused
with the lustful energy of adolescence, feelings of guilt
flooded in with equal intensity. And when his headmaster
spoke of sin and insisted on clean habits and mastery over
sin, he knew well enough about which sin he was talking.
Few could reach such dizzy heights of dedicated morality,
but many struggled throughout their lives to achieve the
religious ideals inculcated in youth. Furthermore, the teaching of the medical profession reinforced the clergy's sermons.
Sir William Acton insisted that masturbation led to blind-
ness, mental decay, feeble offspring and early death. And the
morality and the fear bit deep enough to make Victorians
ashamed of their backslidings and quickly cover them up
with a blanket of respectability.

In some ways the girl's life was more rigorous, certainly
more sheltered than a boy's, and her innocence was protected
so meticulously that many middle-class brides had no idea
of the consequences of marriage. A boy could not be kept
ignorant, but girls could be and were; and on their honey-
moons they were shocked into frigidity.

The morality the Victorians had learned in childhood,
with its strict taboos and maniac fears, they were expected
to follow throughout their adult lives, no matter what the
cost. Only men and women fortified daily by an ardent
Christian faith could hope to do so – hence the terrible crisis
which all Victorians feared when they had doubts about
religion. For once the sanction of religion no longer operated,
their feet would be on 'the slope of sensual slime'. Hence the
horror in many circles of the new science of Darwin, Huxley
and the rest, which could, and did, lead to *doubt*. The Victorian, therefore, was a man of fear; fearful above all of
temptation, no matter how innocent seeming. Why such
terrors? There had been evangelical Christians in the eighteenth century and in Regency England: there had been
sabbatarians, even a few dedicated to total abstinence, but
they had been minority groups. Why did this rigorous
morality become so dominant?

The causes of change of cultural morals are little understood but in the case of Victorian England there are two very important ones which we can discern; one is quite well known, the other only recently brought home to historians by the publication of *My Secret Life*. The more important, perhaps, was fear. Between 1789 and 1837 Europe had been convulsed by revolution and by threat of revolution: the first eleven years of Queen Victoria's reign were worse rather than better. Year after year it seemed as if Britain itself would not escape from the wave of revolutionary ferment that was rolling over Europe. Chartists preached physical force; the desperate economic situation provoked riots; the structure of society looked both worm-eaten and brittle. Here surely was the hand of God, that retribution which William Wilberforce had told the English would certainly come were the upper and middle classes not to reform their morals. His book, *A Practical View of the Prevailing Religious System of the Professed Christians in the Higher and Middle Classes in this Country contrasted with Real Christianity* (naturally to their detriment), rattled through edition after edition and strengthened immensely the new emerging moral attitude. Lord Liverpool, as prime minister after the Napoleonic wars, provided government funds for new Anglican churches and was quite frank about the reason: religion he regarded as the only possible safeguard against the radicalism of the poor. Indeed the middle classes became infused with proselytizing zeal and they provided the leadership for Sunday schools, societies to reclaim fallen women, for strict sabbatarianism, for the first temperance societies, and for those active works of charity amongst the poor that both Henry Mayhew and Charles Booth (who investigated the London poor with dispassionate insight) thought to be so useless. Nevertheless soup kitchens, shelters, artificially created work, eased the middle-class conscience which was deeply troubled both by the extent and depth of poverty and all its sinful concomitants – gambling, drunkenness, debauchery and prostitution. And they knew that the godly working man worked better and longer than the dissolute. Without cynicism they believed respectability led to profit. And it often did. At the lowest it was a necessary insurance.

The second cause was social and economic. The working class, even the artisans and lower middle class, lived on desperately narrow margins: only a strict frugality which eschewed expense of any kind – drink, smoking, gambling, girls, finery in dress or ostentation in living – could guarantee survival and possible progress up the rickety ladder of economic advancement. Hence anything which might excite the imagination or titillate a natural appetite had to be frowned upon. So the aspiring artisans, like their earnest betters, took to the grimmer styles of religion, built themselves vast, cold, brick temples in which they worshipped their remorselessly puritanical God. The spearhead of lower middle-class godliness joined the Order of Rechabites, pledged to drink only water, banished all profane literature from their houses, Tennyson's poems along with Dickens's novels, would not allow their wives to cook on Sundays, regarded the theatre as a snare of the Devil and any manifestation of sex as a sure passport to Hell.

There is no doubt that between 1830 and 1850 this passionate and rigid puritanism spread as easily as cholera in the new manufacturing towns of the midlands and the north. In one small corner of Lancashire, Preston, there were seventy-seven regular public speakers, dedicated to total temperance. They held meetings for reformed drunkards, sometimes for five nights at a stretch, in which personal experiences, combined with conversion, were recounted as at a revivalist meeting. The town was divided up into areas and each house canvassed and lists of 'intemperates' compiled. According to one authority, by the end of Queen Victoria's reign there were thirteen general societies, eight women's organizations, five juvenile associations, seventeen religious associations, four philanthropic institutions and nine orders and friendly societies dedicated to the war on drink.

But so long as Queen Victoria reigned there were no licensing hours; men and women drank as long as the landlord would supply them, and there was no ban on children quaffing their ale, or if sufficiently affluent and the landlord complaisant, getting blind drunk. One cannot understand, therefore, the rage for temperance without a realization that these reformers were daily confronted by drunken women and children, by homes destroyed by drink and working men made jobless through alcohol. At the same time, the reformers' triumphs were met by furious abuse from the brewers and distillers, who used all the influence they could to prevent Parliament limiting the sale of drink. Emotions were, in consequence, heightened to an extraordinary degree and the social battle about temperance took on political and religious overtones that reflected the deep divisions in society itself, represented in many a Victorian mind as God versus Mammon.

As with drink, so with sex. Innocence, purity, chastity, the sanctity of marriage, were, as we have seen, widely held Victorian ideals: the reality was grosser, much grosser. And one can only understand their intensity if one realizes the fabulous availability of sex in Victorian England. The home, the school, the university, the empire itself, each had its darker side. One has only to read *My Secret Life* or Mayhew or Booth to realize that poverty and destitution were always so close to lower-class Victorian men and women that they easily became the victims of those members of the propertied classes who wished to debauch them. For those middle-class Victorian men who could not square their sexual needs with the conventional pattern of their lives, and they were the majority, their opportunities, based on hard cash, were legion.

The position of the servant girl, often only fourteen or fifteen years old, could be tragic. Usually she was a country girl, more frequently than not without friends or relations in London, dependent therefore utterly on the household which employed her. These were fair game for either the master of the household or his sons. The author of *My Secret Life* and his friends seduced scores of them. If they rejected their master's advances they were liable to be brutalized or dismissed; if they became pregnant, as they usually did, accusation of their masters would frequently lead to instant dismissal without wages or a reference, whereas if they kept quiet, they might collect a month's wages and a future reference, even sometimes secret support from the guilty male.

Yet it would be wrong to suppose all of these girls were innocent victims. Village life was not prudish. As female servants were rarely let out of the houses in which they worked, many enjoyed first the flirtations and then the frolic with their rich masters or their sons. The temptation was not all one way and it is clear from *My Secret Life* that working-class girls, unlike many of their mistresses in Victorian England, were not altogether ignorant of the pleasures of the bed. Nevertheless the situation was usually one of crude power that ended disastrously for the girl.

The major recruitment to the teeming world of Victorian prostitution came from the servant class. The other main source was the factory girl or those employed in seasonal trades. Victorian London possessed every variety of whore, perhaps tens of thousands of them, from the *maîtresse en titre* set up in a beautiful Maida Vale villa, with carriage and servants, to the prostitutes who lurked in the alleys of the Strand, where a sailor might find an ageing woman for a few pence, taking her then and there against the wall. The same shabby area possessed broken-down knocking shops, where rooms could be hired for an hour for the use of prostitutes as young as thirteen or fourteen. Boys were no more difficult than girls: young soldiers, as J. A. Symonds' memoirs show, were always available in Hyde Park and male brothels were common enough in Knightsbridge and elsewhere. When the author of *My Secret Life* wanted a young virgin heterosexual male, he had no difficulty in getting a sixteen-year-old carpenter for half a sovereign. The boy was on the verge of starvation.

Whatever a man might want, no matter how idiosyncratic, it was available in Victorian London. And the reason was poverty. Mayhew talks of the parentless children, some no more than ten or twelve, living in cheap dormitories on money got by thieving or earned by prostitution, yet rioting night after night in sexual orgies. There were tens of thousands of Victorian men, women and children who knew nothing of Christianity and its morality, who only knew the need for bread and survival. And again it would be wrong to think of them drowned in misery and guilt or harrowed in their souls by the work they did. Many of the little whores that the author of *My Secret Life* debauched both loved the work and loved the rewards. And that this was so provided the greatest horror to the evangelical Victorian.

As with London, so with the great towns – Manchester, Bristol, Liverpool, Brighton, Leeds – they too presented similar dangers, though less, perhaps, than London. Unless armed against the world, the Victorian youth was presented with endless opportunity for sexual indulgence. The temptation began in the home, it met him in the world, but he did not escape from it at school. All the great Victorian moralists and evangelists regarded the school years as vital, the time when a boy might be saved or lost. But Victorian boarding schools were cesspits of juvenile delinquency. Bullying abounded, and bullying on an appallingly violent and sexual level. Homosexuality was widespread and openly indulged. An occasional boy might be flogged or expelled or both, but the fundamental conditions were never tackled. Every small boy at Harrow was given a girl's name and they were referred to as the senior boys' 'bitches' – a situation which in the 'decadent' and permissive twentieth century would never be permitted. Around those Victorian boys who were saved, therefore, raged a sea of temptation, hence the anguish of doubt, the terror of losing faith and the need to intensify religion, hence the need for a morality that was absolute and unyielding.

As in the town, as in school, as in the great cities, so the empire presented a similar conflict of attitudes, a typical Victorian schizophrenia. The Christian ideal of Empire was venerated. Christian English gentlemen, models of fair play and decency, would, both by the sense of justice and compassion, bring light to heathen darkness and raise the level of

the pagan world in which they would live their dedicated
lives. The white man's burden was not a sly hypocritical
phrase, but deeply and sincerely meant. Moral priggishness,
an arrogance about their position in the world, was obvious
enough in many of the great imperial proconsuls and in their
dedicated district officers, but the ideal was accepted and
thousands of colonial civil servants attempted to live up to it.
But power and status corrupted others. In India, in Malaya,
in the Southern Seas, even in 'Darkest Africa' men took what
was so easily available, the native girl who could not resist
the temptations either of money or status. By the end of
Victoria's reign India had the problem already of the Eura-
sian, the man or woman of mixed birth, despised by both
races, Indian and British. Money and power wrought their
evil work as with the prostitutes of London. Hence the need
for evangelical missionary enterprise.

Indeed as one explores and probes the dark side of nineteenth-century life and its poverty and its orgiastic opportunities, one can understand the ferocious need that Victorian
men and women felt for a social morality that was as absolute
as it was comprehensive. They might be the leaders of society,
but they were still the minority. And in a nation in which
affluence on the borders of the middle class was so fragile, sin
might be equivalent to economic disaster. Only by a life of
pious frugality could many hope to rise above the filth, the
squalor, the depravity of Victorian England. Many of the
rich and the well-to-do were troubled by conscience in the
face of so much social injustice, and their attempts to win
working-class men and women to temperance and godliness
were also an effort to make them economically viable. And
this having been said, there is no doubt too that respectability in itself became a pursuit. The Victorians became
adepts at disguising the weaknesses, shortcomings and failings
of their heads of society: or they shut their eyes to the obvious. Dr Vaughan's scandal, although known to a few, was
hidden to the world at large for nearly a hundred years.
Skeletons were quickly locked in family cupboards. Although
many Victorians rigorously repressed their sexuality, they

remained haunted by it. And the very conflict in their natures, as in a Ruskin or a Dickens, or even Tennyson, drove them towards that creativity which is also one of the marks of the Victorian age.

It was a society of vivid and startling contrast: of the saccharine innocence of the girls of Millais's academic pictures and the garish whores of the old music halls, of Dean Farrar's sentimental, lofty-minded story of adolescent purity, *Eric, or Little by Little*, and true Harrow, with its 'bitches'. Although it was the world of Mrs Gaskell's *Cranford*, pious, delicate, religious and good, it was also the world in which the author of *My Secret Life* bought or seduced two thousand girls, boys and women. Its sexuality was often more rampant, more wanton and much more gross than our own today, but it refused to accept it and resolutely tried to pursue purity and respectability. It disguised its failures and took refuge in silence. Anything was better than the evil which surrounded them and lured them to damnation. And one can only understand the Victorians and the urgency of their morality if one grasps that they were a minority in a boisterous sea of dire poverty and rampant lust.

3

The Edwardians

She was dead at last. The German Emperor had rushed across Europe to be at her deathbed; the Prince of Wales, an ageing and corpulent *bon viveur*, had broken down and wept as she put out her feeble arms and called 'Bertie'. The nation stood silent and stunned, waiting for the last moments to ebb away. Then her people broke into an orgy of lamentation. Three thousand poems bewailed the passing of Queen Victoria – newspapers in Calcutta, Rangoon, Capetown, Montreal, in cities and countries throughout the world, printed elegies with borders as black and as deep as night. The Reverend R. C. Fillingham, M.A., widely known as the Radical Vicar of Hexton, wrote in *The Echo*,

> It is no time for speaking. Voice, be dumb!
> The darkest day of England's years has come.
> From peers' and peasants' eyes the tear-drops start,
> Each heart in England is a broken heart.

But be dumb the English poets would not be. Even *The Agnostic Review* burst into song, proclaiming for the Queen, if not a heavenly, at least an historical immortality. The peerage had its poet in Lord Burghclere; the House of Commons, not to be outshone, produced an ode by William Allan, M.P.; Ella Wheeler Wilcox rhymed for America; the Poet Laureate, Thomas Hardy, produced one of his more unreadable lyrics, and there was 'a very creditable effort penned by a working man', Mr Egby of Reading.

The refrain, no matter how complex the variation of imagery and prosody, was often the same – the Great Mother of Empire had gone at last; in poem after poem there was a note of doom, of the ending of an age, a sense that the world would never be quite the same again. Mostly they looked back with longing and nostalgia to Victoria's long, long reign. Those few who cast a thoughtful eye on the future usually did so only to exhort the heir, as did A. Clements Baker of *The Illustrated Sporting and Dramatic News* in a dreadful poem entitled 'Farewell':

> Who loves the land, the dear old land that bore us –
> Who holds her honour as no party scheme –
> Who fain would front whatever lies before us,
> From foes who plot or fools who only dream –
> Who loves this country – for the past a debtor,
> And doubtful for the future, dark, unknown –
> Will join the chorus – where could we do better? –
> 'Long may Victoria's memory guide the Throne!'

Indeed the strong current of apprehension that runs like a tide through these lucubrations sprang from a realization that for over twenty years the Edwardians had stood in the wings of history waiting to take over their heritage and enjoy it – openly, publicly and without reproof. But on Victoria had gone year after year, as the Prince of Wales grew older and fatter, more habituated to a restless life of pleasure and yet, quaintly enough, still very nervous in her presence. The Great Mother might stir love and devotion in her subjects, but she scared the wits out of her children and grandchildren.

In fact, she had mothered half the monarchy of Europe, and now splendiferous in uniforms of staggering grandeur they followed on foot the tiny coffin on its flag-draped gun carriage. To the sound of rolling drums and muted fife it moved steadily through the complex ritual of royal death to its last resting place by the side of her endlessly mourned husband. Then the new age began with alacrity. Edward VII knew that at fifty-nine there was little time to lose. He lost none. For ten brilliant years the Edwardian age glittered, alas with more tinsel than gold, but none could deny its sparkle.

Excluded as a youth, excluded as a young man, excluded as a mature man and excluded in late middle age from the affairs of state, Edward VII had been forced to a life of pleasure to which, in any case, he was temperamentally inclined. As regularly as the seasons he moved from the gaming tables of Marienbad and Biarritz to the racecourses of Doncaster and Ascot, during February and May he entertained, went to the theatre and visited his female friends at five o'clock of an afternoon for a '*thé complet*'. With the regularity of a migratory bird he left in March for two months in the sun, in August he was resplendent in naval gear at Cowes Regatta, in October at Balmoral for the deer and grouse, at Christmas and the New Year – Sandringham. As best they might, his ministers pursued him, inured to all-night trains, tempestuous sea-passages and the dank discomfort of Balmoral. The country's business had to go on but at least there was style, laughter, amusement, the clear pursuit of a life of the instincts which his subjects could vicariously enjoy.

Queen Victoria may have had a chilling presence, innate dignity and grandeur that derived from isolation, but there was not much that her subjects could participate in – the glimpse of her at the occasional Jubilee or as she flashed by in the royal train. She might be a symbol of widowhood and motherhood, but hers was a deeply lived private life. Her major palaces were moribund. Only the private houses of Osborne and Balmoral had the deep impress of her personality and her husband's. Edward gave up Osborne and set about the rest. Palaces he intended to live in to the full. He got especial pleasure from breaking up or burying the life-size statues of Victoria's ghillie, John Brown, with whom she shared in later middle age an occasional cigarette and more frequently a dram of whisky – a solecism of taste that Edward was never likely to commit.

His mistresses were pretty, elegant, witty, well-born and usually discreet – and knew their place. At his succession he was firmly in the hands of Mrs George Keppel, a charming and beautiful creature of exceptional social skill, who never exploited the position and managed to be liked by Queen

Alexandra, who invited her to share the vigil by Edward's deathbed. The King's mistress was as much a magnet as the King himself; they never lacked for cronies. Their circle was, of course, at once aristocratic and rich, but also cosmopolitan, and what is so rare for monarchy at that date, in no way anti-semitic, for both the Rothschilds and the Cassells were close friends. Indeed earlier they had rescued him financially and helped to create the circumstances in which he could enjoy untroubled his extravagant life.

Sometimes Edward's entourage was cynically referred to as 'The Bodies' in contrast with the more intellectual segment of English aristocratic social life, led by Arthur Balfour and Margot Tennant who married Asquith, afterwards the Liberal prime minister. Their circle of friends was known as 'The Souls'. The difference between Bodies and Souls, however, lay not so much in their sexual mores, but in their social interests. The Souls loved talk – talk about politics, talk about people, talk about books, talk about theatre, talk about science – and if, at her dinner parties, the talk became too gossipy and private, Margot Asquith would quell the table in a high piercing voice and demand 'general conversation'.

But, like the Bodies, the Souls lived glamorously in public, yet loosely in private, maintaining, however, the discretion and code which was so much a part of the attitude of the Edwardians to life. As one of Edward VII's friends cynically phrased it, 'It does not matter what you do, so long as you don't frighten the horses.' The public must not be shocked. If Balfour slept with Lady Elcho, she nevertheless arrived at country house parties with her husband, and Balfour slipped along to her bedroom in the dark. No one acknowledged their adultery, although everyone knew of it. And so it was with the Bodies, their relationships were passionate; but as they were less intelligent and less controlled than the Souls, sometimes their scandals surfaced. This had been particularly true of the time they were waiting in the wings for Victoria to die; after his accession Edward VII was older, discreeter, more tired and much more firmly under the control of Mrs Keppel.

Nevertheless the gyrations of these gilded creatures, whether Bodies or Souls, were noted at endless length in the social pages (not columns) of the daily press. They were perpetually photographed – at races, at the theatre, at the opera, at garden parties and at play at Biarritz, Nice or Marienbad. Their public function was similar to that of film stars in the twenties and thirties or of pop-stars in the sixties. They projected an image of glamour, sophistication, riches to those for ever denied them. They represented a curious and unique phase in history: a public aristocracy on constant view, constantly photographed, constantly written about. The growth of democratic attitudes had not progressed far enough for ordinary men and women to create their own folk heroes and heroines, except in sport or in the London theatre, and so they looked for glamour where it was traditionally to be found, amidst the aristocratic rich.

And with large segments of the nation the Edwardian nobility was immensely popular. The Prince of Wales's triumph with Persimmon at the Derby in 1896 made the public hysterical. His mistress, Lily Langtry, had her photograph pinned up on thousands of walls. The Earl of Derby was immensely popular, so was the Earl of Lonsdale, with his yellow carriages and footmen in yellow livery, the idol of the prize-fighters. Aristocratic weddings at St George's, Hanover Square, or St Margaret's, Westminster, drew crowds of thousands; they also projected a view of a fun-loving, instinct-satisfying life. After the moral earnestness, the soul-searching and the widow-gloom of the Victorian world, the pleasure-loving Edward VII and his friends cast a radiance over English life. Edwardian England certainly had its darker side, it was not short of men of deep social conscience and radical intentions, but there can be no doubt either that England took to play and pleasure between 1900 and 1914 in a way that it had not done before – these were the boom years of three-day cricket, of football, of daily race meetings, of music halls and theatres and the astonishing mushroom development of the seaside resort, above all of Blackpool and

Brighton with their fun fairs and daring, erotic and intensely vulgar post cards.

That is why there was on the surface a sense of ebullience, of fun, of radiant human enjoyment, at the centre of which stood the King, small may be, fat may be, but dignified and with a style all his own, from the trim of his beard, the tilt of his hat, the angle of his cigar. Like all monarchs who achieve great popularity, he possessed the delight of an actor in self-presentation and also much of a great actor's sense of timing. And popular Edward VII was: Victoria might have been more greatly revered, but no sovereign in modern times has won the warmth or affection of his people as Edward VII did.

And yet, his gilded world, whether of the Bodies or the Souls, was something of a mirage, and even Edward VII's popularity sprang from the coarser, more philistine, more thoughtless elements of English society. The English aristocracy lived on a curious tight-rope of self-deception. Their actions belied their beliefs. Only the very stupid or the very insensitive amongst them could be unaware that this was so. And long before his reign was over, even the horses had begun to neigh and stamp and look bloodshot-eyed. To the critical and the intelligent the behaviour of the rich seemed like an outrageous hypocrisy. Indeed one can trace back to the Edwardians the early beginnings of that voice of criticism which in the last two decades has become a deafening roar.

Of course, there had been self-deceptions in Victoria's age, but at least most men in public life had attempted to live according to the harsh morality of their day and when they failed, some of them, such as Parnell or Dilke, had their careers blighted by the simple fact of their adultery. In Edward's England there was a conspiracy to stop such public ostracism. A. J. Balfour lived with Lady Elcho for years, and probably had a son by her. The King knew it, yet Balfour's public life suffered not at all. And, of course, there were well-known whoremasters, noble pursuers of jockeys as well as of the Turf. As for gaming, and for that matter cheating at cards, it was a part, as the famous Tranby Croft case had shown (a guest had been caught cheating at a house-party when Edward VII, as Prince of Wales, had been a guest), of the gilded world. And, too, there were darker contrasts – the banquets, the lavish and spectacular consumption, the torrent of gold earned so easily and spent so profusely that stood out garishly against a background of poverty, low wages and widespread malnutrition. And worse for Edward VII's world, the Bodies and Souls were not the only Edwardians waiting in the wings of history.

There had always been great tension in Victorian England, a deep concern amongst the sensitive about the contrast between 'the dark satanic mills' and the self-indulgent life of elegance and refinement. There had been worry, too, about the hypocrisy which discreetly sheathed the legs of a grand piano to avoid offence by analogy, yet did nothing about child prostitution. And from the 1880s onwards, the most powerful voices in English intellectual life had begun to criticize their world, either directly, like G. B. Shaw, H. G. Wells, Havelock Ellis, Edward Carpenter and the rest, or by implication, as Wilde and his friends had done in poetry, plays and their style of life. And some, such as Yeats and his friends, retreated into the Gaelic twilight, which rejected the harsh realities of industrial England just as completely.

Indeed at Edward's accession there were few writers, very few intellectuals who took an unalloyed delight in their world. Even Kipling, the arch-poet of empire, in his great poem 'Recessional', written for the Queen's Diamond Jubilee in 1897, was full of foreboding, heavy with the sense of inevitable decay of empire and greatness. Not surprisingly the Boer War, in which the British army singularly failed to cope with South African guerilla forces, and in consequence, *had* committed some foolish atrocities, divided, in a way most reminiscent of Vietnam, English society; the majority of intellectuals, writers and artists being highly disturbed by England's policy. The more thoughtful of them were equally shocked by the revelation that a third of the recruits for the army were suffering from malnutrition.

And no sensitive eye could fail to see the terrible contrasts in London itself – the bitter slums of Bethnal Green, still with earth closets, perhaps one to a dozen families, one water tap set in the street or court for a cluster of houses, the houses themselves alive with bugs and fever; the children dirty, illiterate, unkempt and often debauched; and yet less than three miles away was the glitter of Mayfair, the profusion of food and drink, whoring and gambling, the idle men and women drifting from one extravagant amusement to another. And the contrasts in the country were no less vivid, no less shocking, to those who responded to human need and human justice.

So it is not surprising that the Edwardian age developed a strong streak of middle-class socialism, symbolized by the powerful Fabian Society and led by Beatrice and Sidney Webb, around whom clustered for a time G. B. Shaw, H. G. Wells, Arnold Bennett, Rupert Brooke, G. M. Trevelyan, Bertrand Russell, indeed most of the intellectual aristocracy of England. It started slowly in the 1880s as the Fellowship of the New Life, but by the end of Edward VII's reign it had collected nearly four thousand members drawn from some of the most influential groups – social as well as intellectual – in English life. Bertrand Russell, every inch an aristocrat, was so deeply moved by his socialist convictions that he gave away all his inherited wealth and reduced himself to poverty. Mostly the Fabians were highly intelligent members of the middle class, and this fact has been of enduring importance in the development of English political life, for it has given social respectability to English socialism. It has also helped to give the Labour Party a very considerable middle-class leadership and so helped to moderate the sharp conflict between classes that the social injustices of Edwardian England were fostering. Many of the Fabians found, as Galsworthy did, the pulls of middle-class life stronger than those of socialism and so they drifted slowly back to their natural habitat; but they took with them a sense of social need and of social justice.

Also that great politician of genius, David Lloyd George, the greatest of Edwardians, realized the dangers for the

Liberal Party that the growth of Labour politics would bring – and in a series of masterly budgets he laid down the foundation of that welfare state upon which the Labour Party were to build after the Second World War. Not, however, without a struggle. His measures – old-age pensions, national insurance to cover sickness and unemployment – stirred many of the aristocracy to such unbridled rage that the House of Lords threw out his Finance Bill in 1909 and so precipitated a constitutional crisis of such ferocity that it materially speeded the King's death in 1910 as well as leading to the reform of the Lords in 1911. Nothing highlighted the shallow hypocrisy of Edwardian England as clearly as the bitter opposition of men as inordinately rich as the Duke of Devonshire doing his best to prevent an aged miner securing a pittance from the State. Conflict in politics was made worse by the intractable problem of Ireland that teetered time and time again on the brink of civil war. And yet in spite of the gravity of the problems which faced Parliament, there was more social experimentation, a greater flexibility and originality in politics than England had experienced in decades. Edwardian politics express not only the conflicts of Edwardian society, but also its intellectual vitality and daring, as well as concern for the deepest human values.

Indeed in all aspects of life, the Edwardian age was one of creative conflict that ranged from the plight of women to the censorship of plays, but the burden of every conflict was the same – freedom for greater self-expression, social customs and institutions more in tune with human needs, the removal of restraint and an insistence on justice for all, abolition of prejudice and the end of hypocrisy. Naturally those comfortably entrenched in the lush pastures of privilege and riches viewed such wild and, to them, naïvely self-righteous posturings as the thin end of anarchism, irreligion and pagan sexuality. The plays of Mr Shaw, the novels of Mr Wells, the statues of Mr Epstein, the paintings of Mr Fry and the morals of Mr Lytton Strachey turned many a bishop, many an admiral, many a general and almost all the judges purple with fury and horror. It is hard for us to think of the

Edwardian literary scene as one of immense daring, full of revolutionary attitudes in art and alive with genius of a high order. But so it was. A philistine but stylish king ruled over a country in the grip of a cultural renaissance that only now is beginning to be appreciated to the full.

Then, as now, liberation was what the *avant-garde* intellectuals and artists were after, and they attacked where the restraints and hypocrisies were most obvious and inane – the position of women in society and the attitude to sex in the arts. Indeed the Edwardian age heard the first clear clarion call of Women's Lib. There was a two-pronged attack: an attempt to get easier divorce, in which women were aided, indeed led by men, and a struggle to secure the vote in which they had to fend for themselves, for they secured only a tiny support from the males. For divorce the *cause célèbre* was provoked by Bertrand Russell's brother, Lord Russell, who deliberately committed bigamy because he could not escape from a disastrous marriage. He was tried by his brother peers by the old medieval process in the House of Lords, found guilty and sent to jail for three months, becoming in the process a public hero of the left. In spite of bishops, moralists and Edward VII himself (he loathed divorces as much as he loved adultery), the liberals won through and Parliament made divorce a little easier, a little cheaper, if no less squalid in the publicity and social ostracism that it entailed.

The suffragettes had a tougher fight. They chained themselves to the railings of 10 Downing Street, they starved themselves to death in jail and one martyr flung herself under the galloping racehorses at the Derby in the presence of the King – all to no avail. It required that great liberator, the First World War, to crack male domination in politics. Nevertheless it was these passionate, dedicated, single-minded Edwardian women, led by Sylvia Pankhurst, who heralded that long slow revolution in the position of women which is only now beginning to snowball.

A faint scent of liberty, like a hint of blossom in springtime, began to infuse the cultural air of Edwardian England.

Like so much that flourished in the King's reign, its origins lay in the 1880s and 1890s. Oscar Wilde, Aubrey Beardsley, *The Yellow Book*, had all titillated late Victorian England with their hints of sophisticated sin; Edward Carpenter and Havelock Ellis had led an open assault on the bigotry and hypocrisy of Victorian sexual attitudes, proclaiming not only the widespread nature of male and female homosexuality, but also its naturalness. However, this early dawn quickly ended in disaster. Wilde went to jail; Havelock Ellis's books were prosecuted and suppressed; Carpenter harried. Such results scared the sinners and the sophisticated; the former crossed the Channel, the latter retreated into silence.

But revival came with the new reign and so the voices for freedom were not muted for long. Even two years before the King's accession, Dora Kerr had published a blistering attack on England's sexual morality. Her criticism was twofold and is best expressed in her own vigorous prose:

> We profess ignorance in children, entire sex suppression in girls and youths, full-blossomed knowledge and wisdom at the moment of marriage, unrelieved life-long sex-starvation for half the women of the upper class, and deprivation during the most vigorous years in life of the majority of men. There is (fortunately) *some* difference between what is professed and what is actually done. ... There is a great deal of Free-Love among married people in England, in the refined classes ... the one great drawback to it is the amount of deceit which endangers self respect.

The same themes were taken up and developed by some of the suffragettes who realized that the social position of women could never be changed unless they ceased to be exploited by men either in marriage or prostitution. As Mrs Pankhurst vividly phrased it, 'Votes for Women and Chastity for Men'. And there were minor victories: the best birth-control manual available sold merrily at fifty thousand copies a year; most barbers and some chemists were well stocked with contraceptive devices and were not prosecuted. A plea for the social acceptance of 'bachelor mothers' led only to the vituperation of the author – not jail. And, of course, the new woman was visible, not only in St John's

Wood amongst the literary and artistic bohemians, but also on the stage and in best-selling novels. Indeed the Edwardian writers, Wells, Arnold Bennett, G. B. Shaw and others, developed a new style of heroine, who was sexually alive and sexually frank, 'emancipated' was the word. Such books were regarded by the conservative forces with horror and were thundered against in the press, and attempts were made to suppress them.

The good, the holy and those fearful of social anarchy and national decay closed ranks. The Purity League was formed, the Mothers' Union got up in arms, bishops thundered in the House of Lords on the decay of the nation's morals, there were repeated National Councils on Public Morals, schoolmasters, led by Edward Lyttelton, headmaster of Eton, damned adolescent sexual activity as suicidal to health as well as morals, a theme re-echoed by the medical profession's condemnation of contraceptives. The Circulating Libraries Association, putting the country's salvation higher than private gain, purged their shelves of pornography and set up their own personal censorship as savage and as quaint as that of the Lord Chamberlain over the theatre. Even Henry James's *Italian Hours* was banished and the London County Council refused to allow *Dombey and Son* to be given as a school prize. A clutch of busybodies called the Crusaders hoped to reimpose censorship by law.

But they were like King Canute and the tide: the winds of change were gathering force every year. And, of course, opposed to the stultifying and tortuous censure of the moralists were some of the wittiest and most passionate writers twentieth-century England has known – George Bernard Shaw, H. G. Wells, Arnold Bennett – who all attacked vigorously and brilliantly both the official censorship on the stage and the unofficial one in the libraries.

As with literature, so with art. The early impressionist shows in England in the 1880s had been greeted with bewilderment and disdain. Renoir's nudes sent chills of horror down episcopal spines. Naturally when the post-impressionists arrived in Brighton in 1910 they were abused as the works of lunatics and psychopaths. But the French poison spread – Walter Sickert and Wilson Steer, both converts to Impressionism, started the New English Art Club. George Moore preached the virtues, not only of Impressionism, but also of Realism and Symbolism. And a battle royal began with the Royal Academy which, they insisted, was wasting Sir Francis Chantrey's huge bequest to the nation on academic works of utter banality. Almost every painter of merit, let alone of innovation, had been neglected, the commonplace flattered by high prices. A first-class fight took place in the House of Lords in 1904, when Lord Lytton successfully indicted the Royal Academy and obtained a select committee to investigate the Chantrey Bequest. Alas, the results were puny: all issues were evaded or swept aside and the Academicians pursued their dreary way, and indeed still do. But the damage was done: new attitudes to art had been ventilated, the stuffiness, hypocrisy, self-complacency of the Establishment exposed. The tensions so created were to prove a wonderful stimulus to British art which once more began to flourish, not with the genius of France, but at least with a vigour and freshness and a sense of experimentation that was wholly admirable, and was to lead to Henry Moore and Graham Sutherland.

The story of music was similar to that of art. Banality and mediocrity remained supreme in the social Establishment and England's greatest musical genius for two centuries, Elgar, found his audience mainly in Germany, although his greatest works embodied so much of the spirit of his age – its ebullience, its colour, its sense of space and freedom. But the tensions of Edwardian society were at work in Elgar, too. His spirit darkened and his work lost ebullience but gained in poignancy. His music remained intensely English in mood. Nor was Elgar alone. Other composers of merit – Delius, Holst, Bancroft – brought to the Edwardian age an achievement, as in painting, which was to prove remarkable and lasting.

Indeed wherever we look – at the empire and its fading rituals, at the condition of England, at social and political protest, at the new movements in art, literature and music – the Edwardian age is obviously at war with itself, creating tension and strain within the growing and socially powerful classes. Although there were still myriads of complacent, self-satisfied Victorians about, the more sensitive and intelligent men and women were horrified by the double standards both of life and thought.

It was a society in ferment and in strain – the early dawn of those problems and those attitudes which still grip our world – the great chasm between appearance and reality. How could one reconcile Edward VII's refusing to allow a divorced person convicted of adultery into the Royal Enclosure at Ascot with the known fact that he himself was sleeping with Mrs George Keppel? How could one reconcile the lavish dinners of a noble establishment – with course following course like a feast of Trimalchio – with the terrible discoveries of Rowntree at York where about a third of the population was suffering from malnutrition? How could one reconcile social attitudes to sex – repressive, terrifying, harmful – with the known facts of life and living? How could one reconcile the availability of expensive pornography with the attempt to suppress *Ann Veronica* by H. G. Wells? How could one reconcile the lewd innuendos of Marie Lloyd in the music halls with the banning on the stage of *Blanco Posnet* by G. B. Shaw? More and more men and women could not, and the voice of protest grew from a squeak to a roar. Nevertheless, I am sure that it was the tensions caused in private as well as in public by double standards which provided much of the creative stimulus of an age whose literary and artistic heritage is only just being appreciated.

In the Edwardian age two tides met and created turbulent waters. There was the old stately sweep of traditional England, concerned with preserving the society of status and deference in which, therefore, appearances and conventions were as important as defences against a flood; for believers in the past monarchy, Church, family and the old morality were as sacred as the books of Isaiah. But there was the new tide that was now beginning to run towards its flood – mass education, almost universal literacy, growing lower middle-class affluence, a growing army of men and women who wanted not subjection and a morality which put them in their place, but a taste of the joys which the aristocracy and well-heeled middle class had never denied themselves in private. The old world was cracking and the new, mass consumer society with its tensions and conflicts, its demands for innovation and change, above all its clear call for personal freedom of every kind, was beginning to seep through in an uncheckable stream. And yet there was one quality which derived neither from the past of tradition nor was, alas, to be typical of the future, and that was gusto. Edward VII lived as if he enjoyed every hour of every day, and so did most of his subjects, and that is what, perhaps, gives the Edwardian age its present radiance.

1971

Index

Index

Index

Index

Index

Index

Index

Index

272

Index